At Sundry Times

AT SUNDRY TIMES

An Essay in the Comparison of Religions

by

R. C. ZAEHNER

Spalding Professor of Eastern Religions and Ethics
at the University of Oxford
Fellow of All Souls College

FABER AND FABER
24 Russell Square
London

First published in mcmlviii
by Faber and Faber Limited
24 Russell Square London W.C.1
Printed in Great Britain by
Latimer Trend & Co Ltd Plymouth

for

Daniel and Thomas

REES

Contents

Foreword

The present book is based on the Sir D. Owen Evans Lectures which I was invited to deliver before the University College of Wales at Aberystwyth in January 1957. To compress the whole of what seemed to me to be the *praeparatio evangelica* as manifested in India and Iran into five lectures was no easy task for the author and must have strained the attention of even an audience as receptive and alert as that of Aberystwyth. In deciding to publish, then, I have considerably expanded Lectures II, III and V, and have added an appendix on the Qur'ānic conception of the mission and nature of Jesus Christ. With this additional elbow-room it is hoped that greater justice will have been done to the progressive development of the idea of God in the Indian tradition, and that some advance may have been made in bridging the gap that has hitherto separated the Qur'ānic (I dare not say Muslim) view of our Lord from our own.

I am greatly indebted to the former Principal of the University College, Mr. M. Goronwy Rees, for having invited me to give these lectures, and it is hoped that their publication in book form may contribute, in however humble a way, to a better understanding between the great religions.

R. C. Z.

All Souls College,
Oxford.

CHAPTER I

Comparative Religion

What is comparative religion?

'"When *I* use a word", Humpty-Dumpty said, in rather a scornful tone, "it means just what I choose it to mean—neither more nor less."

"The question is", said Alice, "whether you *can* make words mean so many different things."

"The question is", said Humpty-Dumpty, "which is to be master—that's all."'

So with comparative religion, the question is which is to be master, that's all. In Great Britain the undisputed master in this field is Professor E. O. James; and it is thanks to his pre-eminence that comparative religion in this country has come to mean very largely the comparative study of primitive religions: it has come to mean what is sometimes called social anthropology. Comparative religion, so understood, has paid too little attention to the great religions of the world other than Christianity; yet these, despite the missionary zeal of the Christian Churches, still maintain their vigour and have resolutely refused to disappear. It is these religions in their relationship to Christianity that I propose to study in these lectures.

The Chair in Oxford which, at present, I have the honour of occupying, is unique. Strictly speaking it is not a chair of Comparative Religion at all, and I, therefore, like Humpty-Dumpty, consider myself justified in asserting mastery over those two 'proud' words. The Chair is that of 'Eastern Religions and Ethics'. Its founder, the late H. N. Spalding, was not interested in primitive religion as such: he wished, rather, the Chair to concern itself with 'the great religions and ethical systems . . . of the East', the setting forth of their development and spiritual meaning, and the interpretation of them by comparison and contrast with each other and with the religions and ethics of the West. This is what I too understand by Comparative Religion or, to be more precise, the comparative study of religions.

We have now defined what, for the purposes of these lectures, we understand by comparative religion. Let us now consider how the subject should best be approached. There are many agnostics engaged in this study who would maintain that only agnostics can be expected to achieve complete objectivity in this field because they alone might be expected to be free from religious prejudice. Yet quite the reverse would appear to be true. As anyone who has read the work of Dupont-Sommer on the Dead Sea Scrolls will realize, such a claim is manifestly untrue: for, in his anxiety to make the Teacher of Righteousness of the Scrolls into an almost exact counterpart of Jesus of Nazareth, Dupont-Sommer allows himself to change, emend, and 'complete' the text of the Scrolls in a manner that is shocking in what is supposed to be an academic discipline. There can scarcely be any more unreasonable body of men than these apostles of reason, at least when they are dealing with religion. For religion is basically irrational: at its worst it is below reason, at its best far above it. It can be studied rationally, and should be and must be, 'for reason is God's scale on earth',[1] but it can never be understood by reason alone. Whatever God may be, He is certainly not *only* a rational being: He is a tremendous mystery as Rudolf Otto long ago pointed out: He is a scandal and an offence.

To say that only an agnostic can investigate the phenomena of religion impartially, is nonsense. If you do not know from the personal experience of your own life what it means to pray, your views on prayer will be valueless. This point was clearly

[1] Al-Ghazālī *Mishkāt al-Anwār*, in *Al-Jawāhir al-Ghawālī* ed. Sabrī, Cairo, 1934, p. 122; tr. W. H. T. Gairdner, Lahore, 1952 (reprint), p. 107.

made by the great mystical theologian of Islam, Al-Ghazālī, when he declared that no doctor of Islam, be he never so learned, could offer valid criticism of mystical experience, if he has never had such an experience himself. 'What a difference between being acquainted with the definition of drunkenness —namely, that it designates a state arising from the domination of the seat of the intellect by vapours arising from the stomach —and being drunk! Indeed, the drunken man, while in that condition, does not know the definition of drunkenness nor the scientific explanation of it; he has not the very least scientific knowledge of it. The sober man, on the other hand, knows the definition of drunkenness and its basis, yet he is not drunk in the very least. Again the doctor, when he is himself ill, knows the definition and causes of health and the remedies which restore it, and yet is lacking in health. Similarly there is a difference between knowing the true nature and causes and conditions of the ascetic life and actually leading such a life and forsaking the world.'[1]

Ghazālī is, of course, absolutely right. The agnostic is simply not in a position to discuss religious experience of any kind, whether mystical or not. The Christian too, on his side, must be presumed to suffer from a handicap, for, as a Christian, he knows at first hand only one *type* of religion. He is equipped to understand religions which are basically similar to his own, that is, Judaism, Islam, and Zoroastrianism; but is he quite so well equipped to understand the religions of India with their totally different approach and their totally different background?

It must be admitted that very few Christian writers on comparative religion seem really to understand what the Indian religions are about. Paradoxically enough it would seem to be the most dogmatic and the most uncompromising from among their number, the Neo-Calvinist Hendrik Kraemer who has assessed them best and fitted them into his own essentially Christian theology. He has fitted them in all right and passed appalling judgement on them; yet his analysis of Oriental

[1] Id. *Al-Munqidh min al-Ḍalāl*, tr. W. Montgomery Watt as *The Faith and Practice of Al-Ghazālī*, London, 1953, p. 55.

mysticism is essentially correct, and his violent protest against the Radhakrishnan school of 'indifferentism' which would reduce Christianity merely to a form of *bhakti* or devotional religion, was long overdue. 'The mystic,' Dr. Kraemer says, 'who triumphantly realizes his essential oneness with God, or the World-Order, or the Divine, knowing himself in serene equanimity the supreme master of the universe and his own destiny, and who by marvellous feats of moral self-restraint offers a fascinating example of splendid humanity (cf. the great Yogis of Tibet), nevertheless, in the light of Biblical revelation, commits in this sublime way the root-sin of mankind—"to be like God". In other words: *he repeats the Fall.* In India, for instance, the part of divine reality and truth which has, owing to the initiative of the self-disclosing God, succeeded in shining through to man, is all . . . inevitably vitiated by this monistic tendency, which is regarded as the pride, not as the avowed stumbling-block, of India.'[1]

Dr. Kraemer thus hauls the non-Christian religions up before the judgement-seat of 'Biblical realism' and finds them guilty of a monstrous *superbia*—a pride, indeed, which, in refusing to recognize the specifically Calvinist dogma of the total depravity of man, can in no wise see the necessity for grace. He thus confronts two views of God and man which seem to be radically incompatible. So, though we cannot accept his wholesale condemnation of Indian mysticism as a repetition of the Fall or follow him in seeing the 'mystery of iniquity' in 'the highest expressions of the human mind',[2] we cannot but admit that he has fully understood and faced the extreme Vedāntin claim that man and God are essentially identical, drawn the consequences of this claim and interpreted it in a way that is alone consistent with his own 'Biblical realism'. Thus understood the fully non-dualist Vedānta can, from the point of view of Biblical realism, only appear as man's assertion of his independence of God, as the sin of Lucifer and Original Sin. Anyone whose faith is less toughly uncompromising than that of Dr. Kraemer, might be

[1] Hendrik Kraemer, *Religion and the Christian Faith*, London, 1956, p. 335.
[2] Ibid., p. 227.

tempted to question the validity of Biblical realism itself (since it appears to rest on no authority except that of Dr. Kraemer) —so sweeping does its condemnation of extra-Biblical religion appear to be. In the course of our present inquiry we shall try to see whether the Biblical tradition is indeed so utterly irreconcilable with the witness of the Indian religions as Dr. Kraemer would have us believe or whether there is not indeed some way of bridging the gap.

First, however, we must ask ourselves what is meant by religion; and if we are to know what religion is, we must also find something in common between the great religions of the world. What, to take the extreme case, is there in common between the Judaism of the Old Testament and primitive Buddhism? And it is at this point that we appear to be checkmated even before we have begun our inquiry. For what are the essential elements in these two religions?

The Old Testament is an account of Yahweh's dealings with His people; it is the story of an intensely personal God who reveals Himself progressively to one people which He has chosen out of all the nations of the earth. He instructs them and chastises them, but always He is near to them and they are made almost terrifyingly aware of His presence. In Israel only the 'fool' could possibly say in his heart: 'There is no God'. Such is the religious climate of Jewry. Yahweh speaks through His own chosen ones, the prophets; and who dare gainsay Him? Not even in the Qur'ān does this *mysterium tremendum* make itself so tremendously felt.

At the other end of Asia, in India, we meet with the Buddha, the founder of a religion second in importance only to Christianity. That Buddhism *is* a religion few would now deny; yet there seems to be nothing in common between it and Judaism. In Europe we would normally regard worship of God as at least one of the prime constituents of religion: yet for the Buddha there is no God, nor indeed is there any specific entity you could call 'man'. There is absolutely no idea of any divine plan working itself out in history: as there is no God, so can there not be any divine plan. Judaism, like its offshoot, Christianity, is rooted in history and looks forward to the end of the world. For the Buddha, as indeed for all Indian religions, there is no history and there is absolutely no purpose in the historical process. Religion, for him, is simply not conceived of in these terms. Religion means personal salvation: it is not concerned with time or history, but with eternity. There is this world, a perpetual and meaningless flux, an aggregate of pain or suffering, a never-ending crucifixion: but over against it stands the eternal, *nirvāṇa*, which is the extinction of pain and of desire which is its source, the 'blowing out' of all phenomenal existence. This is the Buddhist's goal.

This is to put the contrast at its starkest; and there seems to be no common element between Judaism of the Old Testament and the most primitive forms of Buddhism we know.

For the believer in any religion the comparative study of religions is dangerous; for if, as would at first sight appear, there is no common ground between two of the greatest and most fundamental religions of the world, how can we be sure that either is true? How can we be sure that any religion is true? Will we not be forced to adopt an agnostic approach and simply treat religion as a branch of psychology? For when we look at the religions of the world, we are faced with two totally different approaches to the whole subject, we are faced with two chosen peoples, not one; for, whereas Europe and the Near East owe their religions directly or indirectly to the Jews, further Asia owes hers directly or indirectly to the Indians: and these two peoples see religion in an entirely different way. Perhaps they do so because they are talking of different things.

In reading the best books of even the best Christian scholars one is frequently astonished at their apparent inability to see through Hindu or Buddhist eyes. Too often they persist in speaking in Christian terms about concepts that are entirely alien to Christianity as usually interpreted. They do not seem to realize that whereas the Christian starts with the idea of God, the Hindu and Buddhist do not: they start with the idea of the human soul. Basically they are not interested in what we would call God at all; they are interested in the realization here and now of a state of existence in which time and space and causation are transcended and obliterated: they aim at the realization, the felt experience of immortality. In Hinduism we meet with different philosophies which seek to explain what this beatitude consists in, and in these we do sometimes run into something very like God: at least we meet with a first cause which is at the same time the ground and support of the universe. The Buddha, however, reduces religion to what seemed to him to be its bare essentials, release from suffering, and by this he means release from the phenomenal world. He had no interest whatever in metaphysics nor in revelation, for he had no belief in God either as a person or as a principle. Astonishing though it may seem to us he would probably not have regarded even the Hebrew God as lying within the sphere of religion. All that was essential he had declared in the four Noble Truths—the truths of pain, of the cause of pain, of the cessation of pain, and of the way that leads to the cessation of pain. All else was unprofitable. For when asked why he had left so many important questions unanswered, he replied that he had declared what was sufficient unto salvation; all the rest 'is not profitable, does not belong to the beginning of the religious life, and does not tend to revulsion, absence of passion, cessation, calm, higher knowledge, enlightenment, *nirvāṇa*. Therefore have I not declared it.

'And what, monks, have I declared?' he asks. 'This is pain, I have declared; this is the cause of pain, I have declared; this is the cessation of pain, I have declared; this is the Way leading to the cessation of pain, I have declared. And why, monks, have I declared it? Because it is profitable, it belongs to the beginning of the religious life, and tends to revulsion, absence of passion, cessation, calm, higher knowledge, enlightenment, *nirvāṇa*. Therefore have I declared it.'[1]

This, then, is what the Buddha considered to be the essence of religion—the diagnosis of the whole cosmic process as pain and the practical steps which can be taken to pass beyond the

[1] *Saṁyutta Nikāya*, v, 437, *apud* E. J. Thomas, *Early Buddhist Scriptures*, London, 1935, pp. 117–18.

world of pain. There can be no question of grace to aid you on your path since there is no god from whom grace could derive. Salvation or the achievement of Nirvāṇa is a purely personal matter and it must be achieved alone. The Buddha's last words to his disciples are reported to have been: 'Decay is inherent in all compounded things. Work out your salvation with diligence.'[1] But beyond the world of coming to be and passing away lies Nirvāṇa, a state which is beyond time and space. 'There is,' the Buddha says, 'an unborn, not become, not made, uncompounded, and were it not . . . for this unborn, not become, not made, uncompounded, no escape could be shown here for what is born, has become, is made, is compounded. But because there is . . . an unborn, not become, not made, uncompounded, therefore an escape can be shown for what is born, has become, is made, is compounded.'[2]

This is the one affirmation the Buddha makes about the state he calls Nirvāṇa: 'There is an unborn, not become, not made, uncompounded.' Alongside this conditioned world there is an unconditioned, that is, an eternal mode of existence to enjoy which is man's ultimate beatitude. This would appear to be the only point at which primitive Buddhism touches Judaism and Christianity: there is such a thing as the eternal. But what an enormous difference separates the two religions. For the Hebrews it is God who is the Eternal Being, and man is not called upon to share in His life. For the Buddhists there is such a thing as an eternal mode of existence and this can be experienced by all who are 'enlightened' enough to find it. Thus, there is no God at all in the Christian sense of the word, but there is eternity which is within the reach of man: man himself is eternal.

This direct confrontation of Judaism with Buddhism, then, shows us one thing. The common ground between the great religions is that they are all concerned with eternity. They are not necessarily concerned with God at all if by God we mean

[1] *Mahā-parinibbāna Sutta*, vi, 10.

[2] *Udāna*, 81 *apud* E. Conze, *Buddhist Texts through the Ages*, Oxford, 1954, p. 95.

not simply an eternal mode of existence, but the sum and summit of all value. *We* mean this, but the Buddhists emphatically do not. Thus it seems a little naïve to say, as Professor James does, that the concept of deity '*must* be the affirmation of a supernatural Reality responsive to human needs, the objective ground and sovereign moral ruler of the universe, the personal source and conserver of value, the ultimate standard of conduct, a worthy object of worship, the guide of man from the cradle to the grave and the hope of immortality'.[1] This amounts to little more than saying that such a Being exists because we want Him to exist. To the Buddhist it might seem cowardly because it is everywhere belied by experience. If the world was indeed created (and few Indians would admit this), it was most evilly created. The world, as we see it, is not good: it is just 'pain', just that and nothing more. No Buddhist would be likely to give James's definition of deity, which he would dismiss as wishful thinking, a second thought. Rather, 'Work out your salvation with diligence'; but work it out yourself and place no reliance on the figments of either your own imagination or that of others.

Christians are all too apt to condemn the Indian religions as inferior because they see no purpose in human life, and Śrī Aurobindo's reaction against the traditional interpretation of Hinduism shows that this criticism has struck home. Yet the more traditionally minded among Indians might well reply that they are simply not interested in whether or not life has a purpose; they are not interested in phenomenal life at all; they are interested in the eternal. If you strike the eternal, all else will be added to you; you will have passed beyond pleasure and pain into a perfect peace where you will no longer even feel the *need* for a God.

These are two points of view: and they would appear to be irreconcilable. The purpose of this book will be to investigate whether there is any system into which the fundamental tenets of all the great religions can be made to fit.

First let us return to consider a little more deeply the contrast between Semitic and Indian religion. On the one side you find

[1] E. O. James, *The Concept of Deity*, London, 1950, p. 152.

claims to exclusive truth through revelation, on the other you find a total indifference to so-called dogma and a readiness to admit truth in all and any religious manifestation. On the one side you find prophets claiming to speak in God's name, on the other sages interested only in piercing through to the immortal ground of their soul. On the one side you find passionate denunciation of error, on the other you find only tolerance and kindliness and anxiety to see the other point of view. On the one side you find a passionate belief in a transcendent God who is 'axiologically other' as Professor Farmer puts it,[1] a God whose will it is desperately important to know; on the other you find a patient search for the 'kingdom of God' which is 'within you'. We of the Christian tradition demand that our God should be good, that He should have a purpose in creating us and the world in which we live, and that He should enable us to know Him and lead us to the Beatific Vision of Him. The Indian tradition does not see things in this way at all: it matters little whether you like to think of the eternal as God or deity, as personal or impersonal, possessed of qualities or devoid of them. Whatever He or it may be, you must find it in yourself. When you have found it you will know that this is eternal life which is your ultimate bliss.

Religions of Semitic origin are for ever proclaiming the Truth—one and undivided. For the Hindu truth is a many-sided affair and can be viewed from many angles. Semitic religions are ideologies: Hinduism and Buddhism are ways of life. The Semitic type of religion inevitably tends to lead to fanaticism, persecution, and ideological war for the simple reason that man remains imperfect and when once he believes that he knows the truth, he must necessarily wish to destroy error even by means that may be at variance with the 'truth' he professes. Hinduism and Buddhism again are—with some sad lapses—just the reverse: since all religions are paths leading to one goal and all are ultimately concerned in seeking out the inmost ground of the soul, intolerance is obviously pointless as well as wicked.

[1] H. H. Farmer, *Revelation and Religion*, London, 1954, p. 78.

These, then, are the two ways, the two attitudes to what is supposedly the same problem: and the second way is without doubt the more attractive, the more human and therefore the more humane. But then the Semites have never even tried to make their God attractive. Attractive He is in a profound sense, but not in the manner of a Raphael Madonna or a Grecian god. When He attracts, it is like a magnet: He is irresistible, and you go to Him whether you like it or not. Many of us do not like it at all.

And here again there is yet another fundamental difference between the Indian and the Semitic approach. In Indian religion, whether it be Buddhist, Jain, or Hindu, enormous importance is attached to the complete suppression of the passions, to the achievement of total *vairāgya*, *ἀταραξία*, or stilling of the affections, whether they be for good or evil. This is as prominent in the theistic Bhagavad-Gītā as it is in the atheistic Sāṁkhya or in Buddhism. Detachment is in itself a goal, for without it there can be no realization of the still centre of the soul. The Christian idea that God *is* Love is unthinkable to the Buddhist and Christ's words at the Last Supper, 'With desire I have desired to eat this passover with you',[1] would most certainly be taken to indicate that He was still a thousand miles from the 'enlightenment' of the Buddha, for a Buddha is, by definition, one who has passed beyond all desire; for craving is the source of suffering, the basic evil that binds us to this hateful world of time and change. Christ's love is passionate, the Buddha's compassion is detached and passionless. Christ enters the world in order to redeem it by His own suffering and passion on the Cross; the Buddha enters the world in order to point the path which overcomes suffering and saves us *from* the world. Christ accepts suffering and thereby brings man and God together in His own tortured body. The Buddha does otherwise: he conquers suffering. For the Enlightened One there is no more pleasure or pain.

The Indian attitude to the world may seem strange to us, but it is basic to every form of mysticism. It is true that the Hindus

[1] Luke xxii, 15.

claim that the Vedas are 'revelation' (*śruti*, lit. 'hearing'), but they are not revelation in the sense that the Old Testament or the Qur'ān are. They are not regarded as a book sent down by a highly personal and sometimes capricious God, but rather as primordial truth about man, the universe, and the soul of man. Nonetheless the principal test of orthodoxy among the Hindus is the acceptance of the Vedas as a revelation of the nature of things. Characteristically the bulk of the Vedas is anonymous; and thus, for the Hindus, the Vedas are impersonal truth just as Brahman is the impersonal ground of all being.

In Buddhism there is nothing corresponding to revelation in any sense. The Buddha discovers the true view of life and proclaims it in his own right as Buddha, that is, one who has 'awoken' from the bad dream of phenomenal existence. In a sense, then, the Buddha is a psychologist rather than a founder of a religion; and this may well explain Jung's interest in the many religions that sprang from his teaching.

Again on the all-important question of what constitutes a man there is no agreement between Semitic and Indian religion. The Hebrews—and in this respect they agree with the Zoroastrians—regarded man as being a single, unified being consisting of soul and body, neither of which could exist without the other; and it was for this reason that they came upon the idea of the survival of the soul after death very late. This Hebrew conception of man passed on into Christianity and Islam, both of which proclaim the resurrection of the body in the last days, though what is understood by the resurrected body is far from clear. Indian religion, on the other hand, very soon developed a wholly dualistic view of the nature of man, the source of which may well have been the doctrine of the transmigration of souls which the Aryan invaders of India seem to have borrowed from the aboriginal population. If there is metempsychosis, then it must follow that the union of the soul with the body is temporary; and so it is that every sect and philosophical school of Hinduism teaches that there are two worlds, not one—two worlds which are never wholly compatible. There is the world of eternal spirit on the one hand and the world of never-ending change on the other. Two eternities face each other—here the eternal 'now' so dear to the mystics, there the eternity of time which never began and which will never end. Not only man, but the animals too, are thus a compound of these two different eternities. The separation of the one from the other constitutes salvation: soul must bid farewell to matter for ever if it is to be free and if it is to recognize itself as eternal. The separation of the eternal from the perishable remains the goal of all Indian religion, however this separation may be conceived of or expressed. That there should be a resurrection of the body must seem to the Indian sage the wildest improbability: and not only is it supremely improbable, it is also absolutely undesirable. The body, and indeed all matter, is of its very nature corruptible; it passes away and can never be reconstituted. The soul is *by nature* eternal and so can only suffer diminution and loss by its association with the body. If there were a resurrection of the body, then this would be the final insult to much that Hinduism and Buddhism stand for. Incarnation and reincarnation are the curses which, for a time, the soul must bear. Death, when, at long last and after millions of years of incarnate existence, it mercifully brings release, is veriest bliss; it is Nirvāṇa, the goal of every Indian ascetic and sage. How very bitter, then, to be told by Christian missionaries that the soul will once again be dragged out of its splendid isolation and imprisoned once again in a loathsome body; and how much more bitter to be told that this is a higher form of religion. So once again do the Hebrews and the Indians clash on the all-important question of what constitutes a man.

So too with personality. Professor Farmer speaks typically as a Christian when he claims that the apprehension of God as personal is essential to the 'living experience' of God. The Christian tends to cling very tenaciously to his personal immortality; and this is really preposterous, for did not Christ Himself say: 'Except a corn of wheat fall into the ground and die, it abideth alone: but if it die, it bringeth forth much fruit. He that loveth his life shall lose it; and he that hateth his life in this world shall keep it unto life eternal'?[1] In the idea of dying to self we do indeed find a link—and an important one—between Christianity at least and Indian religion; and this is one of the ideas we propose to examine in due course. It is an idea that the Indians rigorously follow up, but it is an idea which makes respectable Christians extremely uncomfortable. 'If any man will come after me, let him deny himself, and take up his cross, and follow me.'[2] To the average Christian this is bitter medicine and few would even attempt to take it. The Indian, on the other hand, knows from his sacred books if he is a Hindu, and from the Buddha's central teaching if he is a Buddhist, that without denial of the 'ego', without the destruction of what goes by the name of personality there can be no salvation. To project personality on to the Absolute, as the Semites appear to do, must therefore seem to him utterly illogical.

In this too the two views face each other in stark opposition. On the one side you have Semitic religion proclaiming a personal God with whom a personal relationship is possible because man too is a person and as such has value: on the other you hear the Indian sages declare almost with one voice that personality is ultimately illusory and that final bliss consists precisely in the elimination of personality and in being either absorbed into the Absolute as a river is lost in the sea or in actually realizing oneself as the Absolute, the One without a second. Denying self is taken very seriously indeed by the Indians: it is the whole basis of their ethical system and this system itself is the expression in practice of the belief that an individual self has no real existence. To expect personal survival would appear to them to be both unrealistic and very selfish; and so, of course, it is.

It should be remembered that the Hindus and Buddhists, or at least the most vocal of their exegetes today, base the claim for the truth of their doctrines on experience. In mystical experience, they would say, the human soul reaches certainty that it is immortal since it is merged in the universal spirit or Brahman in which all sense of individuality is lost. This experience, they

[1] John xii, 24–25. [2] Matt. xvi, 24.

would add, is attested in every land and in all epochs of the history of the human race. Its universality is the hall-mark of its truth. The experience cannot adequately be put into words, for it is an experience of eternity, and words can only describe what is limited by time and space. In the mystical experience of *samādhi*, however, subject and object are done away with: knower, knowledge, and known are all one. The experience cannot be seized or fastened down by rational thought, for it is a form of 'knowledge' to which the mere discursive intellect cannot attain.

All this is quite true. There can be no doubt at all that the experience of being at one with all Nature, of being simultaneously oneself and the world, is attested in all lands and at all times. Where there seems to be a misunderstanding, however, is in the assumption that this intimate sense of communion with Nature is identical with the theist's experience of communion with God. We shall have to deal with this all-important point in another chapter.

Indian religion, then, places all its emphasis on the mystical or inward type of religion, what Plotinus called the flight of the alone to the Alone.[1] This is, of course, not true of popular Hinduism; but the advanced Vedānta would maintain that the popular theistic cults were imperfect approaches to the true goal of religion, which is the realization of the eternal. The Indian emphasis on mystical experience seems to us far too exclusive. Mysticism of one sort or another is a widely attested phenomenon, but it is not by any means the only subjective religious phenomenon. The mystic, simply by being a mystic and therefore incapable of giving exact expression to his experiences, can have no message from God to man. According to the Semites God can and does speak to man, and his chosen vessels for this purpose are the prophets. In India there are no prophets; and it is significant that the Bhagavad-Gītā, the most popular manual of teaching in Hinduism, is put into the mouth of Krishna, a mythical hero who came to be regarded as an incarnation of Vishnu. India produces sages, Israel prophets. The

[1] *Enneads*, vi, 9, 11.

message of the first is renunciation of the world in order to partake in an eternal order, the message of the second is the dealings of the Eternal with this world of space and time.

Prophecy, as we understand it, is—with one notable exception—peculiar to the Semites. Among the Semites—again with one enormous exception—it is peculiar to the Hebrews. The mystic sees himself as merged into the eternal or 'oned' with the eternal, but the prophet knows or thinks he knows that the Eternal speaks through him to the world. He is not the passive victim of a supernatural state; he is, willy-nilly, the mouthpiece of an overwhelming power which, through him, makes the heaviest demands on man. In this respect the Old Testament is totally unlike any other sacred book. Basically it is the history of God's dealings with His people, God's message delivered with ever-increasing urgency to mankind through a series of prophets. If, then, the Indians are justified in laying tremendous emphasis on mystical experience, the Semites are no less justified in emphasizing the prophetic experience: for if we, like the Buddhists, are to make experience the basis of religion, then we must concede at least equal validity to the experience of the prophets as to that of the mystics. Mystics make no demands, they merely point a way: prophets make insistent demands, they demand obedience. They are extremely uncomfortable people.

I hope that the religious pattern we are trying to discern is now becoming a little clearer. On the one hand stands India with its quest for the eternity that is in every man; on the other stands Israel, a very late-comer to the idea of immortality, with its personal and overpowering God who makes His will known through prophecy. If both traditions represent an aspect of truth, then the link between them is at present veiled from our eyes.

Israel and India are the 'types' of all higher religion. Outside them we do find the mystical and prophetical types of religion represented, but nowhere else are they so clearly differentiated. In China a mystical immanentism develops in Taoism which is closely akin to the immanentism of the Upanishads. Outside

Israel we find one minor and one major prophet, men who see themselves as the mouthpiece of God and who bear a message to their respective peoples. On the one side we have Zarathushtra, the prophet of ancient Iran, on the other Muhammad, the Prophet of the Arabians. Almost exactly between them in time is the eternal stumbling-block, Jesus Christ, who claimed to be the Son of the Blessed.

To Christians, however, it is Muhammed, *the* Prophet *par excellence*, who is the stumbling-block, and he a stumbling-block that most writers on comparative religion prefer to by-pass. In earlier days it was customary to dismiss Muhammad as an impostor. This is absurd, for there is no criterion by which the gift of prophecy can be withheld from him unless it is withheld from the Hebrew prophets too. The Qur'ān is, in fact, the quintessence of prophecy. In it you have, as in no other book, the sense of an absolutely overwhelming Being proclaiming Himself to a people that had not known Him. However much you may misunderstand or disapprove of the Qur'ān, you cannot ignore it. Not even in the Old Testament do you have such a overmastering insight into Omnipotence. Nowhere else is God revealed—if revelation it can be called—as so utterly inscrutable, so tremendous, and so mysterious. That Muhammad was a genuine prophet and that the authentic voice of prophecy made itself heard through him, I for one find it impossible to disbelieve on any rational grounds—assuming, of course, that God exists and makes Himself known through prophets.

Muhammad *is* a stumbling-block; for if Jesus Christ was the Son of God (which Muhammad hotly denied though he freely granted almost all His other claims), then what possible additional message could God have which He had not transmitted through His Son?

Parokṣapriyā iva hi devāḥ pratyakṣadviṣaḥ: 'the gods love the obscure and hate the obvious', as the *Bṛhadāraṇyaka* Upanishad[1] rightly says. And the second Isaiah agrees; 'For my thoughts are not your thoughts, neither are your ways my ways, saith the Lord. For as the heavens are higher than the earth, so are my

[1] 4. 2. 2.

ways higher than your ways, and my thoughts than your thoughts,'[1] 'because the foolishness of God is wiser than men; and the weakness of God is stronger than men'.[2]

Such seems to be God's answer to us, the students of comparative religion: for it is He who has set the problem, and it is He 'who at sundry times and in divers manners spake in time past unto the fathers and the prophets'.[3] 'Divers manners': there is the crux, and little did St. Paul know how divers the manners were.

So the problem has been stated not so much by us as by Him 'who at sundry times and in divers manners spake in time past unto the fathers and the prophets'. In seeking to solve the riddle propounded to poor man by the divine Sphinx, I shall quite shamelessly assume the existence of the Sphinx, and I shall make the further enormous assumption that the Sphinx reveals Himself in some measure in all the religions of mankind. I am fully aware that to question the ways of Omnipotence and to seek to explain what, of its nature, cannot be explained, is both impossible and impious. I have often censured it in others: I censure it in myself. Yet the problem must be tackled, for the co-existence of living religions as utterly different as are Judaism and Buddhism cries for an explanation. Above all it demands an explanation that will make sense, an explanation on the one hand that is not too obviously based on exclusively Christian values which no one else accepts, and one which, on the other, does not take refuge in metaphysical mystification of the kind now practised by M. Frithjof Schuon.

M. Schuon takes up the sublime position that there is 'metaphysical' truth, which is one, and 'religious' truth, which is many. Orthodoxies, he maintains, are truths on a religious plane, different manifestations of the one 'metaphysical' truth which is inexpressible. Heresies, he adds, are always false in themselves; but as to what *is* a heresy and what is not, M. Schuon reserves judgement to himself. Thus in Christianity, he maintains, 'orthodoxy' is represented by the Roman Catholic (Latin) and Eastern Orthodox (Greek) Churches, while it

[1] Isa. lv, 8–9. [2] 1 Cor. i, 25. [3] Heb. i, 1.

seems to be implied that other denominations are heretical.[1] In Islam, however, the Shīʻa sect, which is separated from the majority Sunnīs as sharply as are Protestants from Catholics, is as orthodox as its rivals. Similarly Buddhism, though regarded by the Hindus as heretical, is for M. Schuon an orthodoxy. For myself, I propose to follow no such method. Primarily I shall concern myself with what sincere men have believed and believe to be revelation, and in the chapters that follow I shall confine myself to revelation as it appears in the sacred books of the Hindus, in the 'enlightenment' of the Buddha, in the non-Jewish prophetic religions, that is, Zoroastrianism and Islam, and lastly in the revelation of God as Man in the person of Jesus Christ, the son of Mary.

I am fully aware that to attempt this in the compass of five chapters is the height of presumption. 'Let the potsherd strive with the potsherds of the earth. Shall the clay say to him that fashioneth it, What makest thou? or thy work, He hath no hands?'[2] To which the clay has no answer except that 'the Lord God . . . breathed into his nostrils the breath of life; and man became a living soul'.[3] And so, if man tries to seek out the ways of God, it is because the breath of God is in him, and this breath will not be stilled.

In this introductory chapter I have stated the enigma in the baldest terms. In the following chapters perhaps we shall stumble on an answer, or perhaps we shall not.

[1] F. Schuon, *The Transcendent Unity of Religions*, London, 1953, p. 116.
[2] Isa. xlv, 9.
[3] Gen. ii, 7.

CHAPTER II

The Indian Contribution, I

The problem that the comparative study of religions sets for Christianity and, indeed, for all faiths that make exclusive claims, has now been stated. We saw that two distinct types of religion face each other, the Judaic on the one hand, which is concerned with a transcendental God experienced by prophets as an objective fact; and the Indian on the other, which is primarily concerned with the eternal as experienced as a *state* within the human soul. The prophet confronts the mystic: and each speaks a different language that is not comprehensible to the other.

In this and the following chapter we will be considering the nature of Indian religion both in its Hindu and its Buddhist manifestations.

The earliest literary monument of Indian religion is the Rig-Veda. In this we find a polytheism which is recognizably Indo-European and readily comparable to the earliest phases of the religion of the Greeks and Romans and the other Indo-European peoples. Even at this stage, however, this polytheism slips over into something which Max Müller called 'henotheism' or 'kathenotheism'; that is to say, the poet's attention became so exclusively fixed on the particular god he was addressing that he attributed to him all the divine characteristics that had previously been divided among the various gods that went to make up the pantheon. Thus, to take but one example, Indra who seems originally to have been a warrior god and god of the storm, takes on all the attributes of the just sovereign normally associated with the 'high-god' Varuṇa, the guardian of the cosmic law. Originally a genial war-lord with no marked moral characteristics, he becomes the upholder of the law[1] who speaks no falsehood.[2] While formerly he had represented the irresistible power both of nature and of a conquering race, he now takes over the moral order too from Varuṇa, although there is no evidence that he originally had any connexion with that order. The peculiar properties of individual gods, then, imperceptibly pass from one into another so that the distinction between them comes to be blurred. So a tendency away from clarity and away from the drawing of sharp distinctions becomes apparent in even the earliest Indian thinking. 'They call' the divine 'Indra, Mitra, Varuṇa, Agni, or it is the celestial bird Garutmat. What is but one the wise call [by] manifold [names]. They call it Agni, Yama, Mātariśvan.'[3] Thus, as the gods tend to merge into one another, the divine power or cosmic order usually called *ṛta*, *vrata*, *dharman*, or *dhāman* in the Rig-Veda, remains the same, and by attaching itself to an individual god, endows him with that supernatural something, which, since it is that which makes the universe a cosmos rather than a chaos, makes him truly a god. The cosmic law thereby becomes more important and more fundamental than the individual who presides over and operates the law. The nature of this law will henceforth be the prime preoccupation of the early philosophers.

Towards the end of the Rig-Vedic period the old polytheism is more directly questioned, and speculation about the beginnings of the world begins. This may be regarded as the beginning of Indian philosophy which, throughout its history, has remained firmly rooted in religion. In the later hymns of the Rig-Veda various cosmological myths appear, the purpose of which is to account for the origin of the world, the development of multiplicity out of unity. From these early hymns on-

[1] e.g. *Rig-Veda*, III, 51, 2: cf. Bergaigne, *La Religion Védique* (4 vols., Paris, 1878–97), vol. iii, pp. 246–8.

[2] e.g. *Rig-Veda*, III, 32, 9: cf. Bergaigne, ibid., p. 244.

[3] *Rig-Veda*, I, 164, 46.

wards the theme of Indian philosophy has been the relationship of the one to the many, and the possibility of restoring the primal unity through mystical insight.

The creation hymns of the Rig-Veda represent the transition from the theism—whether polytheism or henotheism—of the earliest period to the pantheism of the later. Creation is regarded as the transition from a chaos to a diversified order which may involve a pre-existent creator-god or not. Yet, however the process is conceived of, there is never any idea of creation *ex nihilo* as there is in the Semitic religions. In the two hymns to Viśvakarman,[1] the 'All-Creator', God and the *materia prima*, primal matter, are regarded as being distinct. 'What was the basis, what the beginning, how was it—that from which Viśvakarman, the all-seeing, generated the earth and unfolded the heavens in their greatness?'[2] the poet asks. It is Viśvakarman who 'welds them together with his arms and wings', or who, varying the metaphor, carves them out of the primal *wood*—a word which, strangely enough, corresponds exactly to the Greek *hylè* or primal matter. Here the former and the formed are still distinct; and as 'creator' (*dhātā*) and 'orderer' (*vidhātā*)[3] God stands aside from primeval matter and carves it out as a carpenter might carve out his wood.

This is perhaps the last stage in primitive Indian religion in which God as efficient cause of the universe is considered to be distinct from its material cause. In other creation hymns the supreme principle appears as both, or it is the 'seed' which fertilizes the water from which the 'One' is born,[4] the 'golden seed' (*hiraṇyagarbha*) which is born as the only Lord of Creation[5]—a god as yet unknown to men: for 'Who is this God,' the seer asks, 'to whom we should bring sacrifice?' Alternatively, as in the famous *Puruṣasūkta*,[6] the first principle is regarded as being a gigantic male, from one quarter of whom all earthly creation originates, while the remaining three-quarters constitute what is immortal in heaven (§ 3). The creation of this world pro-

[1] *Rig-Veda*, X, 81 and 82.
[2] Ibid., X. 81. 2.
[3] Ibid., X. 82. 2.
[4] Ibid., X. 82. 6.
[5] Ibid., X. 121. 1.
[6] Ibid., X. 90.

ceeds from the sacrifice of the primal giant's mortal part; and the universe is therefore only a small part of the whole divine substance. This is pantheism in the sense that the world is not distinct from God, but it is not pantheism in the sense that God transcends the world by those three-quarters of Him which are immortal. This distinction is usually maintained in the later 'pantheistic' period.

But perhaps the whole spirit of reverent inquiry which is so typical of these hymns, is best illustrated by an equally famous hymn (*Rig-Veda* X. 129) with its obscure groping after the One, which, it felt instinctively, must underlie all the diversity of an everchanging world.

'Then neither Being nor Not-being existed, neither atmosphere, nor the firmament, nor what is above it. What did it encompass? Where? In whose protection? What was water, the deep, unfathomable?

'Neither death nor immortality was there then, no sign of night or day. The One breathed windless by its own power. Nought else but this existed then.'

Then, as if unsatisfied with this solution which brings all things back to the One, the poet starts again:

'In the beginning was darkness swathed in darkness: all this was but unmanifested water. Whatever was, that One, coming into being, hidden by the Void, was generated by the power of heat.

'In the beginning desire which was the first seed of mind overcovered it. Wise seers, searching in their hearts, found the bond of Being in Not-being.

'Their cord was extended athwart. Was there anything above or anything below? Givers of seed there were, and powers; beneath was energy and above impulse.

'Who knows truly? Who can here declare whence it was born, whence is this emanation? By the emanation of this the gods came afterwards.

'Who knows then whence it has arisen? Whence this emanation has arisen, whether it was created or not, only He knows who surveys it in highest heaven. He only knows, or perhaps He does not know.'

It is not our intention to offer an explanation of this dark hymn here. Suffice it to say that the author, throughout his changing terminology, seems to conceive of primal existence as a formless and moving mass (water, darkness, the Void, or Not-being)—the *materia prima* or female principle of alchemy and Jungian psychology.[1] From this utterly undifferentiated chaos the One, that is, in this context, God as manifest in creation, appears either 'by its own power' or 'by the power of heat' (*tapas*, a word which later came to mean creative austerity)—through a principle of illumination or differentiation usually associated with the male principle. Creation, then, is regarded, as in so much of primitive religion, as the result of the union of a primeval male and female, or rather as the self-fertilization of a still androgynous first cause:[2] 'Beneath was energy (?) (or "Nature" *svadhā*)[3] and above impulse'; beneath the female and above the male, from the union of which the whole universe proceeds. This type of myth will occur again and again in the later literature and can be found throughout the world's mythologies. But the interest of our hymn lies not so much in this as in the last stanzas which, contrary to all expectation, suddenly introduce a God who stands outside the whole process of the generation of the world and 'surveys it in highest heaven'. He alone is master of the riddle; He only knows . . . or, terrible thought, 'perhaps He does not know'.

This hymn sets the stage for the further development of Indian philosophy as does no other. The Rig-Veda had presented the religious mind with a galaxy of deities, largely an-

[1] See especially C. G. Jung, *Psychology and Alchemy*, in *Collected Works*, vol. xii. For similar myths in Iranian mythology cf. R. C. Zaehner, *Zurvan, A Zoroastrian Dilemma*, Oxford, 1955, pp. 72–78.

[2] Cf. in Judaism the Kabbalist idea that Adam was originally androgynous.

[3] The meaning of this word is doubtful, but it is understood in the second sense by Sāyana.

thropomorphized, it is true, but all to a certain degree transcendent in that they are distinct from the impersonal powers that control Nature. The highest of these was Varuṇa, who guards or protects the impersonal law—his own law which is immutable[1]—and who is therefore regarded as the author of that law, a fully transcendent god then. This idea recedes ever more into the background and the 'law' of Nature gradually ousts its author in importance. God and Matter, the former and the formed, coalesce into a single androgynous One, which, as chaos and female, is the material cause of the universe, and as divisive principle, however expressed, is its efficient cause. For the last time perhaps until the resurgence of theism in the Bhagavad-Gītā this Vedic hymn which we have just quoted, appeals to a principle 'in highest heaven' who alone 'perhaps' knows the riddle of this universe. The Vedic hymns form the grand introduction to the history of Indian theism; but there are many movements in the 'Fantastic Symphony' of Indian religion before the initial theme is again announced.

The Rig-Veda is the oldest portion of the whole corpus of sacred literature which goes by the name of Veda. Beside it there exist three other Vedas; and to each of the four are attached later writings known as Brāhmaṇas, Āraṇyakas, and Upanishads. The first two we can safely ignore since they deal almost exclusively with the sacrificial ritual, the incredibly complex theories that purport to explain it, and the sympathetic magic attached to it. Moreover, these documents, whatever they may have meant to their original authors, are wholly incomprehensible to the modern mind. The Upanishads, however, we cannot ignore; for when the Hindus speak of the Vedas, it is primarily the Upanishads that they mean. The Upanishads constitute the *Vedānta* or 'end of the Veda': they are the basis on which almost all subsequent Indian religious thought is built up.

Unlike the Rig-Veda the Upanishads are philosophical in content, but they do not form a single 'system': they neither give a single consistent interpretation of the universe, nor do they

[1] See A. A. Macdonnell, *Vedic Mythology*, Strassburg, 1897, p. 26.

claim to do so. They are rather the first gropings of the Indian mind in its attempt to find the ultimate ground of the universe. This simple fact has been obscured by the medieval Indian philosophers, each of whom has tried to force consistency on to the Upanishads—a consistency that is always the philosopher's own and into which he vainly tries to force the unwilling texts. It is then refreshing that Professor Surendranath Dasgupta, the foremost authority on Indian philosophy today, has expressed the following view. 'It is necessary,' he writes, 'that a modern interpreter of the Upanishads should turn a deaf ear to the absolute claims of these [ancient] exponents, and look upon the Upanishads not as a systematic treatise but as a depository of diverse currents of thought—the melting-pot in which all later philosophic ideas were still in a state of fusion.'[1] No one who has made a study of the Upanishads without reference to the later commentaries which so obviously distort them, is likely to quarrel with this eminently sound judgement. It is, however, encouraging that India's foremost scholar should state the case so plainly; for the Indian tendency which we have already noticed, to regard different interpretations of reality merely as aspects of one 'truth', has in recent times monopolized Indian thinking in so far as it is popularly presented to the West.[2]

The Upanishads themselves are the reverse of dogmatic, and in them we find the first strivings of the Indian mind towards the formulation of metaphysical concepts. In the history of Indian thought they correspond to the phase represented by Hesiod and the pre-Socratics among the Greeks. The difference, which is enormous, is that the Upanishads became a sacred book, whereas the pre-Socratics did not. One can, however, imagine how great the confusion would have been if the pre-Socratics had been anonymous and if their joint productions had been gathered up into a sacred canon in which Heraclitus

[1] Surendranath Dasgupta, *A History of Indian Philosophy*, Cambridge, 1951, vol. i, p. 42.

[2] This is equally true of the Neo-Vedāntins who derive from Vivekananda, of Coomaraswamy and his disciples Guénon and Schuon, and of Radhakrishnan.

and Parmenides, for instance, would enjoy an equally infallible authority.

The Upanishads, then, can be regarded as the beginning of Indian philosophy. Yet they are more than this, for in them we find insights which cannot possibly be attributed to reason, however primitive, but which must reflect experiences wholly at variance with our normal sense data and anything deducible from them. Take, for example, the following passage:

> 'This Self is the honey of all creatures, and all creatures are the honey of this Self. The Person, composed of brilliance and immortality, who indwells this Self, and this Self, composed of brilliance and immortality, which is [identical with] this Person —this very Self is this immortal (neuter), this Brahman, this All.'[1]

Seemingly this is pantheism with a vengeance:[2] the human soul experiences itself as co-terminous with the whole universe; it is the universe, and the universe is the soul. To the reflecting consciousness this is nonsense, and no amount of meditation on the nature of things could possibly lead to so irrational a conclusion. We can, then, only conclude that such passages as this arise from a radical alteration in the mode of consciousness itself; and because such passages occur again and again throughout the Upanishads, we must again conclude that transformation of consciousness was deliberately sought out with a view to gaining intuitive knowledge of reality. How, then, was this achieved?

India is the homeland of Yoga; and the object of Yoga is, precisely, to produce a radical transformation of consciousness in which our normal perceptions are wholly transcended and in which 'a father becomes no father, a mother no mother, the worlds no worlds, the gods no gods, the Vedas no Vedas'.[3] The Upanishads are primarily philosophical and metaphysical in nature, concerned with the discovery of the eternal ground of the changing universe: Yoga is the practical technique that

[1] *Bṛhadāraṇyaka* Up., 2. 5. 14. [2] But see p. 67.
[3] Ibid., 4. 3. 22.

claims so to transform consciousness that the Yogin can experience a state of being which transcends space and time. The authors of the Upanishads frequently interpreted this state as meaning that the soul, so delivered from the trammels of space and time, *must* itself *be* the ground of all contingent being, thereby drawing a purely metaphysical conclusion from an experience which can, in fact, be more rationally accounted for, as we shall see.

The practice of Yoga most probably preceded the Aryan invasion of India, for among the recent discoveries at Mohenjo Daro there are figurines of a deity sitting in the Yoga position of meditation, reminiscent of later statues of Śiva as the great ascetic. The existence of Yoga as a technique is therefore indisputably very ancient, and although it is rarely mentioned in the Upanishads themselves, it forms, from the beginning, part and parcel of the technique of salvation practised by both the Buddhists and Jains[1] whose philosophy of existence differed substantially from that of the Upanishads. Thus it would appear that Yoga techniques were current in India from the earliest times and were practised by all religious sects. Philosophy took due account of the transformation of consciousness that Yoga could produce and pressed Yoga experience into its service; and the Yogins themselves evolved an empirical philosophy of their own which was far different from that of the Upanishads and runs directly counter to many of their more extravagant conclusions. But basically the aims of Yoga and Upanishadic speculation are poles apart. The one is a psychological technique, the other metaphysical inquiry.

In the Upanishads we have a quasi-rational investigation into the nature of things, the search for the eternal ground of the universe. Simultaneously, in Yoga, we have the search of man for the eternal essence of his own soul, which, it is claimed, can be and actually is experienced by the Yogin in trance. It seems to have been the combination of a rational and reverent inquiry on the one hand and the experiences of Yoga on the

[1] Cf. E. J. Thomas, *The History of Buddhist Thought*, London, 2nd ed., 1951, p. 43.

other that led to the ultimate conclusion, which is undoubtedly the purport of a majority of Upanishadic texts, that the eternal element in the human soul at its deepest level is identical with the ground and origin of the universe. God is man; and man is God, and between the two, as they are in their essence and when stripped of all that is accidental, there is no difference at all. This is the basic conclusion of the Vedānta philosophy in its extreme non-dualist form as interpreted by Śankara in the ninth century A.D.; and this absolute monism is regarded by many in India as being the bald statement of absolute truth. It is as foreign to the Judaic conception of deity as it is possible to be.

In ancient India nothing is datable; nor is it possible to judge the comparative age of a given doctrine even from an approximate dating. Thus we cannot be sure what philosophical system, if any, the Yoga technique was originally designed to serve. We do know, however, that from the earliest times both the Buddhists and Jains made use of this technique, and that within orthodox Hinduism it came to be so closely linked with the Sāṁkhya philosophy that the two were normally classed together as the Sāṁkhya-Yoga. This is significant: for all three systems—Buddhist, Jain, and Sāṁkhya—are atheistical; and for all of them *mokṣa*, 'deliverance', 'emancipation', or 'release' consists simply and solely in freeing the soul from all its physiological and psychological adjuncts. Primitive Buddhism has no metaphysics, and the Buddha therefore refused to speculate on the nature of the released state though he let it be understood that it partook of immortality. Neither the Jains nor the Sāṁkhya-Yogins, however, were so non-committal. For both of them 'release' constituted the release of the individual soul, which was regarded as an eternal monad, having its being outside space and time, from all that is not eternal, that is, from body, emotion, and discursive thought. The bliss of release, then, consisted in isolation (*kaivalyam*), the isolation and insulation of the soul within itself, a timeless enjoyment of a timeless essence. Yoga, then, seems originally to have been a psychological technique for uncovering the immortality of one's own soul in distinction and separation from both the empirical 'ego' and the objective world.

Now, while there is every reason to believe that the Yoga technique started in a milieu that was essentially atheistical, there is little reason to believe that it was adopted into the monistic or pantheistic Vedānta as a means by which the individual could realize himself as Brahman or the 'All' until much later. In the earliest Upanishads there is only one reference to Yoga,[1] and what is meant by the word in that context is quite unclear. The first clear reference to Yoga as a technique appears in the *Kaṭha* Upanishad. 'When the five senses and the mind are stilled,' we read, 'when the intellect is no longer active, that, they say, is the highest course. This they consider to be Yoga, the firm control of the senses. Then does one become undistracted. Yoga indeed is the origin and the end.'[2]

For the *Kaṭha* Upanishad, then, Yoga simply means the 'rigid control of the senses' through which the immortal soul (here called *puruṣa* or 'person') can be uncovered. Similarly in the later *Śvetāśvatara* Upanishad[3] a detailed description of Yoga[3] practices appears for the first time in Upanishadic literature. Here it is claimed that Yoga enables the adept first to see visions:

'Fog, smoke, the sun, fire and wind,
Fireflies, lightning, crystals, the moon—
These are the preliminary forms
Which in Yoga cause revelation in Brahman.'[4]

Then (§ 15) he sees 'the nature of Brahman through the nature of his own soul (*ātman*) [acting as] a lamp'. What precisely is meant by *Brahman* in the *Śvetāśvatara* Upanishad, we shall have to discuss later; but it seems clear that the object of Yoga in

[1] *Taittirīya* Up., 2. 4: Speaking of the 'self that consists of understanding' the Upanishad says: 'Faith is its head; the right its right side; the true its left side; Yoga its vital part (or body, *ātman*); might its lower part or foundation'.

[2] *Kaṭha* Up., 6. 10–11.

[3] 2. 8–15.

[4] § 11:

these Upanishadic passages is the same as that of the atheistical Yoga of the Buddhists, Jains, and Sāṁkhya—namely, the freeing of the immortal substrate of the soul, the *ātman*, from all distractions caused by the bodily senses and the mind, and the consequent experience of a timeless state. For Yoga this is primary, and the partially pantheistic and partially theistic ideology of the two Upanishads in question is largely irrelevant. In time Yoga, as a technique, is used by all the different philosophical schools.

As classically formulated, however, Yoga appears as the technique used for realizing the truth of the so-called Sāṁkhya philosophy: it is the technique whereby it is possible to separate the eternal soul from all its mortal trappings. It is not concerned with God, for there is no God in the Sāṁkhya system. It is truc that in Patañjali's *Yoga-Sūtras*, a being called 'the Lord' is introduced; but this 'Lord', *īśvara*, is not at all what we would call God. Like all other souls he is eternal, but he is not the creator and sustainer of the universe, nor anything like it. He is simply the only soul that never comes into contact with matter and who is thereby able to help other souls out of their bondage to the body. Yet though the *īśvara* of Patañjali is certainly not God, he does prefigure, however dimly, the fully developed divine figure of the Bhagavad-Gītā.

How, then, does the Sāṁkhya-Yoga consider other souls? The Sāṁkhya is as radically dualistic as is Manichaeanism. Reality is two, not one. On the one side is *puruṣa*, the human soul, or rather an infinity of human souls; on the other is *prakṛti*, the world, Nature, matter, or whatever you want to call it. The *puruṣas* or souls are timeless monads: *prakṛti* or Nature has no beginning or end; it is never-ceasing change, the world of time and space as we know it. The two principles should never have come into contact, but they did, though how and why is left absolutely vague. This is an unnatural state of affairs since a timeless being has no business in a temporal world. When in the world it is blinded to its true nature; it identifies itself with the body and this in turn involves it in the endless round of reincarnation. Only when circumstances are favourable will it become aware of its true identity and then it will strive to realize itself in isolation from all that moves in time and space. Its blessedness is described by Patañjali, as by the Jains, as *kaivalyam* 'isolation'—a state in which it contemplates itself as it is, an immortal soul, splendidly isolated and enjoying its own eternity. There is no question of any union with the 'Lord', for he is simply one of many *puruṣas*, though unique in that he never was or can be defiled by contact with Nature.

The Sāṁkhya-Yoga is usually classed as one of the six schools of Indian philosophy. This may lead to misunderstanding; for in so far as the Sāṁkhya analyses the nature of the universe, it falls more properly within the sphere of cosmology, and in so far as it concerns itself with the nature of human personality, it must be classed as a branch of psychology. Indeed the whole idea of the 'self' as distinct from the 'ego' (*puruṣa* and *ahaṁkāra* in the Sāṁkhya system) has now received the blessing of C. G. Jung and the whole school of psychology to which he has given his name. There is, of course, a fundamental difference between Jung and the Sāṁkhya-Yoga since, in Jung's sense of the word, the 'self' is seen indeed as the immortal centre of the human personality, but the aim of his psychological method is not only to bring the self to light and enable it to displace the ego as the directing principle of the total psyche, but also to harmonize the rest of the psyche around this new centre, whereas the aim of the Sāṁkhya-Yoga is to divorce for ever the immortal self from all purely spatio-temporal elements in the psyche. Jung sees the process as 'individuation' or 'integration of the personality': the Sāṁkhya-Yogin sees it as the 'isolation' of the 'person'—for that is what *puruṣa* means—from the psychophysical envelope which surrounds him. However, Jung, without any reference to revealed religion, declares that 'the self as such is timeless and existed before any birth'.[1] 'This,' he adds, 'is not a metaphysical statement but a psychological fact.'

By 'psychological fact' Jung appears to mean that the immortality of the soul is not something that we merely accept on

[1] C. G. Jung, *Psychology of the Transference*, in *Collected Works*, xvi, p. 184.

trust from religion or metaphysics; it is something that can be experienced here and now. Jungian psychology, in fact, revives ancient Indian religion; and this will serve to illustrate the point we have already made, namely, that Indian religion, at least as it appears in Buddhism and the Sāṁkhya-Yoga, is not interested primarily in the nature of God but in the nature and immortality of the human soul. The Indians were trying to systematize an experience which may occur to anyone, which frequently does occur to people when undergoing the manic phase of a manic-depressive psychosis, and which can on occasion be artificially produced by the use of drugs—the experience of a second self within one which is quite distinct from the ego and is felt to be immortal. All higher Indian religion is concerned with this experience; and what Indian religion is for ever trying to do is to forge a link between the objective world and the consciousness of immortality which is latent in all men. This consciousness is called *mokṣa* or 'release' by the Hindus, *nirvāṇa* or 'blowing out' by the Buddhists. In each case it means release from, or the blowing out of, phenomenal existence. 'Personality' is not integrated as with Jung: it is released from the embrace of the phenomenal world and the ego. This, for the Indian, is the prime function of religion: the question of the existence and nature of God is, when all is said and done, of secondary importance.

In most forms of mysticism this discovery of the immortality of the soul plays an important part, but it can never be the final goal of Christian mysticism as it is of Sāṁkhya-Yogin or Buddhist 'mysticism'. For Christian and indeed all theistic mystics claim to experience not only the immortality of the individual soul but also the union of that soul with God, who is not, as in the non-dualist Vedānta, identical with the soul. The realization of the immortality of one's soul is not the same as what is sometimes called nature mysticism. The latter is a phenomenon which is widely attested throughout the world and is basic to much Upanishadic thought. The former is basic to Buddhism and the Sāṁkhya-Yoga and has recently been restated by Jung. Examples of it are not very common in Wthe est, but they are not unknown. The clearest example that has crossed my path is that of Proust.

I have dealt at some length with the case of Proust elsewhere,[1] but it is so illuminating that I venture to quote some of the relevant passages again.

Throughout the length of Proust's great novel passages occur which seem unconnected with the main theme of the book, but which nevertheless are intensely significent, for they are sure intimations of immortality. It is only at the end of the book, however, when the author describes how he is about to enter the Hôtel de Guermantes that this feeling of certain immortality strikes him with such force that, in retelling the story, he is forced to step back and pause, to take the measure of this wonder, and to try to analyse its nature.

The first occurrence of the theme is in the episode of 'la petite madeleine' in *Du Côté de chez Swann.* Very little is said, but that little is enough to make the attentive reader sit up with a renewed interest, for Proust seems to be describing precisely what Jung was later to analyse and what the Indians had long ago systematically formulated, I mean, the discovery of the immortal 'self' or soul as an experienced fact beneath the transitory, officious ego.

The occasion of the experience is trifling as it so frequently is; and it is worth mentioning in this connexion that one school of Zen Buddhists in Japan teaches that quite trivial causes may serve as the occasion for the coming of that sense of ineffable bliss in an eternal 'now' which they call *satori*. Be that as it may, all that happened in Proust's case was that he dipped a bun into his tea and raised it to his lips. In so doing 'at the very moment when the mouthful [of tea] mixed with the crumbs of the cake touched my palate, I shuddered, taking note, as I did so, of the strange things that were going on inside me. An exquisite pleasure had invaded me—isolated—I had no idea what its cause might be. Immediately it had made the vicissitudes of life seem indifferent, its disasters harmless, its brevity illusory—operating much as love operates, filling me with a precious

[1] R. C. Zaehner, *Mysticism Sacred and Profane,* Oxford, 1957, pp. 50–61.

essence: or rather this essence was not *in* me, it *was* me. I had ceased to feel mediocre, contingent, or mortal. Whence should this strong joy have come to me? I felt that it was connected with the taste of the tea and the cake, but that it transcended it infinitely and could not be of the same nature. Whence did it come? What did it mean? How to lay hold of it?'[1]

Let me emphasize the words: 'It had made the vicissitudes of life seem indifferent, its disasters harmless, its brevity illusory . . . filling me with a precious essence; or rather this essence was not *in* me, it *was* me.' Here Proust describes what Jung was later to call the 'transference'—the surrender by the ego of the control of the psyche to a higher centre which he calls the self. Proust's 'precious essence' is none other than this 'self', the immortal centre of the human psyche. This is seen or rather felt to be the real self or personality, the discovery of which makes 'the vicissitudes of life seem indifferent, its disasters harmless, its brevity illusory'. The discovery of this precious essence, which is our second self, is nothing less than the experienced certainty of our own immortality. That Proust himself felt this to be so is clear enough from the passage we have just quoted. It becomes even more clear in *Le Temps Retrouvé* in which he tries to analyse the nature of the experience more closely. Meditating on a later experience in which nothing more extraordinary than the unevenness of some paving-stones at the entrance to the Hôtel de Guermantes was enough to bring to life in him, in its full actuality, an answering sensation felt on the steps of the Baptistery in Florence in days long past, Proust realizes that the subject experiencing the identity of these impressions as if they were both equally present here and now, must be different from the subject of normal sense-experience which is conditioned by time and space and the outside world. 'This' strange 'being', he says, 'would only appear at a time when, through one of those identities between the present and the past, it could exist in the only atmosphere in which it could live and enjoy the essence of things, that is to say, outside time. That explained why my pre-

[1] *A la Recherche du Temps perdu*, Paris, Bibliothèque de la Pléiade, Gallimard, 1954, vol. i, p. 45.

occupation with death should have ceased at the moment when, unconsciously, I recognized the taste of the little bun; for at that moment the being that I had been was an extra-temporal being and therefore careless of the vicissitudes of the future.'[1] 'This being,' Proust goes on to say, 'feeds on nothing but the essence of things, in them alone it finds its subsistence and its delight.... It suffices that a sound once heard before, or a scent once breathed in, should be heard and breathed again, simultaneously in the present and the past, real without being actual, ideal without being abstract; then, immediately, the permanent essence of things which is usually hidden, is set free, and our real self, which often had seemed long dead, yet was not dead altogether, awakes and comes to life as it receives the heavenly food now proffered to it. One minute delivered from the order of time creates in us . . . the man delivered from the order of time. How easy to understand that this man should be confident in his joy, even if the mere taste of a bun may not seem, logically, to contain within itself the reasons for that joy. It is understandable that the word "death" can have no meaning for him: situated, as he is, outside time, what could he fear from the future?'[2]

In this experience Proust had transcended time and space. It is understandable, then, that for such a one death can have no meaning, for in an eternal present, an eternal 'now', there can be neither before nor after, there can be neither birth nor death. Moments such as these are experienced more often perhaps than is generally realized. People who have experienced them feel a natural reticence about them, for who would understand what was meant—who, that is, in a Christian and post-Christian Europe where the experience of immortality is no longer considered the proper province of religion? Yet any practising Buddhist or Hindu would know, immediately and instinctively, what Proust was trying to say. How evident it would be to the Buddhist that this state in which the word 'death' could have no meaning could only be that 'deathless-

[1] Ibid., vol. iii, p.871.
[2] Ibid., pp. 872–3.

ness, peace, the unchanging state of Nirvāṇa',[1] 'the utter extinction of ageing and dying'[2] described by their Master. In this state, too, the Sāṁkhya-Yogin would recognize the freeing of the immortal *puruṣa* from the cloying embrace of *prakṛti*, that is, the body, the senses, intellect, and mind. That this state is one of bliss is attested not only by the unanimous witness of the Hindu and Buddhist scriptures but by all the nature mystics who have enjoyed similar experiences. Many such experiences have been listed in my *Mysticism Sacred and Profane*, and more could without difficulty be adduced.

Proust's experience, however, is not by any means identical with that of the nature mystics: for in his case there is no sense of the loss of personality, there is rather the sense of one personality being replaced by another, of the empirical ego handing over control to the eternal 'self', or, in Sāṁkhya terms, the *ahaṁkāra* handing over to the *puruṣa*. And it is not without significance that the immortal soul is called precisely *puruṣa*, that is, the 'Person'. This is what Jung calls 'integration', whereas nature mysticism, as usually experienced, denotes rather an expansion of the personality in which the distinction between subject and object seems to be obliterated. This Jung calls positive inflation. Proust, on the other hand, claims to have realized another 'self' distinct from the ego as being immortal; and his experience, so far from giving him an inflated idea of his 'ego', caused him to doubt the very existence of that entity.[3] This seems to be the authentic Sāṁkhya-Yogin experience, the separation and isolation of the self or soul from all temporal things, both from the world and from carnal man. The achievement of such a state as this is the goal of the Yoga technique; and seen in this light, it is not difficult to understand why the Indians have persisted in this practice for at least three thousand years.

[1] *Suttanipāta*, 204, *apud* E. Conze, *Buddhist Texts through the Ages*, Oxford, 1954, p. 93.

[2] Ibid., 1094, *apud* Conze, ibid.

[3] *A la Recherche du Temps perdu*, vol. iii, p. 873: 'Instead of taking a more flattering view of my ego, I had, on the contrary, almost doubted the actual reality of the ego.'

Proust's experience may be taken as an example of the realization by a modern European of the state of immortal isolation which is the goal of the Sāṁkhya and Jain, and probably of the Buddhist too. The Upanishads, on the other hand, in so far as they are dependent on experience and not merely metaphysical speculation, seem to be far more akin to nature mysticism proper or what I have elsewhere called the pan-en-henic experience, in which the experiencing subject seems to merge into the experienced object, often generalized as the 'All'. Cases of *this* experience could be quoted from all over the world and from all periods of history; and the basic element in the experience seems to be that the sense of mortal and individual life is lost in the everlasting life of Nature as a whole. By identifying himself with the totality of living things the mystic thereby partakes in the undifferentiated life of all things and achieves an immortality which is in no sense personal, as it emphatically is in the Sāṁkhya-Yoga, but which seems to dissolve personality in an infinitely greater whole. These two distinct 'intimations of immortality' seem to meet in the following experience which is described in a letter from Tennyson to William James:[1]

'A kind of waking trance—this for lack of a better word—I have frequently had, quite up from boyhood, when I have been all alone. This has come upon me through repeating my own name to myself silently, till all at once, as it were out of the intensity of the consciousness of individuality, individuality itself seemed to dissolve and fade away into boundless being, and this not a confused state but the clearest, the surest of the surest, utterly beyond words—where death was an almost laughable impossibility—the loss of personality (if so it were) seeming no extinction, but the only true life.'

It is worth noting in passing that this state of blissful depersonalization was produced in Tennyson by the repetition of his own name. This religio-magical technique is known to all

[1] William James, *The Varieties of Religious Experience*, revised ed., London, 1919, p. 384.

religions, and is used to empty the mind of all worrying distractions, thereby stilling consciousness and making way for the emergence of the contents of what Jung calls the collective unconscious and William James called the mystical or cosmic consciousness. The Hesychasts achieved much the same result by the repetition of the name of Jesus, the Muslim mystics or Ṣūfīs by the perpetual recitation of the name of Allah, whereas the Hindus preferred to repeat the sacred syllable 'Oṁ' or some more extended magical formula or *mantra*. The same effect can be produced in Catholics by the recitation of the Rosary. The result consciously or unconsciously desired is to empty the conscious mind of all distracting thought in order to allow free entrance to the divine or what is held to be such.

In the case of Tennyson we have the same sense of immortality that we have already met with in Proust, the same state in which 'death was an almost laughable impossibility', and in addition we have the loss of personality ('if so it was', as Tennyson cautiously adds). This loss of personality, interpreted as a dissolving and fading away into boundless being, clearly distinguishes Tennyson's experience from that of Proust. In Proust's case the 'ego', that is, the *ahaṁkāra* of the Sāṁkhya system, gives way to 'un autre moi', another ego or self 'which feeds on nothing but the essence of things', dwells 'outside time', and is therefore immortal. But, for Proust, this *alter ego*, though distinct from the everyday subject of sense experience and discursive thought, is none the less personal. It is Proust's own *puruṣa*, his own 'Person', experienced as it is—eternal. It is quite exactly what the Sāṁkhya-Yoga understands by *puruṣa*—an eternal monad that has its essential being outside the phenomenal world of space and time. In Tennyson's case, on the other hand, personality seems to 'dissolve and fade away into boundless being', the individual soul is lost in the 'All', in the everlasting life of Nature in which it shares. This is quite foreign to the categories of the Sāṁkhya-Yoga, but finds the closest parallels in the Upanishads as we shall very shortly see.

This type of experience which generally goes by the name of nature mysticism and which I have elsewhere classified as 'pan-en-henic'—the experience of all as one and one as all—is so characteristic of much Upanishadic writing that we will allow ourselves to quote one contemporary example. Anyone interested in further instances of this well-nigh universal phenomenon may refer to William James's chapter on mysticism in his *Varieties of Religious Experience* and to chapters III–V of my own *Mysticism Sacred and Profane*. The following, however, may be taken as typical:

'I sat up in bed to look out of the long window directly opposite, and I watched the lights reflected in the narrow muddy streets of this little town. I thought of Charles Lamb's pleasure in lamplight and wet streets, when suddenly—a translucent, glowing, white-blue mist had blotted out this world and all experience of my sojourn on it. With the mist came ineffable peace and joy.

'I was unaware of personality. I didn't think: thought is limited by language, words and condition. I was all consciousness, feeling, awareness, but unconditioned, if "I" could be called "I" then.

'One can hardly describe an experience in which one is caught up into—what? Something I had never read of, meditated on, or knew existed—as an unborn child couldn't realize a description of this world.

'The mist became denser, and with the deepening the knowledge, reassurance, radiance, peace—in fact ecstasy also deepened, until "I" seemed to be "It" and "It" seemed to be "I". We were merged, transfused, interpenetrated.

' "I", my personality, had fallen away—where? A puzzle, leaving a throb of bliss within a throb. *Satisfying* is the embracive word.

'All consciousness, awareness, and yet when I came back there were no incidents to relate. When merged, I was in all that had been, was, and would be; I realize now that man measures space and time, nothing is after or before but simultaneous, it is all there.

'Suddenly, the mist, the glow, had disappeared as it came.

I was still sitting upright in bed holding the sheet, my eyes wide open, and gazing at the lights in the street.

'My first thought was: "Well, beneath everything there is this calm, joy, assurance; perhaps it is the 'everlasting arms'?" Then a curious thing happened. I looked at the world outside my window, felt the furniture in my room, and said "How queer, this is a shadow world. I have touched the Real and what is always 'there'—all this world I have known will now be unreal. Why is it here? To experience what?" I lay down to sleep and awoke unusually rested. Body and mind were refreshed, I understood the feeling "as though cleansed in dew". All events on this planet will be as ripples on the sea, the calm is ever beneath. How is it possible to be perturbed again? (Needless to say, I often am perturbed, maybe not so much as formerly.)'[1]

To anyone at all familiar with the Upanishads and the later writings that depend on them this passage must appear as striking confirmation of what they say, for we find here, in a letter written by a lady in the twentieth century in England, not only the basic doctrine laid down in the Upanishads, but the very terminology used by them to describe the state of ultimate bliss. 'Brahman is the Real, knowledge, infinite',[2] we read. So too our source experienced 'It' as 'the Real', knowledge', and as 'all that had been, was, and would be'. Again the classic formulation of Brahman in the later Vedānta is *Sac-cid-ānanda*, 'Being, awareness-consciousness-knowledge, bliss'; and in our present text we read: 'The mist became denser, and with the deepening the *knowledge*, reassurance, radiance, peace—in fact *ecstasy* also deepened until "I" seemed to be "It" and "It" seemed to be "I".'

All the salient words go straight into Sanskrit, representing as they do the key conceptions of the Upanishads; yet, as she herself informs us, the lady in question had never read about or meditated on what she now directly experienced. In her case it is significant that there is absolutely no sense of the presence of

[1] From a letter of Miss Dorothea Spinney of Felden, Boxmore, Herts.

[2] *Taittirīya* Up., 2. 1. 1.

a personal God: she seems to be 'It', not 'He', and in the Upanishads the Brahman, when not mentioned by name, is simply referred to as *tat*, 'that' or 'it'—'That art thou'.[1] So too when she speaks of 'knowledge' she plainly means intuitive knowledge beyond discursive thought, a concept that appears in the Upanishads as *jñāna*, *vijñāna*, or *prajñāna*. 'Reassurance' again is *niścaya* which means 'certainty of a truth experienced'. 'Radiance' is *tejas*, and 'peace' *śānti*, a term with which Mr. T. S. Eliot has familiarized us and which is the keynote of the Upanishads.

The symbolism of light is, of course, common to all mystics, and Miss Spinney's experience is heralded by a 'translucent, glowing, white-blue mist'. So too we read in the Upanishads:

> 'In the highest golden sheath
> Is Brahman without stain or part:
> Brilliant is It, the light of lights;[2]
> Who knows the Self knows It.
>
> The sun does not shine there, nor yet the moon and stars,
> Nor do these lightnings shine [there], much less mere fire.
> It shines and all things shine in its reflected light;
> Its light illumines this whole [world].'[3]

It seems then plain that what Miss Spinney experienced was Brahman. But what is Brahman? In the purely speculative passages the Upanishads try to find a concrete and definite answer, but in those passages which identify the 'self' or soul with Brahman, the latter is usually left undefined, or is identified with the 'All'. The Upanishads are strewn with these intimations of a cosmic immortality, a break-through into the individual consciousness of a 'cosmic consciousness'—of what Jung perversely persists in calling the collective *un*conscious.[4] To

[1] *Chāndogya* Up., 6. 8. 6 ff.

[2] Cf. *Bṛhadāraṇyaka* Up., 4. 4. 16.

[3] *Muṇḍaka* Up., 2. 2. 9–10. Cf. *Kaṭha*, 5. 15: *Śvetāśvatara*, 6. 14.

[4] Samadhi, an ecstatic condition that seems to be equivalent to an unconscious state. The fact that they call our unconscious the universal consciousness, does not change things in the least. . . . They do not realize that a "universal" consciousness is a contradiction in terms.' *The Integration of the Personality*, London, 1940, p. 26.

show how exactly parallel their thought and feeling are to that of the passage we are now considering, we cannot do otherwise than quote at some length.

On the identity of 'I' and 'It' we read:

'In the beginning this [world] was Brahman. It took cognizance of itself, "I am Brahman". Therefore it became that All. Whosoever of the gods became aware of this, became that [Brahman]. So too in the case of seers, and so too in the case of men. . . . This is so now also. Whoso knows, "I am Brahman", becomes this All. Not even the gods have the power to prevent him becoming thus, for such a one becomes their own self (or soul, *ātman*).[1]

Here the phenomenon of nature mysticism in which individuality is lost and merged into the 'All' is projected on to mythology. This merging into the infinite, so characteristic of Upanishadic thought, is interpreted by Jung as a repetition of an essentially infantile phenomenon in which the child, conscious of itself as a separate entity for the first time, sinks back, blissfully, into a state of undifferentiated oneness with its mother;[2] this, it appears, is the significance of 'becoming the All'. It seems, however, far more likely that this type of experience is rather to be interpreted as what Jung himself calls the integration of the personality, the subsuming of the purely mortal parts of the psyche—ego, feeling, thought, etc.—into the immortal self or *ātman*. This would appear to be the obvious interpretation of the following passage, for example. 'He who recognizes that radiant imperishable [essence] which has neither shadow, body, nor blood, attains to that imperishable [essence]. He becomes omniscient and whole. . . . He who recognizes that imperishable [essence] on which the conscious self with all its powers, the life-breaths, and the elements rest, becomes omniscient and penetrates all.'[3] This seems more comprehensible than the passage from the *Bṛhadāraṇyaka*, for the text does not say

[1] *Bṛhadāraṇyaka* Up., 1. 4. 10.
[2] *Psychology of the Unconscious*, London, 1919, p. 199.
[3] *Praśna* Up., 4, 10–11.

'becomes this all (*idaṁ sarvam*), but 'becomes all, entire, or whole, (*sarvo*, masc. agreeing with the subject). 'This can surely only mean the integration of the conscious mind with what Jung calls the self, here called 'the imperishable'. That the experience is not a simple retroversion to embryonic unconsciousness seems proved from what the nature mystics have always said from the Upanishads to the present day. According to them there is nothing blurred or indistinct about this experience; it is not a lapse into the unconscious, but 'the only true life', 'the Real', for 'Brahman is consciousness (*prajñāna*)',[1] or again it is 'intelligence (*vijñāna*) and bliss',[2] 'the Real',[3] and 'the Real of the Real';[4] and this Real is one's true self.[5]

Modern Hindus interpret this experience as being a shift to a 'higher' form of consciousness—super-consciousness as they sometimes call it—in which all is seen as one. Yet, obviously, to say 'I am this All' at any level of consciousness is really nonsense. It can only mean that the objective world is so thoroughly grasped and 'seen' by the mind that the latter makes the 'seen' image part of itself. The problem was not unknown to Aristotle and he solved it in the following way.

'Let us repeat,' he says, 'the soul is in a certain sense all existing things, and existing things are either objects of sense or objects of intellection. The understanding is in a sense the objects understood and sense-perception is the things perceived. Just how this is so, must now be investigated.

'Intellection and sense-perception share between them all objects, potential intellection and perception relating to things potential, actual to things actual. Now the faculties of sense-perception and intellection in the soul are potentially their objects, that is, objects of perception and intellection respectively. They must then be identical either with the objects themselves or with their forms (εἴδη). But they cannot be identi-

[1] *Aitareya* Up., 5. 3.
[2] *Bṛhadāraṇyaka* Up., 3. 9. 28.
[3] Ibid., 5. 4. 1.: *Chāndogya*, 6. 8. 7., etc.
[4] *Bṛhadāraṇyaka* Up., 2. 1. 20.
[5] *Chāndogya* Up., 6. 8. 7 ff.

cal with the objects themselves, for it is not the stone [itself] which is in the soul, but the form [of the stone].'[1]

Seen in this light the well-nigh unanimous testimony of the nature mystics to the effect that 'I am this All' or that 'without and within are one' becomes a little more comprehensible. The 'All', or rather the 'form' of the All is directly—existentially, if you like—grasped by the mind or senses, and a powerful sense of ontological identity thereby arises: knower and known become one.

Identity of subject and object, of Brahman and *ātman*, is usually considered to be the general purport of the Upanishads, but even in the passages we have quoted, we have seen that this is an over-simplification. This seems particularly true in the passage quoted from the *Praśna* where the recognition of the imperishable results in personal integration rather than in self-identification with the external world. Yet in many passages this self-identification is undoubtedly there; and this is not surprising, for however we may choose to explain the problem, it reflects a fully authenticated and world-wide experience. Perhaps its clearest and most extreme formulation is to be found in *Kauṣītakī* Upanishad I. 6. The soul of the recently dead is being questioned by the god Brahmā (not to be confused with the neuter Brahman):

'Him Brahmā asks: "Who art thou?" To him he should reply: "I am a season, connected with the seasons, produced from the womb of space as seed for a wife, as the brilliance of the year, as the soul (*ātman*) of every being. Thou [thyself] art the soul of every being. What thou art, that am I."

'To him he says, "Who am I?"

'He should say: "The Real."

' "What is the Real?" . . .

' "It is co-extensive with this All. This All art thou." '

This is pantheistic monism with a vengeance, the *reductio ad absurdum*, almost, of the natural mystical experience. God, the

[1] Aristotle, *De Anima*, iii, 8, 1–2 (431b).

world and the human soul are all one and the same: everything is everything else, and there is no distinction anywhere. Yet it is fatally easy to interpret these experiences in this way, for the nature mystic has the overwhelming conviction that this is what the experience actually is. This he further rationalizes by comparing his experience to that of sleep in which the world, which at the time of dreaming appears to be objective, is really part of himself.[1]

The collocation of Upanishadic passages with the actual experiences of modern nature mystics shows beyond the possibility of reasonable doubt that nature mysticism was at least one of the things with which the Upanishads were vitally concerned. There is no reason at all to suppose that this type of experience which, as we have seen, so often comes unheralded and unasked, was ever peculiar to India. What does, however, distinguish India from other lands is that the Indian sages saw in this experience the ultimate goal of religion, and in Yoga perfected a technique by which both this pan-en-henic experience and the experience of the isolation of the eternal in man (the experience of Proust) could be achieved. Both experiences are varieties of self-realization, the realization of the vast potentialities of the human psyche.

In the Christian West, on the other hand, religion has been primarily concerned with what is deemed to be a divine revelation and with the correct interpretation of the content of that revelation. The quarrels of historical Christianity have always been quarrels of interpretation: they have been dogmatic quarrels. It is true that the Eastern Church has laid less stress on the business of defining mysteries than has the Church of Rome and that it fostered the contemplative life far more actively in the early Christian centuries. In this respect Christian life has been greatly weakened by the Great Schism, for Latin clarity was just as much in need of the Greek contemplative spirit as was this of the Latin love of order. Had the Orthodox Church remained in union with the Great Church of the West,

[1] Cf. *Praśna*, 4. 5 etc. A discussion of the Upanishadic theory of sleep would unfortunately lead us too far from our present theme.

it would have made our approach to Indian religion very much easier; for whereas no religion in which revelation is not married to direct experience, can be fully satisfying, so can experience, when divorced from revelation, often lead to absurd and wholly irrational excesses.

This is perhaps the great weakness of Hinduism, and it is a weakness which tends to become more heavily emphasized by the Hindus themselves as they once again become conscious of the intrinsic worth of their religious inheritance. I have called lack of precision in religious belief a weakness; and the mere fact that I speak in this way shows that I am conditioned by my own beliefs. To the Hindu it would seem quite otherwise. Instinctively he reacts against the divisive, categorizing function of the intellect, against what Jung calls the male principle in the human psyche. For him religion is primarily a matter of experience, and religious ceremonies are useful only in so far as they promote experience, in so far as they release psychic energy, to use the Jungian phrase. It is true that revelation also has its part to play; but it is never felt that the revealed texts are in conflict with Yogic experience; they merely supply a convenient variety of philosophical interpretation of that experience, since the Upanishads themselves are also concerned with experience. They do not teach you very much about God, but they do teach you a great deal about the immortality of the soul and the Absolute.

The Hindu often starts from the assumption that the ultimate truths of religion are not expressible in words and that the goal of all religions is therefore probably the same. 'With numerous coherent symbols the same knowledge is revered. All people, whatever their cult, station, or way of life, who are inwardly at peace, attain to the same state (*bhāva*), as rivers (flowing into) the sea.'[1] Hence their large tolerance and their genuine puzzlement at the furious controversies that have from time to time wracked the whole fabric of Christianity. Though the philosophic interpretation of religious experience may vary, and though the philosophers may have some hard things to say

[1] *Anugītā*, 918–19.

about one another, it is rarely felt that a rival philosophy is wholly false: rather it is another point of view, another way of looking at the same truth. This large tolerance is dictated by the nature of the Hindu sacred books themselves; for the Upanishads which concern themselves primarily with the nature of the universe and of its first cause, offer not one but many solutions to this vexatious riddle. Revelation is not consistent with itself.

The principal solutions propounded by the Upanishads are as follows:

(a) the universe and human souls proceed from God as their material cause and are pervaded by God. God is the 'Inner Controller'[1] of the universe and of human souls;

(b) soul, God, and the world are identical;

(c) the human soul and God are identical, and the universe is an illusion.[2]

The Upanishads, then, are primarily theological treatises if by God we understand the First Cause or Divine Ground of the universe. In this respect their approach to reality is radically different from that of the Sāṁkhya-Yoga; for the Upanishads are for ever searching for the unifying principle of the universe, whereas the Sāṁkhya-Yoga, which is unabashedly dualistic, declares that no such unifying principle exists and that salvation consists in disentangling and isolating the immortal soul from everything that goes to make up 'this All'. True, the Upanishads too are interested in self-realization, but the self for them is not an isolated monad but is, in some sense, 'one' with the Absolute, the ground of the universe from which all else proceeds. What the Absolute is and what is the nature of this 'oneness' is the object of inquiry which the Upanishads set themselves.

What is Brahman? That is the question from which all the

[1] *Bṛhadāraṇyaka* Up., 3. 7. 3–23.

[2] This is the theme of the late *Māṇḍūkya* Upanishad where it is explicit. In no other Upanishad is this theme clearly enunciated. The doctrine of an illusory world is foreign to the earlier Upanishads.

Upanishads start. The original meaning of the word *Brahman* is still hotly disputed, and it would be immensely interesting and important if comparative philology could settle once for all the etymology of the word, for we would then be in a position to understand with some precision what it was that these earliest sages were seeking. Since none of the etymologies offered, however, has met with universal acceptance, we can say little more than that the word, in the earliest period, is used to mean 'sacred action', 'ceremony', 'rite', and by extension 'prayer'. 'In India the word was narrowed to "the ceremonial behaviour and acts of priests at sacrifices", or briefly "rite"; it was further restricted to "the recitations that accompanied and formed part of ritual acts", whence "sacred texts".'[1] As in the period immediately preceding that of the Upanishads, that of the Brāhmaṇas, the sacrificial rite came to be regarded as a re-enactment of the primal sacrifice of the Supreme Being from which all creation and all multiplicity proceeded, the *Brahman* came to mean the process of the cosmic sacrifice itself and therefore, by extension, the mysterious power that keeps the universe in being. By the time of the Upanishads *Brahman* means the unchanging law that subsists throughout change. In the Upanishads themselves it is also charged with that quality which Rudolf Otto called the 'numinous' and which writers on comparative religion, universalizing a Melanesian concept, habitually call *mana*.

For the writers of the earlier Upanishads it is plain that the word was also understood in the sense of the primal *matter* of the universe. The idea is very much nearer to the 'primal matter' of Aristotle than it is to the Judaeo-Christian concept of deity. This becomes quite clear when we consider the earliest definitions of Brahman; for sometimes we find that it is identified with food, at other times it is identified with breath. Obviously if one starts with the preconception that Brahman means an immanent God, the identification of it with food will appear

[1] W. B. Henning, 'Bráhman', in *Transactions of the Philological Society*, 1944, p. 116. Henning makes out his case by comparing the etymological cognates in Iranian languages.

grotesque. This is, however, not the way that theology starts in India. The Upanishadic sages, having dethroned the ancient gods, started off with no idea of God at all; they simply felt instinctively that the multiplicity of the phenomenal world could not be ultimate, that beneath diversity there must be unity of a sort. In some ways they were more 'scientific' than the earliest Greek thinkers, for they did not arbitrarily select a given natural element and assert, contrary to all the evidence, that that (fire, water, or air or whatever it might be) was the primal matter of all things. Rather they sought a constant in change, and such a constant they found in the never-ending process of eating and being eaten.

This groping after a material Absolute seems to be the result of Indian man's first realization of himself as a separate conscious entity. It is his first attempt to re-establish the broken link between a newly self-conscious individual and the world from which he has sprung. For, according to the anthropologists and psychologists, primitive man is very much less aware of his distinction from his environment than we are; and this would seem to be true. The primitive Indians certainly felt this strongly. Where, however, they seem to differ from other primitives is that when once they became fully conscious as individuals, they were not prepared to accept the fact. Individual consciousness did not seem to them the unqualified good it so often seems to us. The primitive state of what Lévy-Bruehl called *participation mystique* was altogether to be preferred. Individuality means responsibility, and it must be a shattering experience for primitive man to stand for the first time outside the tribe and realize that he is an individual living soul, alone. The experience is movingly recounted in mythical form in the *Bṛhadāraṇyaka* Upanishad:

'In the beginning this [world] was a Self (*ātman*) alone in the form of a man (*puruṣa*). Looking round he saw nothing other than himself. First he said: "I am." . . . He was afraid.'[1]

Here is depicted the decisive moment in the psychological

[1] *Bṛhadāraṇyaka* Up., 1. 4. 1–2.

history of Indian man, the moment when individuality is realized and the fear that that realization engenders. So far from welcoming the discovery, the Indian sages lost no time in seeking to restore the shattered unity. And so it was that from the earliest Upanishadic times they sought for some principle which was eternal and which transcended individuality: for individuality means individual life, and individual life leads always and inevitably to its opposite, death, whereas to revert to the primal state where all was one means eternal life; and eternal life was, from the earliest Upanishadic period right up to the present day, the prime concern of Indian religion. So we read in what must be one of the earliest passages:

> From the unreal lead me to the real;
> From darkness lead me to light;
> From death lead me to immortality.'[1]

How utterly different from the Book of Genesis! For in Genesis Adam is created immortal and loses eternal life for himself and his descendants by sinning. Once sin has entered the world, history begins and in history there is no immortality. To the authors of the Upanishads the problem appears quite differently. Man suddenly realizes that he is mortal; but this is a condition he refuses to accept. 'From death lead me to immortality' is not a cry of despair: it is a prayer heavy with hope. For early Indian man was aware, even at this stage, that there is something in man that does not die. This something cannot be the body or the ego which experiences through the bodily senses, for both these obviously do die. It must then be sought elsewhere. In the earlier Upanishads we witness, perhaps for the first time in history, the search of man for his immortal soul.

As might well be expected his first gropings are sometimes childish. Sometimes they are quite incomprehensible to the modern mind; yet always they are gropings after something that does not perish. To us the proposition that 'Brahman is food' sounds outrageous or ridiculous, depending on our mood. It is neither: for in it we can discern the effort of primitive man

[1] Ibid., I. 3. 28.

to find something in life that does not die. Life, he correctly saw, depends on food, and when any living creature stops eating, it dies, and in its turn is devoured by some other living thing. So, they thought, though individuals ever perish and are reborn in another form, the principle that keeps them in existence is food. Eating means to assimilate and to be eaten means to be assimilated into another and greater whole: it is to transcend individuality and therefore death. 'One should not despise food. That is the rule.' as one passage half-humorously points out.[1]

The following passage is typical of this type of speculation. It is childish if you like and sometimes quite incomprehensible to our modern minds, but the underlying idea is clear:

'When the Father engendered the seven kinds of food by intellect and austerity, one kind was common to all, two he distributed to the gods, three he made for himself, and one he bestowed on animals. On this [food] are all things grounded (*pratiṣṭhitam*), both what breathes and what does not. Why is it that these things do not perish though they are being eaten all the time? He who knows this imperishableness eats food with the mouth. He goes to the gods; he lives by strength.'[2]

Food is the mystery of imperishableness or immortality; it is the ground of all things. On it 'all things are grounded, both what breathes and what does not'. In the *Taittirīya* Upanishad the same idea is further developed, much of the Upanishad being devoted to Brahman as food:

'From food indeed are creatures engendered,
Whatever creatures dwell on earth.
Then again by food they live
And again pass into it at the end.
For food is the chief of beings,
Whence it is called the elixir of all things.
Whoso reverences Brahman as food
Gains all food:

[1] *Taittirīya* Up., 3. 7. [2] *Bṛhadāraṇyaka* Up., 1. 5. 1.

For food is the chief of beings,
Whence it is called the elixir of all things.
From food are [all] creatures engendered;
When born by food do they grow up.
It is eaten and eats [all] creatures.
Therefore is it called food (an-na=eatable).'[1]

Food is basic to all life; it is an eternal process of eating and being eaten. It is the material and essential substrate of the universe whence breath, mind, intelligence, and bliss, all of which are in turn identified with Brahman, proceed.[2] Breath depends on food and therefore '*is* food. The body is an eater of food. The body is dependent (*pratiṣṭhitam*) on breath, and breath is dependent on the body. So food is dependent on food.'[3] Food, then, is little more than another word for matter, and is the *material* absolute from which life (*prāṇa*, 'breath') and mind proceed. The *Taittirīya* Upanishad is the first known document in which the principles of dialectical materialism are sketched out millennia before Marx and Engels were ever heard of. 'Brahman is food.'[4] This, for the primitive Indian as for the modern Marxist, is an electrifying message. It means that all things are in mutual relation and that there is no death since the death of one individual gives life to another in a whole that is continuously alive. When this is realized, death becomes, as Tennyson said in another context, 'an almost laughable impossibility', and those who realize this are then free to join in that extraordinary paean of joy with which the Upanishad concludes:

'O rapture, O rapture, O rapture!
I am food, I am food, I am food!
I am an eater of food, I am an eater of food, I am an eater of food!
I am a maker of verses, I am a maker of verses, I am a maker of verses!

[1] *Taittirīya* Up., 2. 2.
[2] Ibid., 2. 2–5: 3. 1–6.
[3] Ibid., 3. 7.
[4] Ibid., 3. 1.

I am the first-born of the universal order,
Earlier than the gods, in the navel of immortality!
Whoso gives me away, he, verily, has succoured me!
I, who am food, eat the eater of food!
I have overcome the whole world!'[1]

Thus when Indian thought first comes to grips with the serious problem of what Brahman actually is, it grasps at what is most concrete—food, the 'bread of life' on which life itself is dependent. Indian theology, then, starts as dialectical materialism, and proceeds progressively from materialism to idealism in stages that can with little difficulty be traced. Life, it is true, is impossible without food or nourishment; but is not breath even more essential to life than food? That this may be so is illustrated by a very simple parable.

The bodily functions hold a contest, the object of which is to see which of them is the most essential to life. Speech departs, and the body is dumb but still lives. The eye departs, and the body is blind but still lives. The ear, the mind, and the seed do likewise but the body still lives. Breath then threatens to depart, but all the other bodily functions are seized with panic, realizing that, once breath leaves, they, one and all, will die.[2] Breath, then, is even more essential to life than is food. Breath, the 'spirit of life', *is* life—and one is here reminded that in the Nicene creed Christians confess their belief *in Spiritum Sanctum, Dominum et vivificantem*, 'in the Holy Spirit, Lord and *Giver of Life*'. Breath, therefore, is Brahman. Moreover, breath and consciousness are inseparable: when breath goes consciousness must follow. Thus Indra, one of the old Vedic gods chosen in the *Kauṣītakī* Upanishad to speak as the Absolute, declares:

'I am the breathing spirit (*prāṇa*, "breath") whose self is consciousness. Reverence me as such—as life and immortality. Life is the breathing spirit, and the breathing spirit is life indeed.

[1] Ibid., 3. 10. 6.

[2] *Bṛhadāraṇyaka* Up., 6. 1. 7–14: *Chāndogya*, 5. 1. 6 – 5. 2. 2. *Kauṣītakī*, 2. 14 (9). Cf. *Bṛhadāraṇyaka*, 1. 3. 1–19: *Chāndogya*, 1. 2. 1–9: *Kauṣītakī*, 3. 2–3: *Praśna*, 2. 2–4.

The breathing spirit is immortality indeed. For, as long as the breathing spirit remains in the body, so long is there life. By the breathing spirit one obtains immortality in that (var. this) world—by consciousness and true conception.'[1]

The breathing spirit and consciousness are mutually interdependent: 'the breathing spirit is consciousness indeed; and consciousness is indeed the breathing spirit. The two dwell together in this body, and together they depart.'[2] Both are 'bliss, ageless, and immortal'.[3] As wind in the objective world and as breath in the body the breathing spirit is the source of consciousness and the one true life: it is the living spirit and the immanent God. 'Which is the one God?' a teacher asks. 'Breath', the pupil replies.[4]

From these materialistic and semi-materialistic beginnings the Indian quest for the immortal substrate to the phenomenal world groped its way. But neither of these two formulations satisfied them. They searched for something more subtle still—a Brahman which would be the unitary power underlying all phenomenal existence and residing at the same time deep down in the soul of man. This doctrine, which was to have such immense influence on Hindu thought and which probably developed simultaneously with the doctrines of food and breath, was very early formulated in the so-called *Śāndilya-Vidyā* or 'Wisdom of Śāndilya':

'All this [world] is Brahman. Let one worship it in all quietness as *tajjalān*. [This word, which has no meaning, is interpreted by the commentators as meaning "that from which one is born, into which one is dissolved, and that in which one breathes and acts".] . . . He who consists of mind, whose body is breath, whose form is light, whose idea is the real, whose self (*ātman*) is space, through whom are all works, all desires, all scents, all tastes, who encompasses all this [world], who does not speak and has no care—He is my self within the heart,

[1] *Kauṣītakī* Up., 3. 2.
[2] Ibid., 3. 4.
[3] Ibid., 3. 9.
[4] *Bṛhadāraṇyaka* Up. 3. 9. 9.

smaller than a grain of rice or a barley-corn, or a mustard-seed, or a grain of millet, or the kernel of a grain of millet; this is my self within my heart, greater than the earth, greater than the atmosphere, greater than the sky, greater than these worlds. All works, all desires, all scents, all tastes belong to it: it encompasses all this [world], does not speak and has no care. This my self within the heart is that Brahman. When I depart from hence I shall merge into it. He who believes this will never doubt.'[1]

This is one of the most important passages in the Upanishads: it is perhaps the first formulation of the Hindu idea of God; for here we have passed far beyond a purely materialistic formulation of the Absolute as an eternal physical process as we have passed beyond a simple identification of the human soul with all Nature on pantheistic lines. The formula is indeed capable of a pantheistic or monistic interpretation, but not necessarily so: for not only is Brahman called 'this whole [world]', It also transcends the world, for It is 'greater than the great' and indwells the human soul as what is 'smaller than a grain of rice'. It both transcends the world, sustains it, and indwells it. This is not yet pantheism or monism, but a definition of the simultaneous transcendence and immanence of God that would scarcely have been rejected by St. Thomas Aquinas. It is the discovery of God as the only true and deathless reality, the only self-subsistent Being, from whom all contingent being derives and without whom the whole phenomenal world would sink into pure nothingness.

Yet, in these early Upanishadic passages in which the idea of God as origin, sustainer, and indweller of the universe and the human soul is beginning to emerge as something distinct from them, the old identification of Him with the 'All' persists, though the passages themselves show that a real distinction is now being drawn between the indwelling Brahman, Ātman, or 'Person' and the created order. The Ātman-Brahman, the God who ensouls all things, though still, quite illogically, described

[1] *Chāndogya* Up., 3. 14. 3–4. Cf. *Śatapatha Brāhmaṇa,* 10. 6. 3.

as 'this All', is the hub of the wheel of existence and holds it together. Furthermore it is the King of all creation.

'This Self is the honey of all things, and all things are honey for this Self. This shining, immortal Person who is in this Self, this shining, immortal Person who exists as Self, who is this Self, is this Immortal, this Brahman, this All.

'Verily, this Self is the overlord of all things, the king of all things. As all the spokes are brought together in the hub and felly of a wheel, so are all things, all gods, all worlds, all breathing spirits, all these selves, brought together in this Self.'[1]

The great Self or Person, then, is the eternal axis which keeps the universe in being: He is the God who controls the world from within, the ground on which all existence is woven. The latter theme is beautifully expressed in a famous colloquy between Yājñyavalkya and Gārgī:

'She said: "That, Yājñavalkya, which is above the sky, that which is beneath the earth, that which is between these two, sky and earth, that which people call past, present, and future—across what is that woven, warp and woof?"

'He said: "That, Gārgī which is above the sky, that which is beneath the earth, that which is between these two, sky and earth, that which people call past, present, and future—across space alone is that woven, warp and woof."

' "Across what then, pray, is space woven, warp and woof?"

'He said: "That, Gārgī, Brāhmans call the Imperishable. It is not coarse, not fine, not short, not long, not glowing, not sticky, without shadow and without darkness, without air and without space, unattached, without taste, without smell, without eye, without ear, without voice, without mind, without energy, without breath, without mouth, without measure, without inside and without outside. It eats nothing whatever and no one whatever eats it." '[2]

Brahman, then, is no longer considered as 'food' and the 'eater of food', as an eternal process within matter. He trans-

[1] *Bṛhadāraṇyaka* Up., 2. 5. 14–15. [2] Ibid., 3. 8. 6–8.

cends matter wholly and nothing can truly be predicated of Him which can be predicated of phenomenal existence. 'Woven across' phenomenal existence 'warp and woof' He nevertheless transcends it entirely. Because of His transcendence the world does not know Him, but He is, for all that, the 'Inner Controller', the 'Immortal' who holds all mortal existence in the hollow of His hand. He is 'He who, dwelling in the earth, yet is other than the earth, whom the earth does not know, whose body the earth is, who controls the earth from within—He is your Self, the Inner Controller, the Immortal'.[1] Similarly He dwells in all things, yet is other than all things, whom all things do not know, whose body all things are, and who controls all things from within. 'He is the unseen seer, the unheard hearer, the unthought thinker, the ununderstood understander. Other than He there is no seer. Other than He there is no hearer. Other than He there is no thinker. Other than He there is no understander. He is your Self, the Inner Controller, the Immortal.'[2]

Thus at a very early stage the Hindus had worked out a clear concept of deity as being both transcendent and immanent, distinct from the universe though indwelling it. This idea, despite frequent lapses into pantheism and monism, they were steadily to develop. What principally distinguishes them from the Christians is that they never developed a clear idea of contingent being, and tended therefore to identify God either with the world or with the human soul or both. In the first case you get pantheism, in the second monism. Yet the old idea which finds its first expression in the *Śāndilya-Vidyā* is never lost sight of, and in the Bhagavad-Gītā, where transcendence and immanence meet in Krishna, the incarnate Lord, the rights of God as against the sum-total of creaturely existence on the one hand and the immortal human soul on the other are clearly maintained.

[1] *Bṛhadānaṇyaka* Up., 3. 7. 3. [2] Ibid., 3. 7. 23.

CHAPTER III

The Indian Contribution, II

It can now be said with some confidence that there are three main trends in early Indian religion—the purely practical attempt made by Yogin ascetics to lay bare the springs of the immortal individual soul manifesting itself in the Sāṁkhya-Yoga and in Jainism; the experience of nature mysticism or merging of the individual soul into the All which we found in certain passages of the Upanishads; and lastly the purely theoretical speculation on the nature of Brahman found elsewhere in the same works. In none of these trends did we find anything at all comparable to the Old Testament idea of an intensely personal God operating in and through His people in history. The Old Testament is revelation in the strictest sense: God progressively reveals His purpose to His chosen people, and there is always a looking forward to the coming of the Kingdom of God at the end of time, when Israel will be restored to its rightful greatness. The Eternal stands apart from the world, but nevertheless guides and leads it on to its consummation. The Eternal operates in time; but the Eternal and the temporal, God and His people, are not opposed, but complementary concepts—the Lord and His servant. The relationship between the two is intensely personal, what Martin Buber calls the confronting of an I and a Thou. And because the Eternal Thou is alone the Lord of Heaven and earth, the human 'I' is called upon to obey the divine command in fear and trembling. God reveals Himself to man as Lord, and as Lord He demands unquestioning obedience. He is not concerned with the personality of man, far less with his psychology. He does not reveal man's immortal 'self' to his empirical 'self' as Indian religion does; rather He reveals Himself as an objective and fiercely ethical reality.

The Hindu sacred books—and in practice this means the Upanishads—are also revered as a revelation by the Hindus. In fact the recognition of the Veda as eternal wisdom is one of the things that makes a Hindu a Hindu; and it was because the Buddha refused to recognize anything of the kind that he was rejected by the orthodox. There is, however, the sharpest possible distinction between what the Jews understand by revelation and what the Hindus do. In Judaism the personal relationship existing between God and His people is fundamental: there is a two-way traffic between an I and a Thou, both terms of which must remain always distinct.

In Hinduism things are very different, for there is no creation *ex nihilo*; and man, therefore, as he exists apart from God, is not pure nothingness, he is not utterly and wholly dependent on God for his very existence. Between man and God there are no gulfs fixed. So even when, in the late *Śvetāśvatara* Upanishad and the Bhagavad-Gītā, the idea of a personal God is developed, that God always tends to become identified with the sum-total of the universe; and even when it is said that he transcends the universe and is its sovereign Lord, he never stands apart from it as Yahweh stands apart from His creation and immeasurably above it. In the earliest Upanishads there is no revelation of a truly personal God at all. There are gropings in this direction, as we have seen, but because of the very nature of natural mystical experience which so obviously occasioned those pantheistic passages we quoted in the last lecture, these first tentative strivings towards what 'is other than earth, other than heaven, other than breath, other than mind, other than understanding, other than all things',[1] are so often swept into the all-comprehensive 'All'. The seed falls among thorns, and the thorns spring up and choke it; seeds and thorns become in-

[1] *Bṛhadāraṇyaka* Up., 3. 7. 3, 8, 16, 20, 22, 15.

extricably entangled so that we can no longer tell the one from the other. The impersonal Brahman is at the same time a 'Person', He is all this world as well as the 'self' of the human soul. Impersonal and personal, 'greater than the great' yet 'smaller than a grain of rice' this 'overlord of all things, and king of all things'[1] exercises lordship only for a moment before He once again sinks back into Nature which is the 'All'. This is the *Deus sive Natura* of Spinoza, the identification of God both with the world and with the human spirit.

Now, in studying the Upanishads, it is both possible and necessary to distinguish those passages which speak of an immanent God who indwells both the world and the human soul yet transcends them both, from those which simply identify either the human soul with Brahman or the world, or the world with Brahman.

Many passages, some of which we have already quoted, emphasize the distinction between Brahman and the phenomenal world. The first is the *cause* of the second as fire is the cause of smoke,[2] or the spider of its web. 'As a spider might prolong itself in the threads [of its web], or as small sparks rise up separately from fire, even so do all breathing spirits, all worlds, all gods, all beings rise separately up from the Self. The secret interpretation (*upaniṣad*) of this is "the Real of the Real". Living spirits are the Real. He [the Self] is their [own most] Real.'[3] This is neither monism nor pantheism, but a description by analogy of God as First Cause. Similarly God (the Self) as final cause is compared to the ocean into which all rivers must inevitably discharge themselves,[4] or He is that which pervades all things yet is other than they just as salt dissolved in water will make the whole mass of water salty.[5] All this shows clearly enough how these early sages, with an amazingly sure instinct, were fighting their way towards a conception of God—whether He be called Brahman, Self, or Person—as efficient, material, final, and formal cause of the universe.

[1] Ibid., 2. 5. 15.
[2] Ibid., 2. 4. 10.
[3] Ibid., 2. 1. 20.
[4] *Chāndogya* Up., 6. 10.
[5] Ibid., 6. 13

Against this tendency runs always the tendency to identify everything with everything else. The resulting confusion is appalling, and it is made worse by the fact that not only are the two tendencies weightily represented throughout the Upanishads, they co-exist in the same Upanishad. Thus it is the *Bṛhadāraṇyaka* from which we have drawn most of our 'theistic' texts that declares: 'Whoso knows: "I am Brahman", becomes this All. Not even the gods have the power to prevent him becoming thus, for such a one becomes their own self.'[1] Such glaring contradictions would seem to be explicable only on the assumption that no Upanishad (except perhaps the very shortest) is the work of a single author. This is certainly true of the two 'great' Upanishads, the *Bṛhadāraṇyaka* and *Chāndogya*: it is probably equally true of the other classical Upanishads. The *Māṇḍūkya*, a monist polemic, is an obvious exception; opening with the words, 'This whole [world] is Brahman: the self is Brahman', it maintains consistently the strict Parmenidean position that all is indivisibly and absolutely one. This is monism, pure and simple, and here also wholly divorced from pantheism. The *Māṇḍūkya* is alone among the Upanishads to maintain this position consistently. The nature of the experience underlying this doctrine we shall have to examine later.

Meanwhile, since this whole category of religious experience is so completely foreign to contemporary theology, both Catholic and Protestant, let us summarize again what has gone before.

Early Indian spirituality falls under three distinct heads. The first is represented by the Sāṁkhya-Yoga within the Hindu fold, and by the Jains outside it. The basic teaching of both is that the human soul is an immortal monad which has its being outside space and time. Its connexion with the body is not adequately explained, but is, from the soul's point of view, disastrous; and its salvation therefore consists in severing, once and for all, all attachment to the whole apparatus of earthly life—body, emotion, *and mind*—and in returning to its original isolation, to a state of pure consciousness of self, in which there is no

[1] *Bṛhadāraṇyaka* Up., I. 4. 10.

awareness of anything except this isolated, *personal* soul. For the soul *is* a person (*puruṣa*)—one of an infinity of such persons—existing always in an eternal 'now'. In such a system there is no room for God since each 'person' or soul is sufficient unto itself. The Yoga system of Patañjali, indeed, as opposed to the classical Sāṁkhya, does introduce a personal God or 'Lord'; but this 'Lord' is distinguished from other 'persons' or souls only in so far as he is eternally free and undefiled by matter. He is not the origin of other souls or of the phenomenal world; he is simply the souls' exemplar—the only soul which is eternally undefiled and thereby the model which all entangled souls must strive to imitate. For the Sāṁkhya proper, however, as for the Jains, there simply is no God.

In terms of experience 'salvation' or 'release' for the adept of the Sāṁkhya means realizing oneself as an eternal being *in isolation.* It is not the loss of personality described by Tennyson, but rather the *realization of personality—pauruṣya* or *puruṣa*-hood—in isolation from all that is other than itself. It is what Proust referred to as the awakening of the 'second self'—'our real self which often had seemed dead for a long time yet was not dead altogether'[1]—a 'self' totally distinct from the ego, the reality of which Proust, when in this beatific condition, almost doubted.[2]

So much for this experience—what we will call the Sāṁkhya experience—the isolation of the individual, personal soul *which is experienced as eternal* from all that has its being in space and time.

The second experience which we have called 'pan-en-henic' has already been dealt with at some length. But once again, since the experience is so rarely taken into account by Christian theologians, let us say a few more words about it and see if we cannot somehow grasp it a little more firmly in its ever-elusive essence.

In our earlier discussion of this topic we quoted almost exclusively from the Upanishads and confined ourselves to one example only from modern times. The essence of the experience has, however, in recent times been summed up by Karl Joel in

[1] See above, p. 46. [2] Above, p. 47, n. 3.

the words 'without and within are one',[1] and this amounts to the *felt* identification of the experiencing subject and the experienced objective world. And in this connexion I must ask leave to quote again a beautiful description of this same experience which seems to me to convey its distinctive flavour more satisfyingly than any other passage from literature I know:

'It was as if I had never realized before how lovely the world was. I lay down on my back in the warm, dry moss and listened to the skylark singing as it mounted up from the fields near the sea into the dark clear sky. No other music ever gave me the same pleasure as that passionately joyous singing. It was a kind of leaping, exultant ecstasy, a bright, flame-like sound, rejoicing in itself. And then a curious experience befell me. It was as if everything that had seemed to be external and around me were suddenly within me. *The whole world seemed to be within me.* It was within me that the trees waved their green branches, it was within me that the skylark was singing, it was within me that the hot sun shone, and that the shade was cool. A cloud rose in the sky, and passed in a light shower that pattered on the leaves, and I felt its freshness dropping into my soul, and I felt in all my being the delicious fragrance of the earth and the grass and the plants and the rich brown soil. I could have sobbed with joy.'[2]

This again is the same experience of 'without' and 'within' being one, of 'being the whole world' as the Upanishads sometimes say, and, by being the whole world, of being the Brahman that pervades it all and at the same time inheres in the human soul. This is one of the things which the Hindus understand by *mokṣa* or 'release'. It means the dissolution of the bonds of the ego and the expansion of the released personality to such an extent that it comprises and embraces all Nature. The experience is always overpowering and brings with it a sense of unutterable wonder and breath-taking joy which the subject of the experience can never even hope adequately to describe.

[1] See R. C. Zaehner, *Mysticism Sacred and Profane*, pp. 38, 41, etc.
[2] Forrest Reid, *Following Darkness*, London, 1902, p. 42.

'Have I not said the state is utterly beyond words?' Tennyson wrote.[1] 'I could have sobbed with joy', Forrest Reid confirms. The Upanishads, when they speak of it, let the experience speak for itself.

Both this state, in which subject and object coalesce, and that of the isolation of the personal and eternal soul from all that is other than itself are authenticated experiences, differing, obviously, from each other widely, but sharing this at least in common, that in them normal sense-perception is quite transcended. They are both concerned with a mode of being that eludes and defies both sense-perception and ratiocination.

The question now arises whether such experiences are, either of them, identical with mystical experience as understood by Christians. Nature mystics, because their experience is so overwhelming and, to them, so profoundly real and so inherently meaningful, tend to claim that their experience is, to all intents and purposes, identical with that of the theistic mystics. I have tried to show elsewhere[2] that this can hardly be so, and, in order to demonstrate that Indians too have felt this, I propose to call the great Indian philosopher, Rāmānuja, as principal witness for the defence.

Before, however, proceeding to our main theme which will be the development of theism in India, we must try to come to grips with the nature of these experiences. As we have seen, certain passages in the Upanishads, notably *Kauṣītakī* I. 6.,[3] can only be explained as a description of what the nature mystic conceives is happening to him. Forrest Reid writes: 'It was *as if* everything that had seemed external and around me were suddenly within me. The whole world *seemed* to be within me.' The qualifying 'as if' and 'seemed' he adds because, as a civilized Occidental, he knows that if he omitted them, he would be laughed out of court. Had he lived in the still semi-primitive environment of the Upanishads, he would have written: 'Everything that is external and around me *is* within me. This whole world *is* within me. [I am this all.]' He would have written so

[1] See above p. 48. [2] In *Mysticism Sacred and Profane, passim.*
[3] See above, p. 55.

because this would have seemed to him to be the literal truth: there would have been no 'as if' about it.

It is only when human consciousness has shaken itself free from this curious sense of identity with Nature which Lévy-Bruehl called *participation mystique* that man can see by the use of his unaided reason that such an identification cannot be literally true on *any* plane of consciousness; though even this would be denied by the Neo-Vedāntins and Neo-Buddhists. All he can say is that in these states 'the soul is *in a certain sense* (πως) all existing things. . . . The understanding is *in a sense* (πως again) the objects understood and sense-perception is the things perceived.'[1] Aristotle too adds the vital qualifying πως because he refuses to admit that a man can *literally* be the world. That would be nonsense. Therefore these immediate apperceptions, in which subject and object form a single synthesis, in which knower and known form, so to speak, a single knowing, must admit of some other explanation which is not in flat contradiction to everything that reason teaches us. Had Aristotle come to the conclusion through a natural mystical *experience* that 'it is within me that the trees wave their green branches', he would have verified by the sense of touch the objective reality of a given tree 'experienced within him', and once he had collided with it, would have concluded that after all there was a distinction (πως!) between the physical tree outside and the tree within him; and this would apply to 'the whole world within him' too. Therefore, he would conclude—and indeed did conclude—the tree waving its branches within me is only a 'form' or image of the objective tree out there. The tree is indeed in me—not absolutely though, but πως, that is, in a certain sense; and this sense is that I am identified with the form of the tree, not with the actual physical tree which is still really outside me. This is precisely what Nicolas of Cusa meant when he spoke of man as the *imago mundi* as well as the *imago Dei*.[2]

In his interpretation of this experience Aristotle, it would appear, does not differ substantially from Jung. The terminology is different, that is all. And on the whole I find Aristotle's

[1] See above, p. 54. [2] See below, p. 88.

the simpler as well as the more intelligible. Jung interprets this experience as the union of the ego with the unconscious; and his unconscious is the *imago mundi* of Nicolas of Cusa. 'The union of the conscious mind or ego-personality,' he writes, 'with the unconscious personified as anima produces a new personality compounded of both—"ut duo qui fuerant, unum quasi corpore fiant".[1] Not that the new personality is a third thing midway between conscious and unconscious, it is both together. Since it transcends consciousness it can no longer be called "ego" but must be given the name of "self". Reference must be made here to the Indian idea of the *ātman*, whose personal and cosmic modes of being form an exact parallel to the psychological idea of the self and the *filius philosophorum*. The self too is both ego and non-ego, subjective and objective, individual and collective. It is the "uniting symbol" which epitomizes the total union of opposites. As such and in accordance with its paradoxical nature, it can only be expressed by means of symbols. . . . Hence, properly understood, the self is not a doctrine or theory but an image born of nature's own workings, a natural symbol far removed from all conscious intention. I must stress this obvious fact because certain critics still believe that unconscious phenomena can be written off as pure speculation. But they are matters of observed fact, as every doctor knows who has to deal with such cases. The integration of the self is a fundamental problem which arises in the second half of life.'[2]

In speaking of the 'idea of the *ātman*' Jung is, of course, referring to the classic Vedāntin identification of the *ātman* as human soul with the Brahman as cosmic principle. The classical texts for this concept, usually called *mahāvākyāni* or 'great utterances', are four in number, of which only three are relevant to our present purpose. These are (1) 'Thou art That':[3] (2) 'This *ātman* is Brahman':[4] and (3) 'I am Brahman.'[5] All three state-

[1] 'So that what had been two should become as one in body.'

[2] C. G. Jung, *Psychology of the Transference*, in *Collected Works*, vol. xvi, p. 264.

[3] *Chāndogya* Up., 6. 9 ff.

[4] *Māṇḍūkya* Up., 2.

[5] *Bṛhadāraṇyaka* Up., 1. 4. 10.

ments in fact mean the same since 'that' in the first case also refers to Brahman. How each is to be interpreted in its context, however, is quite a different matter.[1] For our present purposes, however, we may accept the interpretation of the extreme non-dualist Vedānta which takes these words to mean that the human soul *quâ* eternal essence is identical with the ground and source of the universe, the latter being, from the point of view of this ground and source, an illusion caused by *avidyā* or cosmic ignorance—a kind of dream-construction that is inherent in the Absolute itself. In his refutation of this thesis in his commentary on the *Brahma-Sūtras* Rāmānuja exposes its inherent absurdity,[2] and, in his commentary on the Bhagavad-Gītā, he has, to my mind, assigned it its proper place in a wider scheme of mystical theology.[3] Jung, however, like Aristotle before him, has helped to throw light on the nature of these monistic utterances by translating them from the realms of ontology and cosmology, where they make little or no sense, to that of psychology. The feeling of identity that the nature mystic, along with the Upanishadic passages inspired by natural mystical experience, feels with all Nature, and which he feels, in Tennyson's words, to be 'not a confused state, but the clearest, the surest of the surest', is something happening within the human psyche, and has nothing to do with objective Nature as such. What the Upanishads, along with more modern nature mystics, mean by *idaṁ sarvam*, 'this All' or 'the whole universe' has nothing to do with the objective universe: it is the universe which exists within the human soul, which is normally deep down, outside and beyond consciousness, and which emerges from time to time with such overwhelming force that the subject of its visitations is convinced beyond doubt of its overriding reality. So overpowering is the experience that those who undergo it not infrequently interpret it as a direct experience of God. This is particularly true of persons who have no clear conception of

[1] On (1) see above, pp. 54, 71: on (2) see above, p. 58 and below pp. 89–90: on (3) see above, pp. 53, 77.

[2] See Thibaut's translation in *Sacred Books of the East*, vol. xlviii, especially pp. 96–119.

[3] See below, pp. 120 ff.

the nature of God, and it is the great merit of the Indian systems—Sāṁkhya, Buddhist, and Jain—that they interpret the 'released' state in purely psychological terms without reference to God in any shape or form. This is equally true of Proust, of Tennyson, and of Forrest Reid. All of these were brought up in a traditionally Christian society, yet none of them associates his experience with God. The same is true of Richard Jefferies.

Jefferies is perhaps unique among nature mystics in that he contrives to preserve a healthy scepticism throughout his ecstasies. On the purely intellectual plane he is a typical nineteenth-century rationalist with an intense dislike of traditional religion and particularly of the Judaeo-Christian belief that an all-wise God directs the course of the universe. The existence of suffering belies any such belief, and to assert that this suffering world is guided by a wise intelligence is purblind wickedness. 'The whole and the worst the worst pessimist can say is far beneath the least particle of the truth,' he says, 'so immense is the misery of man. It is the duty of all rational beings to acknowledge the truth. There is not the least trace of directing intelligence in human affairs.'[1] In his pessimism and his view of the world as one mass of appalling suffering, Jefferies is, without knowing it, a very good Buddhist; and he is a Buddhist too in that, having diagnosed the world as a conglomerate of pain, he finds the way of escape from this cramped and cramping existence to another mode of being which this world cannot touch, for it is utterly outside time. When he has reached this 'imperishable abode' he speaks as a soul for whom time has lost all meaning:

'The great clock of the firmament, the sun and the stars, the crescent moon, the earth circling two thousand times, is no more to me than the flow of the brook when my hand is withdrawn; my soul has never been, and never can be, dipped in time. Time has never existed, and never will; it is a purely artificial arrangement. It is eternity now, it always was eternity, and always will be. By no possible means could I get into time

[1] Richard Jefferies, *The Story of My Heart*, London, new ed., 1912, pp. 104–5.

if I tried. I am in eternity now and must there remain. Haste not, be at rest, this Now is eternity. Because the idea of time has left my mind—if ever it had any hold on it—to me the man interred in the tumulus is living now as I live. We are both in eternity.

'There is no separation—no past; eternity, the Now, is continuous. When all the stars have revolved they only produce Now again. The continuity of Now is for ever. So that it appears to me purely natural, and not supernatural, that the soul whose temporary frame was interred in this mound should be existing as I sit on the sward. How infinitely deeper is thought than the million miles of the firmament. The wonder is here, not there; now, not to be, now always. Things that have been miscalled supernatural appear to me simple, more natural than nature, than earth, than sea, or sun. It is beyond telling more natural that I should have a soul than not, that there should be immortality; I think there is much more than immortality. It is matter which is the supernatural, and difficult of understanding. Why this clod of earth I hold in my hand? Why this water which drops sparkling from my fingers dipped in the brook? Why are they at all? When? How? What for? Matter is beyond understanding, mysterious, impenetrable; I touch it easily, comprehend it, no. Soul, mind—the thought, the idea—is easily understood, it understands itself and is conscious.'[1]

The escape into the eternal Now, so dear to the mystics, here it is, possessing Richard Jefferies so completely that our world of space and time and change and matter has become not non-existent but utterly incomprehensible. In the other world time is a word without meaning, just as eternity or Nirvāṇa or Brahman is for us. And just as a man born blind cannot conceive what colour is, let alone what red, and green, and russet, and yellow are, so with the man who has never tasted of the other world. He cannot conceive of existence outside time, let alone of the different forms of life that must exist there. For 'there is much more than immortality'. Immortality as such is a mere

[1] Ibid., pp. 31–2.

first step because it is open to all men if they can but 'fall out' of the bondage of time. Immortality is the starting point of the mystic, not his goal; for Jefferies was 'fully convinced that there is a vast immensity of thought, of existence, and of other things beyond even immortal existence'.[1] This surely is natural enough; for what reason is there to suppose that the world of eternity, in comparison with which, as all mystics agree, this world is but the shadow of a shade, is less rich in content than this poor temporal world of ours? This is surely the error of the monists, as Rāmānuja clearly saw.

This other world, 'the supernatural miscalled, the natural in truth, is the real. To me everything is supernatural. How strange that condition of mind which cannot accept anything but the earth, the sea, the tangible universe! Without the misnamed supernatural these to me seem incomplete, unfinished. Without soul all these are dead. Except when I walk by the sea, and my soul is by it, the sea is dead. Those seas by which no man has stood—by which no soul has been—whether on earth or the planets, are dead. No matter how majestic the planet rolls in space, unless a soul be there it is dead.'[2]

To Jefferies what is 'miscalled supernatural' but is really inherent in Nature itself—the world of thought, idea, consciousness—alone gives life to external Nature. Until the sea is ensouled by man, it is a dead thing. Here again he helps to throw light on the phenomenon of nature mysticism, a subject on which few can speak with greater authority. The experience is all in oneself; the sensation of comprising all nature is simply the ensouling of the 'form' of Nature in man himself. Actual objects present to the field of vision can only modify the arrangement of the internal 'form', not its total content. This 'form' is in every man and constitutes part of his eternal 'Now', and it is the activation of this form or *imago mundi* which gives rise to all the marvels and transports of the nature mystic. But this internal image of the world is still not man's deepest being, his 'self' maybe in the Jungian sense, but still not the deepest centre of

[1] Ibid., p. 102. [2] Ibid., pp. 32–3.

his 'self'. This 'conglomerate abode'[1] Jefferies also tried to plumb.

'Sometimes I have concentrated myself,' he writes, 'and driven away by continual will all sense of outward appearances, looking straight with the full power of my mind inwards on myself. I find "I" am there; an "I" I do not wholly understand, or know, something is there distinct from earth and timber, from flesh and bones. Recognizing it, I feel on the margin of a life unknown, very near, almost touching it: on the verge of powers which if I could grasp would give me an immense breadth of existence, an ability to execute what I now only conceive; most probably of far more than that. To see that "I" is to know that I am surrounded with immortal things. If, when I die, that "I" also dies, and becomes extinct, still even then I have had the exaltation of these ideas.'[2]

Here we meet once again that 'second self', the 'autre moi' of Proust, the *puruṣa* of the Sāṁkhya, surrounded now by immortal things. If one could but discover it, Jefferies thought, he would be able to execute what, under normal circumstances, he could only conceive. This is, I think, the common experience of artists: nothing can even be begun unless there is some visitation from the other 'immortal' world. Proust's novel needed this impetus before it could be started. But though Jefferies had more vivid insights into the world of 'Now' than are usually granted to even the most gifted, he could not regard death as 'an almost laughable impossibility', as did Tennyson and Proust, for Jefferies' mysticism was a mysticism of the whole man, of body and of soul. 'I believe, with all my heart,' he writes, 'in the body and the flesh, and believe that it should be increased and made more beautiful by every means. I believe—I do more than think—I believe it to be a sacred duty, incumbent upon every one, man and woman, to add to and encourage their physical life, by exercise, and in every manner. A sacred duty each towards himself, and each towards the whole of the human

[1] *Bṛhadāraṇyaka* Up., 4. 4. 13.
[2] *The Story of my Heart*, pp. 34–5.

race. Each one of us should do some little part for the physical good of the race—health, strength, vigour. There is no harm therein to the soul: on the contrary, those who stunt their physical life are most certainly stunting their souls.'[1]

Jefferies thus had no use for the Indo-Platonic view of man as an almost fortuitous amalgam of a mortal and an immortal part, and it therefore seemed to him not at all impossible that the immortal 'I' might perish along with its perishable partner, though he knew full well that 'immortal' means precisely what cannot die. How this can be he does not begin to explain; but because he will not split the human personality in two he accepts total death, which would mean falling out for ever from the eternal 'now' into absolute non-existence. Even so it would have been worth it since he had tasted of immortality in life.

Jefferies had no use for Christianity. Had he been more sympathetically disposed, he might have seen that Christianity puts the mortality of the body and the promise of an eventual immortality in the forefront of its beliefs. For Christians bodily death comes into the world with original sin, when man, compounded of spirit and clay—of *puruṣa* and *prakṛti*—has the folly to seek to be 'like God'. In fact this is precisely what Jefferies believed: death for him is simply an 'inherited weakness or flaw'.[2] And Jefferies is by no means alone in believing this: it has been the common belief throughout the ages of the Taoists in China and the Haṭha-Yogins in India, both of whom strive to prolong life indefinitely by physical Yoga and magical practices. It is part and parcel of the legacy of the human race that it looks back to a golden age when man was still immortal, and it is this belief that leads him, against all the evidence, to look forward to a new age in which the body, once again ensouled, will live on eternally. For Jefferies, sceptic and rationalist though he was, death was no supernatural event. 'It is an event of the most materialistic character, and may certainly be postponed, by the united efforts of the human race, to a period far more distant from the date of birth than has been the case during the historic period. The question has often been debated

[1] Ibid., pp. 87–8. [2] Ibid., p. 109.

in my mind whether death is or is not wholly preventible; whether, if the entire human race were united in their efforts to eliminate causes of decay, death might not also be altogether eliminated.'[1]

Jefferies's instinctive feeling that the immortality of the body is after all possible is not the only thing that brings him close to traditional Christianity. He had probed the mysticism of Nature and his own immortal soul as deeply as have few others, but he was still unsatisfied. He could not consciously draw nigh to God, for he did not believe in the Christian God as currently expounded in England. Convinced none the less by his own unforgettable experience that such a Being must exist, he was forced to call it the 'higher than deity', and in This, with all the force of his unquiet soul, he passionately believed.

'I conclude,' he solemnly declares, 'that there is an existence, a something higher than soul—higher, better, and more perfect than deity. Earnestly I pray to find this something better than a god. There is something superior, higher, more good. For this I search, labour, think, and pray. If after all there is nothing, and my soul has to go out like a flame, yet even then I have thought this while it lives. With the whole force of my existence, with the whole force of my thought, mind, and soul, I pray to find this Highest Soul, this greater than deity, this better than god. Give me to live the deepest soul-life now and always with this Soul. For want of words I write soul, but I think that it is something beyond soul.'[2]

This cry from the depths of Richard Jefferies to a power 'higher than deity' and 'better than god', is in fact an affirmation of his belief in the Christian God than whom none other is good. It bears witness to his yearning for the One True God of whom a Laodicean and self-satisfied pseudo-Christianity had given him no adequate picture. His is the cry of the nature mystic who has savoured the secrets and tasted the beauty of the universe around him and the universe within him, but longs only for the 'better than god', in whom alone, he instinctively

[1] Ibid. [2] Ibid., pp. 51–2.

feels, can peace and endless satisfaction be found. If I have dwelt on him for longer than might seem justified, it is because he mirrors on a small scale the Indian experience of God which we are about to consider.

And what of Nature and the rapturous communion with her that Jefferies enjoyed? How does this prince of nature mystics explain his natural mystical experiences? Certainly they had nothing to do with the 'higher than deity' whom Jefferies never found, nor had they anything much to do with Nature as it is when objectively considered. Jefferies had no illusions at all about this and was as conscious of the cruelty and the apparent senselessness of Nature as anyone else. As an objective fact he abhorred it and its insensate, even hostile, indifference to the lot of man.

'All nature, all the universe that we can see,' he writes, 'is absolutely indifferent to us, and except to us human life is of no more value than grass. If the entire human race perished at this hour, what difference would it make to the earth? What would the earth care? As much as for the extinct dodo, or for the fate of the elephant now going.

'On the contrary, a great part, perhaps the whole, of nature and of the universe is distinctly anti-human. The term inhuman does not express my meaning, anti-human is better; outre-human, in the sense of beyond, outside, almost grotesque in its attitude towards, would nearly convey it. Everything is anti-human.'[1]

Everything anti-human, utterly without purpose, mindless, and unconcerned with good and evil.

'There being nothing human in nature or the universe, and all things being ultra-human and without design, shape, or purpose, I conclude that no deity has anything to do with nature. There is no god in nature, nor in any matter anywhere, either in the clods on the earth or in the composition of the stars. For what we understand by the deity is the purest form

[1] Ibid., p. 45.

of Idea, of Mind, and no mind is exhibited in these. That which controls them is distinct altogether from deity. It is not a force in the sense of electricity, nor a deity as god, nor a spirit, not even an intelligence, but a power quite different to anything yet imagined. I cease, therefore, to look for deity in nature or the cosmos at large, or to trace any marks of divine handiwork. I search for traces of this force which is not god, and is certainly not the higher than deity of whom I have written. It is a force without mind. I wish to indicate something more subtle than electricity, but absolutely devoid of consciousness, and with no more feeling than the force which lifts the tides.'[1]

It seems well-nigh unbelievable that one who could write so rapturously about his communion with sun, sea, stars, and earth, could at the same time coldly pronounce judgement on Nature, the occasion for his ecstasies, as mindless, as 'without design, or shape, or purpose', and as 'grotesque in its attitude towards humanity'. And the mindless 'force more subtle than electricity' 'quite different to anything yet imagined' is the animating principle of the universe, something very like the eternal laws of Nature which Engels declared to be the one abiding reality behind a constantly changing world,[2] something even more like the *prāṇa* or 'breathing spirit' we have already met with in the Upanishads, the spirit which is not above boasting of its evil deeds, in that it claims to have delivered ascetics over to wild dogs, to have transgressed compacts, to have impaled gods and demons in the three worlds, and to have emerged from these exploits wholly unscathed.[3] Such is the spirit animating all Nature, and such too is Brahman or the 'breathing spirit' in its terrible aspect. It is a terrible, a ruthless, and a mindless spirit, whose first products, according to the *Chāndogya* Upanishad,[4] were fire, water, and food—a *material* absolute which we have already discerned in Upanishadic writings. This absolute, this aspect of Brahman, which is the

[1] Ibid., pp. 49–50.
[2] See Engels, *Anti-Dühring* and *The Dialectics of Nature*, *passim.*
[3] *Kauṣītakī* Up., 3. 1, 2.
[4] 6. 2. 3–4.

animating principle of the non-rational universe, is what Jefferies experienced as a 'force more subtle than electricity'; and, of itself, it is totally indifferent to man. Yet it is this that calls forth in the mind of man a response which issues in an ecstasy of communion, but it is the mind of man alone that creates and experiences this ecstasy. 'The mystery and the possibilities are not in the roots of the grass, nor in the depth of things in the sea; they are in my existence, in my soul. The marvel of existence, almost the terror of it, was flung on me with crushing force by the sea, the sun shining, the distant hills. With all their ponderous weight they made me feel myself: all the time, all the centuries made me feel myself this moment a hundred-fold.'[1] It was, then, the impact made by the force of Nature inherent in sea, sun, and earth on the human soul that revealed the marvel and the terror of existence. The nature mystic's experience arises from the union of a 'force more subtle than electricity', the force that animates mindless matter, with the human soul. The result is a boundless expansion of the soul itself: 'Whoso thus knows, "I am Brahman", becomes this All.'[2]

Jefferies knew very well that by communing with Nature you did not thereby 'become' Nature. This would have appeared disgusting and degrading to him. But he did concede that Nature had the power so to act upon the soul as to enlarge it infinitely so as to enable it to draw some of its own power into itself. What Jefferies never did, however, was to confuse Nature or the 'breathing spirit' in Nature with the 'higher than deity', which is his name for God. This the earlier Upanishads constantly did, for the authors of those remarkable works were pioneers in man's pilgrimage to God, and the mysteries they were reverently probing remain, obstinately, mysterious still, however much we may submit them to the dissecting knife of reason. It was, after all, they who were first conscious of the mystery and took the first steps in unravelling it.

But Jefferies, too, deserves all honour for refusing to make the Spinozan confusion between Nature and God. Communion

[1] Richard Jefferies, *The Story of my Heart*, pp. 24–5.
[2] *Bṛhadāraṇyaka* Up., 1. 4. 10.

with Nature, for him, had nothing at all to do with communion with God. Nicolas of Cusa spoke of man in the following terms: *Homo enim Deus est, sed non absolute, quoniam homo. Humane igitur est Deus. Homo etiam mundus est, sed non contracte omnia, quoniam homo. Est igitur homo μικρόκοσμος*: 'For man is God, though not absolutely, for he is man. He is therefore God in a human way. Man is the world too, not indeed all things compressed into a small compass, since he is man. He is therefore man as microcosm.'[1] So when the *Kauṣītakī* Upanishad says,[2] 'You are the self of every being', it can only mean that man as microcosm is the *imago mundi*, and that he can establish a physico-psychic *rapport* with the macrocosm which enables him to experience himself as being co-terminous with it: the 'form' of the 'All' is impressed on the individual 'one'. Indeed it seems more than likely that the mysterious identity of macrocosm and microcosm which we meet with in successive civilizations all over the world is based on this same natural mystical experience. Translated into Jungian terminology the position could be stated thus: the collective unconscious is the common inheritance of the whole human race, and therefore its contents are as various and as limitless as the whole world. To experience an uprush of the unconscious, then, appears to the nature mystic as an identification with the whole world. This is to mistake the microcosm for the macrocosm, the 'form' of the universal thing for the thing in itself.

Nature mysticism, however, is only one type of mysticism. In India every type is represented. Besides nature mysticism of the pan-en-henic type and the Sāṁkhya, a theistic mysticism develops and finds its most perfect expression in the Bhagavad-Gītā. Alongside this and quite at variance with it, develops a fourth type, different at least in its philosophical formulation from all of these. For this type of mysticism, which finds its classical expression in the *Māṇḍūkya* Upanishad and Gauḍapāda's *Kārikā* on the same, the human self or soul is not 'this All', for that is dismissed as being ultimately illusory, nor is it

[1] *De Conjecturis*, II, 14, *apud* Jung, *Collected Works*, vol. xvi, p. 318.
[2] 1. 6.

one of many *puruṣas*, souls, or 'persons', it *is* the Absolute, Brahman, One without a second. Quite naturally the soul that claims to have experienced *this* must, of necessity, consider that it has reached the ultimate ground of all being, illusory though all being other than the One may be. He has, therefore, realized himself as the ground of all that we call contingent being, as the utterly unknowable Brahman which is devoid of all quality.

The *Māṇḍūkya* Upanishad starts with the bold assertion that 'this self is Brahman'. This identity, however, is not immediately apparent. The self can be considered in four different ways—as awake, as dreaming, as immersed in deep sleep, or as being in a fourth state which is utterly indescribable but which is that of Yogic trance. Sense experience tells us that waking experience alone is real. According to Gauḍapāda's verse commentary on the *Māṇḍūkya*, however, this is the exact reverse of the truth. In it there is only experience of what is gross, whereas in dream there is experience of subtle matter which is nearer to the well-springs of the soul. 'The state of deep sleep,' on the other hand, 'is a unified state, a mass of wisdom (*prajñāna*), composed of bliss: it experiences bliss; its mouth (or head) is thought; it is wise; this is the third part. This is the Lord of all, the knower of all, the inner controller, the source of all, the origin and end of creatures.'[1]

It must come as a rude shock to Europeans who are not versed in Upanishadic lore to find God, considered as omnipotent and omniscient Creator, identified with dreamless sleep of all things. It should not, however, be forgotten that, in the religion of the Upanishads, God—whether he appears as Brahman, *Puruṣa* as Supreme Person (as distinct from the Sāṁkhya use of the word), or as Supreme Self—is always the *material* as well as the efficient cause of the universe: he is the ground from which the universe emanates or grows. Further, in the *Māṇḍūkya* Upanishad the identity of microcosm and macrocosm is taken for granted. To the four states of man, the microcosm, correspond four states of the universe, the macrocosm. Being awake corresponds to gross matter because in this state there is com-

[1] *Māṇḍūkya* Up., 5–6.

plete duality between perceiver and perceived (matter). Dreaming corresponds to subtle matter, the stuff of dreams, which, in this state, is the object perceived. Dreamless sleep, on the other hand, is a unitary state prior to dream: it is that from which dreams issue. What in the macrocosm corresponds to dreamless sleep then? Plainly, the one God of whom earlier Upanishads had spoken as being both the material and the efficient cause of the universe. As dreamless sleep gives rise to dreams, so does the one God give rise to creation; and if microcosm and macrocosm are *literally* one, it follows that God and dreamless sleep are identical.

Identity, however, is not enough. Beyond identity lies absolute Oneness, the impersonal One which this Upanishad calls Brahman. This is prior both to God and to dreamless sleep: it is the completely unqualifiable Absolute, the fourth state which 'has cognizance of neither what is inside nor what is outside, nor of both together: it is not a mass of wisdom, it is not wise nor yet unwise. It is unseen; there can be no commerce with it; it is impalpable, has no characteristics, unthinkable; it cannot be designated. Its essence is its firm conviction of the oneness of itself; it causes the phenomenal world to cease; it is tranquil and mild, devoid of duality. Such do they consider this fourth to be. He is the Self; he it is who should be known.'[1]

Thus, once the literal identification of microcosm and macrocosm is made, there is no alternative left except to identify the human soul with God. 'I am Brahman', is now experienced as the literal truth; what is only an 'image of God' claims to be God. This, according to Dr. Kraemer, is to repeat the Fall,[2] it is original sin. And if by sin we understand the Greek ἁμαρτία, the original meaning of which is 'missing the point', he is undoubtedly right; but since the point is, in this case, God, the missing of it is the most serious intellectual error it is possible for a creature to commit.

That this error would inevitably be made by the great major-

[1] Ibid., 7. [2] See above, p. 14.

ity of persons who thus experience the deep unity of their souls, was fully understood by Martin Buber, and he has issued a solemn warning against it.

'Sometimes I hear it said,' he writes, 'that every *I and Thou* is only superficial, deep down word and response cease to exist, there is only the one primal being unconfronted by another. We should plunge into the silent unity, but for the rest leave its relativity to the life to be lived, instead of imposing on it this absolutized *I* and absolutized *Thou* with their dialogue.

'Now from my own unforgettable experience I know well that there is a state in which the bonds of the personal nature of life seem to have fallen away from us and we experience an undivided unity. But I do not know—what the soul willingly imagines *and indeed is bound to imagine* (mine too once did it)—that in this I had attained to a union with the primal being or the godhead. That is an exaggeration no longer permitted to the responsible understanding. Responsibly—that is, as a man holding his ground before reality—I can elicit from those experiences only that in them I reached an undifferentiable unity of myself without form or content. I may call this an original pre-biographical unity and suppose that it is hidden unchanged beneath all biographical change, all development and complication of the soul. Nevertheless, in the honest and sober account of the responsible understanding the unity is nothing but the unity of this soul of mine, whose ground I have reached, so much so, beneath all formations and contents, that my spirit has no choice but to understand it as the groundless. But the basic unity of my own soul is certainly beyond the reach of all the multiplicity it has hitherto received from life, though not in the least beyond individuation, or the multiplicity of all the souls in the world of which it is one—existing but once, single, unique, irreducible, this creaturely one: one of the human souls and not "the soul of the All"; a defined and particular being and not "Being"; the creaturely basic unity of a creature, bound to God as in the instant before release the creature is to the *creator spiritus*, not bound to God as the creature to the *creator spiritus* in the moment of release.'[1]

Thus, according to Buber, who is speaking from personal experience, this feeling of absolute oneness which induces the monist to claim that in trance or what Mircea Eliade and Louis Gardet call 'en-stasis', he *is* God, means nothing more than that he is himself; he has experienced the deepest ground of his own creaturely being, 'an original pre-biographical unity', maybe, 'which has remained hidden unchanged beneath all biographical change'. This original pre-biographical unity is, of course, nothing else than the 'other self', *l'autre moi*, with which Proust has familiarized us and 'which had often seemed dead for a long time yet was not dead altogether'. Moreover, if the Hindu monist wishes to appeal to scripture, the two texts, 'I am Brahman', and 'This self is Brahman', are really either devoid of precise meaning or are tautologous, since the word 'Brahman' may mean almost anything. We have seen that it is equated now with 'food', and now with the 'breathing spirit'. Again it is progressively identified with speech, breath, sight, hearing, mind, and heart.[2] Elsewhere, in the *Chāndogya*,[3] it is progressively name, speech, mind, conception, thought, meditation, understanding, strength, food, water, heat, space, memory, hope, and finally the breathing spirit. Later, as in the Bhagavad-Gītā, it comes to be identified with 'the imperishable', that is to say, the condition of immortality in which the 'released' soul has its being. For the Buddhists, as for the Gītā, 'Brahman' means that which conditions existence in Nirvāṇa, just as space and time condition existence in this world. To say, 'I am Brahman', need mean no more than that 'I am, in my deepest essence, a being who exists outside space and time'. We will

[1] M. Buber, *Between Man and Man*, London, 1947, pp. 24–5. A similar, though less convincing refutation of the monistic mystic's claim to be identical with God is found in Ibn Ṭufayl's *Ḥayy ibn Yaqẓān*, E.T. by Simon Ockley, revised by A. S. Fulton, London, 1929, pp. 143–4. The monist interpretation of the experience Ibn Ṭufayl calls a 'misguided conceit'.

[2] *Bṛhadāraṇyaka* Up., 4. 1.

[3] 7. 1–15.

have to return to the use of the term 'Brahman' later since the relation of Brahman to God in the Bhagavad-Gītā is of prime importance to the understanding of Indian theism.

When the non-dualist Vedāntin claims that he can experience himself as the sole existent One without a second from which a literally imagined[1] universe arises, he is really referring to nothing but an experience of absolute oneness from which all multiplicity is excluded. The aim of the soul in the Sāṁkhya system is, as we now know, complete isolation from the whole world of space and time, subjective as well as objective, so that it has no experience of anything whatever except its immortal self. The goal of both systems is the isolation of the immortal spirit: *but* in the one case this is explained as the isolation of the soul not only from a really existing Nature but also from really existing brother-souls. These continue to exist but are no longer perceived. The Vedānta, on the other hand, maintains that to realize oneself as Brahman means to realize that the phenomenal world is an illusion with no existence of itself at all; for in the state of trance called *samādhi* there is consciousness of the immortal and eternal self only. This is the old quarrel between the idealists and the realists—but on an eternal plane. And that makes all the difference. For though I may be now quite uncertain that Oxford exists in my absence, I certainly propose to return there and very much hope that it will still be there on my return. If, on the other hand, I had cut off all links with that venerable city, it would be a matter of total indifference to me what the philosophers might say about its existence or non-existence. So it is with the Sāṁkhya-Yoga and the Vedānta. For the first Oxford still exists, but there is no awareness whatever that it does exist; whereas, for the second, it never had any existence except in my own imagination. Whether or not it exists is purely a matter of philosophical speculation. All agree that for the inhabitants of Aberystwyth it might just as well not exist. So with the phenomenal world, once isolation in the eternal self is attained, its existence is quite done away with as far as the isolated soul is concerned. However you interpret the

[1] See Gauḍapāda's *Kārikā* to the *Māṇḍūkya*, especially 2. 12–19.

experience philosophically, the experience remains one and the same. Since you experience nothing but absolute oneness, and since you are not conscious that you have ceased to exist, you are experiencing nothing but your self at its deepest level.

The early Upanishads are primarily metaphysical treatises concerned with identifying the Brahman, the ground of the universe. They are not consistent with themselves, nor are they consistent with the Sāṁkhya-Yoga which probably developed at much the same time. Yet wide as is their range, they are never concerned with a personal God in our sense of the word. That was an aspect of the older Vedic religion which they had almost entirely lost sight of. The later Upanishads and above all the Bhagavad-Gītā were to reverse this trend: they were to grope towards a personal, omnipotent, and omniscient God to whom even the neuter Brahman would be subjected. Before this was to happen, however, Buddhism was to intervene.

The essence of early Brahmanism is the search for the Absolute, and its natural development is in Vedāntin monism which claims that the soul is identical with the Absolute. We have seen that, in terms of experience, this probably means no more than the realization of the immortality of the soul. This experience was of supreme importance to the Brāhmans: it was technically referred to as *mokṣa* or *mukti*, meaning 'release' from temporal existence, but in the Upanishads 'release' from temporal existence tends to be supplemented by self-realization as Brahman, or the All, or simply as the 'Self'. The Upanishads, however, remain primarily metaphysical, although the quite irrational elements of nature mysticism and monistic mysticism are certainly present, though always they try to explain these experiences metaphysically. This might be regarded as their greatest weakness. Be that as it may, they are not content to leave things unexplained.

The Buddha started from quite different premises. He is the complete empiricist. Unlike the Hindus he refused to admit (or deny) the existence of the Absolute; he is not even looking for one. He starts rather from the empirical standpoint and affirms that so far as anything is real, this world in which we live is real—and a very unpleasant world it is. Only one thing is empirically verifiable, and that is that all things are in a perpetual state of flux, not staying the same for a single moment. This is not only true of the universe in general; it is even more true of the human being, for the body is an ever-changing organism, never for two minutes the same. This is so obvious that even an ignorant man would conceive an aversion to the body as a loathsome, because a perishable, thing. Only one degree less foolish than the man who is not disgusted with his body is the man who thinks that there is any stability in mind or consciousness; for mind, so far from being more stable than body, is less so. The body may last a hundred years, but the mind 'keeps up an incessant round by day and night of perishing as one thing and springing up as another'.[1] Since there is no permanence in either body or mind, such a thing as a centre of consciousness in the shape of an ego or self cannot exist. Impermanence is the one basic fact of existence in the physical and mental world, and impermanence can be construed as pain or suffering. All existence is suffering—pain without beginning and without end.

The Buddha knew very well that his conviction that there is no such thing as a self or personality was not likely to be shared by the great majority of his contemporaries. The only way to convince them was by example, by leading a life in which there was never any thought of self but which was, nevertheless, perfectly serene. Only by example could others be made to understand that beatitude lies in the literal loss of self. Because he believed that the very idea of personality which he expressed in the words, 'This is mine; this am I; this is my self', was the source of all evil and was what made the attainment of Nirvāṇa impossible, he preached unselfishness in the most literal sense of that word—'There is no such thing as the self'—and at the root of the false idea of self lies the basic evil which keeps this dreadful world in being, concupiscence or desire in all its manifestations, the desire to be as much as the desire to have. Desire is,

[1] *Saṁyutta Nikāya*, xii, 62 in H. C. Warren, *Buddhism in Translations*, Cambridge, Mass., 1896, p. 151.

however, itself dependent on a still deeper cause; and this is ignorance—ignorance, that is, of the true nature of the world, ignorance, above all, that all selves are illusory. To overcome this ignorance, to vanquish desire, and to realize the emptiness of self is to achieve Nirvāṇa. Nirvāṇa means the passing away from the phenomenal world which is compounded of change into 'deathlessness, peace, the unchanging state'.[1] 'From death lead me to immortality', said the Upanishad.[2] 'From life lead me to immortality', would be the Buddha's reply. But perhaps both are saying the same thing, for both traditions are at one with Plato and St. Paul in seeing the body as a tomb, and both cry out to be delivered from 'the body of this death'.[3] Bodily life is not a pleasant thing; with its interminable round of reincarnations it is just an unending stream of suffering—pain, never-ending pain for unenlightened man. This is the first 'noble truth' without which there is no salvation: and salvation means 'immortality', peace, and the passing beyond change.

Buddhist mysticism, then, is akin to that of the Sāṁkhya-Yoga, and consists in the escape from the world of impermanence into a changeless mode of being. But whereas the Sāṁkhya as well as the Vedānta seeks a metaphysical basis for this state, the Buddha refuses to draw any metaphysical conclusions from what he regards as an empirical fact. Hinduism degraded the gods from their high estate and put an impersonal Absolute in their place: the Buddha abolished both and offered what he thought was the only thing worth having—immortality, though who or what was to experience the immortal bliss is never made quite clear, for it did not 'belong to the beginning of the religious life'.[4]

The Buddhist doctrine that there is no such thing as self is usually taken for granted. That this represents the real view of the Buddha is certainly true if by 'self' we understand the empirical ego only. How does it stand with the *ātman*, the

[1] See E. Conze, *Buddhist Texts through the Ages*, Oxford, 1954, p. 92.
[2] *Bṛhadāraṇyaka* Up., 1. 3. 28.
[3] Rom. vii, 24.
[4] *Saṁyutta Nikāya*, v. 437: cf. *Majjhima Nikāya*, i, 431.

'second self' or eternal soul? The Sāṁkhya and Jains, of course, believed in the separate existence of an infinite number of individual souls: neither believed in the existence of a God or Absolute. How do things stand with primitive Buddhism?

There is, of course, no doubt that Buddhism denies both God and Absolute. This seems clear enough from the *Tevijja Sutta*[1] where the Buddha refutes representatives of various Brahmanical schools all of whom claim that the teaching of their own sect 'is the straight path . . . the direct way which makes for salvation, and leads him, who acts according to it, into the state of union with Brahmā (*brahmasahavyatāya*)'.[2] Now, though the grammatical form of Brahmā is here masculine, it is fairly clear, as T. W. Rhys Davids points out,[3] that the Buddha is here referring to all that the Brāhmans meant by the neuter Brahman as well as the masculine Brahmā. In fact 'union with Brahmā' must mean union with the Absolute as understood in the Upanishads, that is to say, as the eternal ground of the universe. The Brāhmans in question further maintain that all their teachings in fact culminate in this same union with Brahmā, which, since they are Brāhmans, must be the Brahman-Ātman synthesis. For them the teachings of all sects must lead to this same goal. 'Just . . . as near a village or a town,' they argue, 'there are many and various paths, yet they all meet together in the village, just in that way are all the various paths taught by various Brāhmans.'[4] They are all 'saving paths', and they all lead to 'a state of union with Brahmā'.

The Buddha will have none of all this. For him union with Brahmā could not be the goal of religion, for none of these Brāhmans had ever met or heard of anyone who had seen Brahmā, knew him by experience, or knew his where, whence, or whither. 'So that the Brāhmans versed in the Three Vedas have forsooth said thus: "What we know not, what we have not seen, to a state of union with that we can show the way, and

[1] *Dīgha Nikāya, Sutta* 13.
[2] *Tevijja Sutta,* § 4 ff.
[3] *Buddhist Suttas* in *Sacred Books of the East,* vol. xi, p. 168, n. 2.
[4] Ibid., § 10.

can say: 'this is the straight path, this is the direct way which makes for salvation and leads him, who acts according to it, into a state of union with Brahmā.' "

'Now what think you, Vāseṭṭha?' the Buddha continues. 'Does it not follow, this being so, that the talk of the Brāhmans, versed though they be in the Three Vedas, turns out to be foolish talk?'[1]

For the Buddha, then, Brahmanical philosophy with its talk of union with Brahman was just silly: it is the old story of the blind leading the blind.[2] Salvation or 'release' has nothing to do with any transcendental principle.

If, however, it is clear that the Buddha had no belief in an Absolute, does it follow that he thereby denied the existence of an individual immortal soul like the *puruṣa* of the Sāṁkhya and the *jīva* of the Jains? He certainly believed in an immortal, unconditioned form of existence as is proved by his famous definitions of Nirvāṇa as an 'unborn, not become, not made, uncompounded'[3] and as 'deathlessness, peace, the unchanging state'.[4]

Of all religions Buddhism is the most elusive, and perhaps we should therefore be satisfied with these two definitions. But if there is such a thing as deathlessness, peace, and an unchanging state, must there not be someone or something that is conscious of this state? Is this not the 'original pre-biographical unity' of the individual soul of which Martin Buber speaks?

In recent times Coomaraswamy has tried to show that the Hindu idea of *ātman* is present in Buddhism also.[5] The evidence he produces seems convincing, but his interpretation of the evidence would appear to be faulty; for, if by the *ātman* we understand a universal Soul, as the Hindus sometimes do, it is scarcely likely that the Buddha would condemn this idea as

[1] Ibid., § 14.

[2] Ibid., § 15.

[3] *Udāna*, 81.

[4] *Suttanipāta*, 204. For further references to descriptions of Nirvāṇa see I. B. Horner in E. Conze, *Buddhist Texts through the Ages*, pp. 82–102.

[5] See his introduction to Miss I. B. Horner's selections from the Buddhist scriptures in *The Living Thoughts of Gotama the Buddha*, London, 1948.

'foolish' in one passage and admit it in the concept of *atta* (the Pali version of the word *ātman*) in others. It is therefore important that we should study these passages with some care.

These have been collected by Miss I. B. Horner in her book, produced in collaboration with Coomaraswamy, *The Living Thoughts of Gotama the Buddha*, and it is her translation that I usually follow. First let us take some of the examples from the *Dhammapada*, though this work is in some ways not typical of the Pali canon, exhibiting, as it does, much more evident signs of Upanishadic influence than does the bulk of the canon. Be that as it may, we know that the Buddha considered human personality, in so far as it is composed of body and mind, to be illusory. He denied that there was such a thing as an ego, that is, a permanent centre of consciousness that remains basically the same throughout life. This is his doctrine of *an-atta*, 'not-self', or selflessness. It comes, then, rather as a shock when we read: 'If one knows the Self as precious (*piyam*, 'dear'), he should guard it well-guarded.'[1] Since this cannot refer to the ego, which is the source of evil[2] and therefore scarcely likely to be referred to as 'precious' or 'dear' by the Buddha or whoever the author of the *Dhammapada* is, *a priori* we must assume that it refers to an immortal self, the *ātman* of the Upanishads at least in so far as that means the immortal ground of the *soul* as opposed to the universe. This seems all the more likely when we remember that the *Bṛhadāraṇyaka* Upanishad teaches that all things are 'dear' (*priya*) 'because of desire for the *ātman*'.[3] 'Not because of desire of a husband is a husband dear, but because of desire for the Self is a husband dear.' It would then seem clear that the Buddha understands *atta-ātman* in these passages as that which is immortal in man. One can even go further than this: the Buddhist 'Self', unlike its Upanishadic counterpart, has moral value, it is very nearly what we call conscience; or so, at least, it would seem in the following two passages:

> 'Desire he should curb for either course,
> Committing nothing that the Self would blame.'[4]

[1] *Dhammapada*, 157.
[2] Ibid., 161, 165.
[3] 2. 4.=4. 5.
[4] *Suttanipāta*, 778.

And again:

> 'Through Self one should urge on the self,
> One should restrain the self by Self.
> That monk, guarded by Self, mindful,
> Will fare along to happiness.
>
> For Self is lord of the self,
> For Self is bourn of the self.
> Therefore restrain the self
> As a merchant thorough-bred horse.'[1]

In this passage the existence of two selves seems clear, the lower self, which is the source of all evil, 'difficult to subdue',[2] and the higher Self, which is 'Lord (*nātho*) of the (lower) self', by which one is purified, and which does not commit evil.[3] Here again there seems to be no doubt that this 'second self' is, among other things, conscience. Obviously, however, it is not only this. The Buddha himself, when predicting his own death, says:

> 'My age is now full ripe, my life draws to its close:
> I leave you, I depart; Self I've made my refuge.'[4]

So too he leaves instructions for the perfected monk:

> Mindful, thoughtful,
> Let him cast off all fetters,
> Let him make of Self a refuge . . .
> Aspiring for the path that changes not.'[5]

The Self that one should 'make a refuge' would therefore appear to be that in man which 'aspires for the path that changes not', presumably then the permanent substrate of the ever-changing human psycho-physical frame. The idea of taking Self as refuge is found in many passages throughout the Pali canon. 'Go along, having Self as lamp, Self as refuge and none other refuge; having *dhamma* as lamp, *dhamma* as refuge and

[1] *Dhammapada*, 379–80.
[2] Ibid., 159.
[3] Ibid., 165.
[4] *Dīgha-Nikāya*, ii, 120.
[5] *Saṁyutta-Nikāya*, iii, 143.

none other refuge,'[1] the Buddha counsels, promising at the same time that he who does this will reach 'the peak of the Deathless'.[2] The Self than which one should have none other refuge, then, would appear to be identical, in some mysterious way, with the *dhamma*. What he means by the *dhamma* (variously translated as 'law', 'truth', or 'doctrine' all of which are misleading) in this context is, however, not nearly so clear. We do, however, read elsewhere[3] that the *dhamma* of good men never ages, and in all its connotations *dhamma* would seem to mean an unchanging something, usually an unchanging law, either of Nature, or of the Buddha. Tentatively, then, one may conclude that this equation of Self with *dhamma* means that the Self is an unchanging something.

This is amply confirmed by the passages illustrating what Self is *not*.[4] It has no material shape, is not body, feelings, perceptions, 'the constructions' or psychological predispositions, or intellect (*viññāṇa*). It has, in fact, nothing to do with the empirical ego or the intellectual and sensual organs through which it operates, all of which are impermanent—and 'what is impermanent, that is ill; what is ill is not the Self. What is not Self, that is not mine, that am I not, that is not my Self. . . . Happy indeed those perfected ones! The thought "I am" eradicated, delusion's net is rent.'[5] The Self, then, is *permanent* in the same way that the *dhamma*, as the eternal law of 'suchness' or truth taught by the Buddha, is permanent, or, as we read elsewhere, as Brahman is permanent. For the man formed by the *dhamma* is described as 'a dhamma-body (*dhamma-kāya*), a Brahman-body; dhamma-become, and Brahman-become'.[6]

This passage is of great importance for our present purpose as it throws light on what the Buddhists understood by the term

[1] *Dīgha-Nikāya*, ii, 100.

[2] Ibid., 101. Horner's translation. Rhys Davids has only 'the topmost height' (*tamatagge* sc. 'beyond darkness').

[3] *Dhammapada*, 151.

[4] See Coomaraswamy and Horner, op. cit., pp. 152–61 where all references are given.

[5] *Saṁyutta-Nikāya*, iii, 83.

[6] *Dīgha-Nikāya*, iii, 84.

Brahman. When the word is used in the early Buddhist scriptures, it appears to have much the same sense as Nirvāṇa—existence outside space and time with no Brāhmanic overtones of identification with anything at all. Buddhaghoṣa's commentary to this passage interprets the word simply as meaning 'the best',[1] a word which is itself used to denote the eternal mode of existence. Similarly it interprets 'Brahman-become' as meaning 'of the same nature as Brahman' (*brahma-sabhāvo*), viz. eternal, permanent, or immortal. On the whole idea of a *dhamma*-body or Brahman-body the same commentary says: 'Why is the Tathāgata (i.e. the Buddha) said to have a *dhamma*-body. Because having devised the Three-Piṭaka-Buddha-word by his mind he conducts it forth by his speech. Therefore his body from having *dhamma*-ness is considered as the *dhamma*, and is so called. And just because of this *dhamma*-body-ness, he has an excellent body, for *dhamma* is also called Brahman in the sense of best, supreme, excellent.'[2] As *dhamma*- or *brahma-kāyo*, *dhamma*- or Brahman-body, a human being is an individual manifestation of the *dhamma* or Brahman, an immortal soul, since the use of the word *kāyo*, 'body', must imply individuation. In so far as he participates in *dhamma*, the Self must be 'intemporal . . . a come-and-see thing',[3] as Miss Horner quaintly translates. In Buddhism, then, it can be stated with tolerable certainty that the 'second' Self can be regarded as something which has its being in eternity. This was as much as the Buddha was prepared to say: he was not prepared to give it a definite name like 'person' as the Sāṁkhya did, or 'living thing' (*jīva*) as the Jains did, nor was he prepared to identify it with anything else as the Brāhmans did. What is affirmed is that the human soul, in so far as it is capable of achieving Nirvāṇa, has an extra-temporal existence which is called *brahman* or *dhamma*. The Self, however, in early Buddhism, is not quite so devoid of quality as it is in some Upanishadic passages. It is a moral entity manifesting itself as

[1] See T. W. and C. A. F. Rhys Davids, *Dialogues of the Buddha*, vol. iii, London, 1921, p. 81, nn. 3, 4.

[2] Ibid., n. 2.

[3] *Saṁyutta-Nikāya*, ii, 199. See Coomaraswamy and Horner, op. cit., p. 204.

conscience, as we have seen, and when it is said that *dhamma* is the 'charioteer'[1] we must infer that it is the directing force of the whole psycho-physical body-emotion-mind complex which constitutes the human personality, but not as a unified whole but as a conglomeration of more or less unrelated parts.[2]

In so far as he admits an extra-temporal self or soul, the Buddha introduces an ethical content into Indian psychology that had not been present before: man's immortal soul is also the principle of righteousness within him—his conscience. It is, moreover, on the ethical side that Buddhism and Christianity, the two numerically greatest religions in the world, come closest to each other; and there is nothing, I think, in the Sermon on the Mount that could not be paralleled in the Buddhist scriptures. There is the same emphasis on compassion, turning the other cheek, divesting oneself of the things of this world, the same dying to self. In both Christ and the Buddha you find the same gentleness and the same impatience with the Scribes and Pharisees on the one hand and with Brahmanical orthodoxy on the other, the same insistence on sincerity of intention and the vanity of ritual automatically performed. But ethics, though an indispensable part of any religion that would wish itself to be considered a 'higher' religion, is not and cannot be the core of any religion. Christ offers to all who believe in Him communion with Himself and, through Him, with the Father ('To day shalt thou be with me in paradise'). The Buddha offers deathlessness and peace independent of any God or Absolute; and this is a personal affair only to be achieved by heroic efforts, for there is no God from whom one may expect help or grace. 'Work out your own salvation with diligence', was the Buddha's last recommendation to his disciples.

In the West we hold that man is a creature and his right attitude to God is one of creatureliness; and creatureliness expresses itself in worship and sacrifice. Neither the Vedānta nor Buddhism accepts this. For the one, man is potentially the

[1] Ibid., i, 33: Coomaraswamy and Horner, p. 199.

[2] *Visuddhi-Magga*, ch. xviii. See H. C. Warren, op. cit., p. 133. The same metaphor occurs in *Kaṭha* Up., 3. 3. ff.

Absolute; for the other, it is simply a question of putting an end to phenomenal existence in order to enter into a bliss which knows neither time nor space. Yet no popular religion can survive on these dizzy heights. Man, by his very nature, needs to worship, and this was later fully recognized both by the Vedāntin Hindus and by the Buddhists; and so it was that the gentle Buddha who sought to guide men to an immortality that was pure selflessness, became himself a god—and not only a god but a god in trinity, consisting of the Dharma-body, which is the self-subsistent reality, the Body of Enjoyment, through which he reveals himself in different guises in all the different universes, and the Body of Transfiguration, which is the incarnate god on earth, the human Buddha who taught and preached the four Noble Truths in the sixth century B.C.[1]

The transformation of Buddhism from an original atheism into a constellation of theistic systems proves not that the empirical psychology of the human Buddha was untrue; it proves only that it was not fully satisfying to the psychological constitution of the average man, for it leaves out of account the psychological needs of the great majority of the human race; it ignores their need to worship.

In Brahmanism we can observe the same development even within the Upanishads themselves. Even in some of the passages we have analysed earlier the idea of God as omnipotent Lord of the universe was not entirely absent. Both the fire-god, Agni,[2] and *prāṇa*, 'breath', or the 'breathing spirit', are spoken of as God (*deva*) or Lord. The breathing spirit 'whose self is consciousness' is called by the *Kauṣītakī* Upanishad[3] protector and sovereign of the world, the Lord of all (*sarveśa*). So too in the *Bṛhadāraṇyaka*,[4] all divinities are finally reduced to one—the breathing spirit.

In the time of the Upanishads the word *deva* or 'god' still

[1] The manner in which Mahāyāna Buddhism came to approximate to Christianity is quite remarkable but cannot be treated here.

[2] *Bṛhadāraṇyaka* Up., 5. 15; *Īśā* 18 (*deva*) = *Rig-Veda*, 1, 189, 1.; *Bṛhad-āraṇyaka*, 6. 3. 5 (*īśāna*).

[3] 3. 9.

[4] 3. 9. 9.

meant *a* god, one of the old gods of the Veda who had by now been reduced to the rank of celestial beings vastly inferior to the Brahman or Ātman. Hence the word *deva* appears very rarely in our sense of the word God. The Supreme Being, whether conceived of personally or impersonally, is called *Brahman*, *Ātman*, or *Puruṣa* ('Person'). All these words may mean an impersonal Absolute, a personal God, or simply the sum-total of existence, depending on whether the author is thinking monistically, theistically, or pantheistically. When the idea of a personal God does develop again, the word *deva* reappears in this sense, and the terms *īś*, *īśāna*, and later *īśvara*, all meaning 'Lord', are all used to represent the personal God. The word *deva* is used in an obscure passage in the *Chāndogya*,[1] where it appears to refer to the breathing spirit, manifest in the macrocosm as wind and in the microcosm as breath. As in the *Bṛhadāraṇyka* it is referred to as the 'one' God. So too 'whatever moving thing there is in the moving world, all this must be enveloped by the Lord':[2] God envelops the universe and therefore stands outside it. Clearer still is the following:

'If one perceives Him as the Self, as God (*deva*), clearly,
The Lord of what was and what is to be,
One will not shrink away from Him.'[3]

The juxtaposition of *ātman* and *deva* shows how very loosely words are used in the Upanishads. *Ātman* is here used not in the sense of a personal soul or as the universal Soul, but as God, 'the Lord' of all things. In these passages we have the first glimpses of the development of a concept of God as universal sovereign and as transcending the universe. Yet Lord of the universe though he is, this God dwells deep down in the depths of the human soul, though he remains distinct from it.

'Him who is hard to see, who has penetrated the depths
Set in the secret place, dwelling in the abyss, eternal,

[1] 4. 3. 6.
[2] *Īśā*, 1.
[3] *Bṛhadāraṇyaka* Up., 4. 4. 15: cf. *Kaṭha*, 4. 5.

Pondering on Him as God while practising the Yoga of Self,
A wise man leaves behind joy (*harṣa*) and sorrow.

'When a mortal has heard this and fully comprehended,
Has cast aside things contingent (*dharmyam*) and found this subtile [God] (masc.),
Then does he rejoice (*modate*), for he has found a meet cause for rejoicing.
I regard Naciketas as being a dwelling open.'[1]

A new conception of God is beginning to emerge. The practice of the Yoga of the Self is first recommended, by which, as in the classical Yoga, the Vedānta, and Buddhism, the opposites of joy and sorrow are transcended and the Self or soul is realized. This is a state of pure contemplation of one's own soul, 'the original pre-biographical unity'. In this state, which is one of denudation, God, who dwells in the abyss, manifests Himself. Finding God the soul no longer rests in the peace that is beyond joy and sorrow, but rejoices, recognizing the 'subtile' immanent God who shows Himself to be other than the soul though hidden in its depths. Naciketas is now a 'dwelling open': the 'dwelling' of his soul is open to the grace of God.

In another passage in the same Upanishad the idea of grace is clearly enunciated. Both the Ātman and God as Creator and dispenser are referred to. It is clear, however, that the Ātman is here regarded as being the immanent aspect of God which indwells the human soul, though distinct from it.

'More minute than the minute, yet greater than the great
Is the Self hidden in the depths of a creature.
Him does one who lets go of his will behold, all sorrow gone,
By the grace of the Creator (*dhātuḥ*) he beholds the greatness of the Self.

[1] *Kaṭha* Up., 2. 12–13.

Sitting, he ranges far,
Lying, he goes everywhere.
Who else than I can know
That God who rejoices without joy?

Bodiless among bodies,
Abiding among things that abide not,
Great, present everywhere (*vibhum*)—
Pondering on Him as Self, the wise man does not grieve.

This Self cannot be found by instruction,
Not by intellect, nor yet by much lore heard;
He can be found only by such as He chooses,
To such does He reveal His bodily form.'[1]

Here God and Self or Ātman are one. As Self God is immanent in the human soul; as God and Creator He is dispenser of the grace which opens the dwelling of the soul to His presence. Yoga practices may help, as we have seen, but it is God's grace alone which can reveal the secret God within. Here there is no trace of monism, for at last we have an I and a Thou: the dialogue between God and man in India has started.

Once the existence of God as Creator and Lord is established and the dialogue between God and man has begun, man is forced to consider what the relationship between God and the impersonal 'Absolute' or Brahman can be. This was never finally settled to the satisfaction of all. The extreme non-dualists maintained that the Lord was merely the first manifestation of the Brahman and, like all other agents in the phenomenal world, was ultimately and from the point of view of Brahman, illusory. The theists, on the other hand, advanced the view that Brahman in *this* sense was nothing but the ideal world contrasted with the world of coming to be and passing away. Both are contingent, and both originate in God. The first clear formulation of this idea is found in the *Muṇḍaka* Upanishad:

'This is the truth.

[1] Ibid., 20–23.

As from a blazing fire sparks
Alike in form issue forth in their thousands,
So from the imperishable, my friend, are beings manifold
Generated, and thither do they return.

Heavenly, not formed is this Person,
Comprising both "without" and "within", unborn.
He does not breathe, nor does He think [discursively]; pure is he,
Beyond the imperishable beyond.'[1]

Brahman is the imperishable, immortal, manifesting itself as breathing spirit, speech, and mind.[2] It is the 'beyond', the other world; but the Person, that is, the personal God, is beyond both this *and* the other world beyond. He is explicitly dissociated from both the 'imperishable' Brahman, from the breathing spirit, speech, and mind, with which in other Upanishads Brahman had been successively identified. He is the Creator of Brahman, the matrix from which it proceeds.

'When the seer sees Him whose colour is gold
The Creator (*kartāram*), Lord, Person, matrix of Brahman,
Then, knowing good and evil, he shakes them off;
Unstained he reaches the highest likeness (*sāmyam*) [to Him].'[3]

God's superiority and priority to the impersonal Brahman is here unambiguously recognized. Brahman corresponds to the ideal world of Plato, it is the stuff of soul and all immortal substances, but created or rather generated by God.

In the *Kaṭha* and *Muṇḍaka* Upanishads, then, the figure of a personal God emerges, Lord of both the ideal world (Brahman) and the world of coming to be and passing away. In the *Śvetāśvatara* Upanishad, however, a fairly consistent theistic doctrine is worked out around the figure of the ancient Vedic God

[1] *Muṇḍaka* Up., 2. 1. 1–2 [2] Ibid., 2. 2. 2. [3] Ibid., 3. 1. 3.

Rudra-Śiva. This is a theistic version of the Sāṁkhya-Yoga, and in it the key ideas of both that philosophy and the Vedānta appear in germ.

The first chapter sets the ontological scene on which the theistic doctrines of the later chapters will be enacted. Various identifications of Brahman with time, fate, chance, etc. advanced by the Brahmavādins, the 'discoursers on Brahman', are summarily rejected. Against these is set the view of the contemplative Yogins (*dhyāna-yoga*) who see the origin of all things in 'the self-power of God' (*devātma-śakti*) hidden in His qualities.[1] God is the One 'who presides over all causes endued with time and self'.[2] He stands beyond time and individuation. God and His power or *śakti* form an indissoluble unity. As God He is unmoved, as *śakti* He is the mover; as God the Self of all things, as *śakti* He who causes motion (*preritāram*).[3] *Śakti* is the creative principle in God[4] 'by whom all things were made'. In later Śāktism Śiva and Śakti appear as the eternally united male and female principles, Śiva the unmoved One, Śakti the ever-productive source of the universe to which all things must return. In the *Śvetāśvatara* the two are not yet separated even in thought. Sexual imagery there is, of course, for God both 'makes the one seed manifold'[5] and is the womb of all,[6] and as the One male (*puruṣa*) he presides over or draws near to (*adhitiṣṭhati*) all wombs.[7] However, the sexual imagery is not at all developed, God being regarded as the unitary essence in which all the opposites, including that of male and female, are resolved and at rest.

Brahman, in this Upanishad, again is the 'imperishable' (*akṣara*) standing over against the phenomenal world, the 'perishable' (*kṣara*).[8] God is the source or 'womb' of Brahman[9] as of all things.[10] Alternatively the imperishable and the perishable, the ideal as well as the phenomenal world, are considered to constitute the city of Brahman,[11] and this is ruled by God,

[1] 1. 3.
[2] Ibid.
[3] 1. 6.
[4] 4. 1: 6. 8.
[5] 6. 12.
[6] 5. 5.
[7] 5. 2.
[8] 1. 7.
[9] 5. 6.
[10] 5. 5. Cf. 3. 4.
[11] 5. 1 reading *brahmapure*.

'who is beyond this [world], beyond Brahman,[1] the Great, hidden in all creatures, body for body'.[2]

> 'In the imperishable, infinite city of Brahman are two things;
> For therein are knowledge and ignorance placed hidden.
> Now ignorance is a thing perishable, but knowledge is a thing immortal.
> And he who rules the ignorance and the knowledge is another.'[3]

Here 'knowledge' is identified with the immortal Brahman, 'ignorance' with the perishable. This is the source of the later Vedāntin theory of *avidyā* as the cosmic ignorance which inheres in Brahman. Brahman, when understood in the sense of both the ideal and the phenomenal worlds must thereby remain permanently imperfect because permanently subject to change in one half of himself. Because, to the theistic conscience this is intolerable, God is seen as the Lord of Brahman, other than it, the Creator of the imperishable as well as the perishable world of matter. He is the Lord who sustains them both.[4]

The classical Yoga, as we have already seen, admits a god, *īśvara*, who, however, is little more than the one pure soul which is eternally exempt from contact with matter, the exemplar, then, of all souls still bound in matter. In the *Śvetāśvatara* Upanishad we have the natural development of this idea. Besides the general distinction drawn between the perishable and the imperishable there is also a distinction between imperishable beings or souls as such. On the one hand there is the Lord God who is omniscient and all-powerful, and on the other are all other souls which, through their union with matter, are ignorant and feeble.[5] To *know* God means to be delivered from existence in space and time, to be released from all 'fetters'.[6] Thus the

[1] This would seem to be the natural rendering of *tataḥ paraṁ brahma-param* taking *param* in the same sense in both cases. Otherwise we would have to render *brahma param* as 'the Supreme Brahman', i.e. a super-Brahman identical with God, the Lord.

[2] 3. 7. [3] 5. 1. [4] 1. 8. [5] 1. 9.

[6] 1. 8: 2. 15: 4. 16: 5. 13: 6. 13.

idea of salvation is not substantially different from that of the Sāṁkhya-Yoga, it is not union with God,[1] but realization of God's nature and His ability to assist the human soul out of its temporal existence into the imperishable world of Brahman. It is still *kaivalyam* or 'isolation',[2] but it is an isolation in which an eternal something is recognized as constituting the real self or soul (*ātmasaṁstham*).[3] This 'something' is the eternal soul-stuff, identical with God in that it shares with Him an eternal mode of existence, but not identical with Him as the creative source of both the eternal and the temporal modes of existence. It is possible to say, in the terminology of the *Śvetāśvatara* Upanishad, that the soul or *ātman* is Brahman because this simply means, as it does in Buddhism, that the soul is eternal or 'imperishable'.

After describing the physical Yoga technique devised for the purpose of liberating the eternal soul from the bondage of matter[4] the Upanishad goes on to describe the nature of release:

> 'Even as mirror stained by dust
> Shines brilliantly when it has been cleansed,
> So the embodied [soul], on seeing soul as it really is,
> Becomes one, its aim achieved, from sorrow freed.
>
> When through the soul as it really is as through a lamp
> A concentrated Yogin (*yukta*) beholds Brahman as it is,
> Unborn, steadfast, from every [transient] nature free—
> By knowing God one is released from all fetters.'[5]

This is the realization of the soul as it is in eternity (which is Brahman) still, it seems, in isolation as in the Sāṁkhya-Yoga. It is achieved by meditating on God and so 'knowing' Him, but it is in no sense a union with Him. The only possible reference to such an idea (apart from 1. 10 just mentioned) is in 6. 13 where Hume translates: 'That Cause attainable by Sāṁkhya-

[1] In 1. 10 *yojanāt*, which Hume translates as 'union with', must surely mean 'concentration on' since it follows immediately on *abhidhyānāt* 'meditation'.

[2] 1. 11. [3] 1. 12. [4] 2. 8–13. [5] 2. 14–15.

Yoga'. But the word he translates as 'attainable' (*adhigamya*) is more naturally translated as 'who can be approached' or 'who can be studied'. There is still no idea of union with God which seems to be foreign to the theistic Sāṁkhya of the *Śvetāśvatara*. God is to be contemplated as the eternal *par excellence*, and by conforming to His nature, the soul realizes itself as eternal too. At the same time, by God's grace,[1] the soul can *see* God both as immanent and transcendent. This is a vision of God, not a union with Him. The element of love is still lacking. Just as with the Muhammadan Ṣūfīs, the soul is seen as a mirror reflecting God and divine in that degree, but the reflection and its source do not here combine.

Strangely enough the *Śvetāśvatara* Upanishad is not directly concerned with God's relationship to the individual soul: it is concerned rather with His relationship to the two contrasted worlds, the perishable and the imperishable. God and soul are both concerned with Nature or the phenomenal world, God as its author, the soul as its victim. God is wholly unaffected by the world, the soul is terribly enmeshed. In a famous passage the difference between them is thus described:

> 'Two birds, fast-bound companions
> Clasp close the self-same tree.
> Of these two the one eats sweet fruit;
> The other looks on without eating.
>
> On the self-same tree a person, sunken,
> Grieves for his impotence, deluded;
> When he sees the other, the Lord, contented,
> And His greatness, he beomes freed from sorrow.'[2]

Here again it is by *seeing* God that the soul is released. God, then, simply by being seen is responsible for the souls deliverance. He is also (more directly) responsible for ensnaring it in Nature in the first place. Nature is at the same time *māyā*, meaning here not yet illusion but what is meant by the word in the Rig-Veda. There it is the great god Varuṇa who is the

[1] 3. 20. [2] 4. 6–7.

possessor of *māyā par excellence*, and the word means 'supernatural or magic power'. The Rudra-Śiva of our Upanishad inherits many of the characteristic features of Varuṇa, notably the fetters with which the latter ensnares the guilty, releasing them only when they repent. This symbolism has passed into the *Śvetāśvatara* where it is God (Rudra-Śiva) who releases the soul not from guilt but from phenomenal existence: 'By knowing God one is released from all fetters.'[1] It is God Himself who ensnares the souls in the phenomenal world and who draws them out again by granting them the vision of Himself.

'He, the possessor of supernatural power (*māyin*) emanates this whole [world] from that (Brahman as the store-house of contingent being):

'In it the other (the soul) is constricted by this supernatural power (*māyā*).

'Now Nature (*prakṛti*) should be known as this supernatural power
And that Great Lord as the author of that power.
This whole world is pervaded by beings which have become fragments of Him.'[2]

The soul, then, is divine since it is a 'fragment' of God[3] rather as the soul is a 'divine spark' for Meister Eckhart and other Christian mystics, yet God Himself remains without parts.[4] This is self-contradictory, no doubt, but for the Upanishads this is not felt to be so. However much you may draw off from the Infinite, it still remains infinite and unimpaired.

'The yon is fulness; fulness this.
From fulness fulness doth proceed.
Withdrawing fulness' fulness off,
Fulness still remains.'[5]

Souls, as fragments of God, must therefore be of the same substance as He, and will be merged into Him at the end of time.[6] And here again, as always in the Upanishads, cosmology

[1] 1. 8, etc. See p. 110 n. 6.
[2] 4. 9–10.
[3] Cf. Bhagavad-Gītā, 15. 7.
[4] *Śvetāśvatara* Up., 6. 5, 19.
[5] *Bṛhadāraṇyaka* Up., 5. 1.
[6] *Śvetāśvatara* Up., 4. 1, etc.

and theology seem to conflict with mystical experience. The experience of release is described as the realization of oneness[1] or isolation,[2] or as merging into Brahman,[3] but not as union with the Lord who is the origin of Brahman. The divine fragments only do this at the dissolution of the world. However, though the theory of salvation in the *Śvetāśvatara* seems to differ little from that of the *Yoga-Sūtras*, its conception is immeasurably grander.

God is no longer the permanently undefiled soul, nor is He an Absolute which can only be indicated by negatives and paradox, as is Brahman in the earlier Upanishads. He has positive qualities and a distinct personality. He is:

> 'The beginning, the efficient cause of the conjoining [of soul and matter],
> Seen as beyond the three times (present, past, and future), without parts too.
> Worship Him who takes on all forms, becomes becoming,[4]
> The adorable God who dwells in your own thoughts, primeval.
> Higher and other than the [world-] tree, time, and form
> Is He from whom this compounded world proceeds.
> Righteousness (*dharma*) he brings, rejecting evil, Lord of good fortune (*bhaga*):
> Know Him as consisting in Himself, the immortal base of all.
>
> Him who is the supreme, mighty Lord of Lords,
> Supreme Divinity of divinities,
> Supreme Master of masters, [utterly] beyond,
> Him let us know as the adorable God and Lord of the world.

[1] 2. 14. [2] 1. 11. [3] 1. 7.

[4] *bhava-bhūta*: 'having become becoming' would appear to be the literal translation. Aliette Silburn, in her translation (Paris, 1948) has 'devenir accompli'. The standard translation 'the origin of all being' seems to be merely evasive.

The effects [He causes] and the tools [He works with]
cannot be known:
No equal to Him is seen, no superior.
His high power is famed as various indeed,
And from His own essence are His works of wisdom (*jñāna*)
and strength.

None is His master in the world,
To lord it over Him. Nor is there any mark of Him.
He is the Cause, Lord of the lords of [all] tools;
He has no progenitor, no Lord. . . .

One God—hidden in all creatures,
Pervading all, Inner Self of all things,
Surveying all deeds, abiding in all creatures,
Witness, thinker, Alone, unqualified.'[1]

Such is the description of the One God who has no equal in the *Śvetāśvatara* Upanishad. This conception of the Deity who is Lord and Creator of the universe, and who loves righteousness and hates evil, appears to us far more advanced than anything we have hitherto met with in the Upanishads. God is supremely transcendent and at the same time absolutely immanent, hidden as He is in the heart of all things. He is the beginning and the end: from Him all things proceed[2] and to Him do they return.[3]

The picture of God painted in the Upanishad is magnificent. To us Christians only one thing is lacking: purpose. If God is the 'cause of phenomenal existence, of deliverance from it, of continuance in it, and of bondage,'[4] what is the purpose of it all? Why does God imprison man in matter, only to release him at his appointed time? Indian religion has no answer to this. The disjunction of body and soul which the earlier pantheism refused to admit, becomes ever more marked. Flesh and spirit were henceforth to remain at war. That matter too could be sanctified was never contemplated by 'higher' Indian religion, and it was left to the despised Tantras to carry on the idea.

[1] 6. 5–11. [2] 3. 4: 5. 5. [3] 4. 1. [4] 6. 16.

'The beginning, the efficient cause of the conjoining.
Seen as beyond the three times, without parts too,
Worship Him who takes on all forms, becomes becoming,
The adorable God who dwells in your own thoughts, primeval.'

The term *bhava-bhūta*, 'become becoming',[1] is arresting, for (if the translation is correct) it implies that God does enter into the phenomenal world. The God, Śiva, however, in glorification of whom the *Śvetāśvatara* Upanishad was written, is never a god who takes on human flesh and blood. In the Śaivite sect devoted to him it is rather man who realizes himself as God and *so'smy aham*, 'I am He', therefore becomes the credo of the whole sect.[2] Incarnation in human form is, however, characteristic of that other great Indian representative of supreme Deity, Vishnu: he becomes incarnate again and again to restore the right order of things in the world.

'Though I am unborn and of unchanging substance, the Lord of [all] creatures . . . I come to be by my own supernatural power (*māyā*). Whenever righteousness (*dharma*) decays and unrighteousness grows mighty, then do I emanate Myself. For the protection of the good, for the destruction of evil-doers, for the re-establishment of righteousness I come to be from age to age.'[3]

'Think not that I am come to destroy the law, or the prophets: I am not come to destroy, but to fulfil,'[4] Christ said of the Old Testament. Similarly the Krishna of the Bhagavad-Gītā did not come to destroy the teaching of the Upanishads, he came to fulfil it. The Gītā does *not* destroy the teaching of the Upanishads—it continues the development that can be traced in the Upanishads themselves from a crude cosmogonism, through the definition of the Brahman as that which 'is greater than the great and more minute than the minute' and the dis-

[1] See above, p. 114, n. 4.
[2] See the Śaivite *Sannyāsa* Upanishads, ed. F. O. Schrader, Madras, 1912.
[3] *Bhagavad-Gītā*, 4. 6–8.
[4] Matt. v. 17.

covery of a Supreme Being higher than the Brahman, to a fuller revelation of a God who is not wholly aloof and wholly inoperative as is Brahman in the world which proceeds from him and again dissolves into him.

Naturally the incarnations of Vishnu differ from the Christian idea of incarnation in several important respects. Christ becomes incarnate in order to vanquish sin and to restore the relationship between man and God which had been severed by Adam's disobedience. His incarnation is unique and He is the sole Mediator. Moreover, in founding the Church He inaugurates the Kingdom of God on earth which in the fullness of time will expand into, and be subsumed by, the Kingdom of God in Heaven at the end of time. There is only one incarnation because, in the Judaeo-Christian view, existence on this earth is a middle stage between creation, the beginning, and the second coming, the end. Life on earth is a progress from Adam's fall which brought about bodily death to the final redemption at the end of time when the body is called upon to share with the soul in immortality and life everlasting. For the Hindu, on the other hand, there is no progress in time: time is cyclical, the world being emanated ever again and in endless repetitive cycles from the matrix of being, which is God, and ever again reabsorbed into it. This endless repetition of the same process is called the day and night of Brahman. In the night of Brahman the world sinks into a state of pure potentiality, and during the day of Brahman it is once again actualized.[1] In such a scheme of things, which the Bhagavad-Gītā accepts,[2] Vishnu's incarnations would seem to have little point. This, however, is not quite true, for Vishnu, in his incarnation as Krishna, promises deliverance from reincarnation not only in this world-era, but also in all world-eras:[3] He calls upon man to share eternally in the life of God.

The Bhagavad-Gītā is the crowning glory of Indian theism, and as such it has largely replaced the older scriptures in popular esteem. The Gītā is not, however, a mere popularization of the principal doctrines of the Upanishads; it is the summit of

[1] *Laws of Manu*, 1, 68–73. [2] Gītā, 8. 17. [3] Ibid., 14. 2.

the mountain which the authors of the Upanishads had, laboriously and with many a fall, been climbing. The process of disentangling God from Nature which we see beginning in the *Kaṭha* and *Muṇḍaka* Upanishads reaches its fulfilment in the Gītā.

I do not propose to argue here as to whether or not the Gītā is a composite production. To define one's position on this most important subject would require a whole volume. I can, then, do no more than state my own view baldly. In general I agree with Rudolf Otto that the Gītā is a heterogeneous collection of treatises which, in the main, have been adapted to the Krishna theology. There are, in addition, some fairly obvious Vedāntin or 'Brahmavādin' interpolations—and by 'Brahmavādin' I understand Vedāntin monists, like Śankara, who see in Brahman the Absolute and who identify this absolute *absolutely* with the human soul or *ātman*. I also agree with Otto that the Gītā, as it originally appeared in the Epic, must have been confined to Krishna's answer to Arjuna as to whether or not it was legitimate to partake in a fratricidal struggle: and this question is only fully answered in the eleventh chapter which is also a theophany of a power and splendour quite unknown elsewhere in Indian religious literature. In that chapter Krishna answers Arjuna as God. Arjuna must fight because that is the divine decree which in any case he is incapable of resisting. If he will not conform himself to the divine will of his own free choice, he will have to submit to God's decree against his will; for God is the sole agent in human affairs, man being no more than His instrument.[1] Krishna's transfiguration in which he is seen as the all-creative, all-consuming, omnipotent Lord, brings Arjuna to his knees in awed adoration. *This* is a description of a direct experience of God fully comparable to those of the Old Testament prophets or to that of Muhammad in the Meccan Sūras of the Qur'ān. The message, too, is the same—God is One, Creator and Destroyer of all that is, and He demands from man absolute obedience. This is the central 'prophetic' point of the

[1] *Bhagavad-Gītā*, 11. 33–34: cf. 18. 60–61. Unless otherwise stated references throughout the rest of this chapter are from the *Bhagavad-Gītā*.

whole Gītā. The rest is philosophy in which there is no trace of this colossal impact of God on man. The philosophical chapters are concerned rather with fitting everything the Hindus had ever thought into the new perspective created by the sudden and authoritative assertion of Himself by the One transcendental God.

We have seen that the main trend of the Upanishads was to regard the first cause of the universe as being an impersonal all-pervading spirit which they called Brahman. In course of time the term *Brahman* came to be used to mean the first cause, however that cause might be conceived. In the later Upanishads we meet with the apparently preposterous assertion that this 'first cause', the inexorable law by which Nature functions and on which Nature is grounded, is itself subject to a higher personal power, God. This means that these early thinkers were beginning to pass beyond the *Deus sive Natura* of Spinoza to the realization that God stands outside and above Nature. The philosophical parts of the Bhagavad-Gītā, under the influence of the tremendous revelation of the eleventh chapter, try to explain God's relationship to the hitherto accepted conception of Brahman as the first cause of the universe and in some sense identical with the human soul.

Despite the Brahmavādin interpolations, if such they are, the Gītā does seem to me to give a fairly consistent account of this relationship, and Rāmānuja's commentary, though it over-simplifies the relationship between *ātman* as individual, immortal soul, and Brahman, which he regards as simply a word for the state of eternity or immortality, is substantially true to the Gītā's line of thought. That Śankara's commentary is a complete perversion of the Gītā is, to my mind, beyond dispute; nor is the situation made one whit better by Radhakrishnan and other modern Hindu translators who frequently, and quite gratuitously, translate Brahman as God. So far is this from being true that one might say that the principal object of the chapters preceding Krishna's transfiguration is to lead up from the concept of Brahman as the immutable substrate of all existence to a concept of God that corresponded to the reality revealed in that transfiguration. This, in fact, is just how Rāmānuja understands the Gītā. The first six chapters are, according to him, devoted to the nature of soul and how to realize it in its eternal essence, for only when the soul is thus integrated and at one with itself, can the true worship of God begin. Yoga, self-discipline, detachment, and renunciation of all that is other than the soul are merely techniques to realize the immortality of the soul. Knowledge of the *ātman*, by which Rāmānuja understands the individual soul (*pratyag-ātman*), is only a department (*aṅga*) of the supreme science (*paravidyā*), by which he means knowledge of God.[1] For Rāmānuja it is not only philosophy but psychology that is the proper *propaideutikon* to theology.

One of the reasons that make the Gītā seem so inconsistent is precisely this, that Krishna leads his disciple imperceptibly on from a more or less straight 'atheistic' Sāṁkhya-Yoga cosmology and psychology to a fully theistic position, and it is only in Chapter viii that God's superiority over the Brahman is more or less clearly enunciated.[2] This emerges fairly plainly from a study of the contents. Of the first six chapters three are concerned directly with Brahman and *ātman* and only secondarily with God. This is true also of the eighth which does however, in one passage, unequivocally state that the Brahman is God's *dhāman* or abode. This word, however, probably still possesses its Vedic sense of 'cosmic law'; and it is not irrelevant to point out that the same word in the sister Iranian languages, with the same root and the same suffix, denotes 'creation', the root itself being identical with that of the Greek *τί-θη-μι*. Brahman, then, in this passage, is the 'thing put' or 'set' by God, the cosmic law of the universe as well as His abode.

It will perhaps be worth our while to present a brief analysis of the first six chapters of the Gītā.

The second chapter teaches that there is an indestructible

[1] Rāmānuja on 6. 46. There is an English translation by A. Govindāchārya, *Srī Bhagavad-Gītā*, Madras, 1898.

[2] 8. 21 'That is my highest abode'. Cf. 14. 3 'The great Brahman is my womb': 14. 27 'I am the support (*pratiṣṭhā*) of Brahman.'

element in man, which does not die when the body is slain and which transmigrates from body to body until it is finally released from all bodily existence. 'This dweller in the body is eternal in the body of all and cannot be slain. Therefore there is no need for you to grieve for any creature.'[1] This being so, death for the soul is a sheer impossibility: the soul merely takes on another body. 'Just as a man discards his worn-out clothes and takes new ones so does the embodied soul discard worn-out bodies and take on others that are new.'[2] The soul is by nature an inhabitant of an eternal world, the sum-total of which goes by the name of Brahman; and to become Brahman is to realize eternity. Brahman as the store-house of immortal souls is referred to briefly: 'Know that (neut.=Brahman) by which this whole [world] is woven; no one can destroy this changeless being.'[3] From Brahman as the totality of souls or ātman-category (*tattva*), as Rāmānuja puts it, the Gītā goes on to consider individual souls:

> 'These bodies which are said to belong to an eternal embodied soul, come to an end, while the soul is indestructible and incommensurable.'[4]

Here it is possible to translate not as '*an* eternal embodied soul' but as '*the* eternal embodied' Brahman, thereby understanding one indivisible soul which pervades the whole world as, of course, Śankara did, for in the genitive case there is no distinction between masculine and neuter. The following stanzas, however, transfer definitely from the neuter to the masculine, from the Brahman to the *ātman*, that soul which 'is not born nor dies at any time, and which will never, having entered the world of becoming (*bhūtvā*), hereafter cease to be. Unborn, permanent, eternal, ancient, it is not slain when the body is slain'.[5]

So much must be considered as of faith. The question, however, is how this eternal soul can be recognized here and now. The answer: by practising Yoga in the widest sense of that word. First one must learn to detach oneself completely from

[1] 2. 30. [2] 2. 22. [3] 2. 17. [4] 2. 18. [5] 2. 20.

the 'fruits' of one's action, abandon all desires, be totally indifferent to good and evil fortune, and withdraw the senses from their objects 'as a tortoise draws its limbs' into its shell.[1] Secondly, one should concentrate one's attention on God (Krishna).[2] 'Then does a man, having abandoned all desires, act without yearning: with all sense of "mine" and "I" departed, he attains to peace. This is the state of Brahman. He who has reached it is not deluded. Taking his stand on this he goes to the *nirvāṇa* of Brahman at the hour of his death.'[3]

God here is not the God who reveals Himself in the eleventh chapter: he is simply the God of the classical Yoga, the soul which remained for ever unsullied by matter, the contemplation of whom leads to no communion with him but simply to the Nirvāṇa of Brahman. Apart from the idea of God which comes from the classical 'theistic' Yoga, both the ideas and the terminology are Buddhistic: the soul passes to a timeless peace. Here Brahman means little more than a timeless mode of existence.

The third chapter, in which Krishna explains the purpose of his incarnations, preaches the same lesson and, in addition, gives practical instruction on how to live in the world. Arjuna is told that he must perform his caste duty of fighting the enemy, but he must do so in a spirit of complete detachment, fighting yet taking no credit for the result 'without expectation or any sense of "mine".'[4] God, however, is no longer just an object of contemplation: He it is who keeps the world in being by his tireless and selfless labour: 'If ever I did not engage in work, unwearying, men would everywhere imitate my behaviour. If I did not do the work that has to be done, these worlds would collapse, and I should be a maker of chaos and the destroyer of these [my] creatures.'[5] Moreover Arjuna should not think that he is personally responsible for his actions; these are done by the *guṇas* or constituents of Nature which are independent of the immortal soul.[6] Better then to leave God to do the work and

[1] 2. 58.
[2] 2. 61.
[3] 2. 71–72.
[4] 3. 30.
[5] 3. 23–24.
[6] 3. 27–29.

fight as if it were nothing to do with him.[1] The import of these two chapters would seem to be that Brahman is the timeless condition which the soul can achieve, while God is the agent who keeps the phenomenal world in being. He is not yet Lord of both Brahman and Nature.

The theme of Brahman is again taken up in chapter v, which is almost identical, as far as doctrine is concerned, with chapter ii, though its exaltation of Brahman as both the goal of Yoga and as an external agency is far more extreme. It is again concerned with the self-discipline of Yoga, and its hero is the *yoga-yukta* or *brahma-yoga-yukt'ātmā*,[2] 'the man whose self or soul is joined together by the joining of Brahman', in other words what we would now call an 'integrated' personality, 'integrated' in the Jungian sense of 'harmonized around the immortal centre or "self" of the total psyche'. Integration (*yoga*) is attained by the remorseless concentration of attention on one point. 'Shutting off external contacts, fixing the eye between the eyebrows and making the in-and-out breathings which pass through the nostrils, equal, the sage who has control of his senses, *sensus communis* (*manas*), and intellect (*buddhi*), and has done with desire, fear and anger, intent on release, is ever released.'[3] Sages such as these realize that the soul or *ātman* is never the author of any action: action is the sphere of Nature (*svabhāva*). They experience no kind of emotion, pleasurable or the reverse, 'established in Brahman'[4] as they are. 'Finding happiness and delight within themselves, illumined by an inner light, such Yogin[s] attain to the Nirvāṇa of Brahman, for they have become Brahman.'[5]

At the same time Brahman is the law which operates in Nature, for the Yogin is bidden to resign all work to Brahman exactly as Arjuna was bidden to leave God to do the work.[6] Rāmānuja explains this by saying that Brahman here means Nature (*prakṛti*) which in a sense is true, since it is certainly Nature (*svabhāva*) that is the agent in § 14. But Brahman in this

[1] 3. 30. [2] 5. 21. [3] 5. 27–28. [4] 5. 20. [5] 5. 24.
[6] 5. 10 *brahmany ādhāya karmāṇi*: cf. 3. 30 *mayi sarvāṇi karmāṇi sannyasya.*

chapter is both the innermost soul, lord (*prabhu*),[1] and pervader of all (*vibhu*).[2] There is no mention of Krishna as God, and it is difficult to resist the conclusion that this is a pure Brahmavādin interpolation, for chapter vi goes over the same ground yet again but does *not* equate Brahman with external Nature as well as the soul, and at the very end it does conclude on a theistic note which leads straight on to the theistic affirmations of the following chapter. The perfect Yogin is he 'who, full of faith, worships Me with his inmost soul (*antarātman*) fixed on Me: him I consider to be the most integrated of all'.[3]

Yet even if chapter v is a Brahmanvādin interpolation, it is interesting that it should have been allowed to stand in a work that is devoted to the glorification of Krishna. The explanation would seem to be that even if you interpret Brahman as being *both* the ideal world *and* the phenomenal world, and even if you cast your actions on Brahman as the agent within the phenomenal world while concentrating on its eternal aspect, this does not in any way conflict with the revelation that is to follow, namely, that there is one upon whom even Brahman is contingent.

The point is perhaps best illustrated from the repeated use of the phrase *yena sarvam idaṁ tatam*, which means literally, 'by whom all this [world] is woven'. Śankara takes *tatam* ('woven') to mean 'pervaded', but it is an obvious reference to the Upanishadic idea of the world issuing from Brahman *qua* Nature or primal matter[4] as a spider's web issues from the spider,[5] or to the similar idea that the world is woven 'warp and woof' on the 'imperishable', that is, Brahman.[6] In the Gītā the phrase occurs (with minor variants) five times. On the first occasion it refers to Brahman as the imperishable source of phenomenal being, as Nature or primal matter, the *prakṛti* of the Sāṁkhya. Similarly in 9. 4 it refers to God in His unmanifest (*avyakta*) form, that is, again primal matter, God's *dhāma*, 'abode' or 'thing set';[7] but in 8. 22 it is the supreme Person, that is, God as

[1] 5. 14. [2] 5. 15. [3] 6. 47. [4] So explicitly in *Śvet.*
[5] *Bṛhadāraṇyaka* Up., 2. 1. 20: *Muṇḍaka*, 1. 1. 7: *Śvetāśvatara*, 6. 10.
[6] *Bṛhadāraṇyaka* Up., 3. 8. [7] Gītā, 8. 21.

distinct from Nature, as the supreme *Puruṣa* or *Iśvara*, the Lord of the classical Yoga 'by whom the whole world is woven'—an idea which is, however, quite foreign to that system. Here there is a distinct shift of emphasis, for the Sāṁkhya idea of *puruṣa* and *prakṛti* appears in 8. 21–22 in a novel form. Formerly the world was regarded as emanating from 'unmanifest' primal matter as a spider's web issues from the spider. Now it is woven by God, the supreme *Puruṣa*, the Lord of the classical Yoga who now ceases to be a *Deus otiosus* and emerges as the Creator of the world. God, as supreme Person and Lord, weaves the world, as in the *Bṛhadāraṇyaka* Upanishad, across primal matter, the 'unmanifest' (*avyakta*, a Sāṁkhya expression) or the 'imperishable' (*akṣara*, a Vedāntin expression).[1] Finally in his profession of faith in the transfigured Lord Arjuna exclaims:

> 'Thou art the *Urgott*, the ancient Person,
> Thou art the resting-place of all.
> Thou art the knower and the known, supreme abode (*dhāma*):
> By Thee are all things woven, O Thou of infinite form.[2]

Thus the idea of God in the early chapters of the Gītā develops from the *Deus otiosus* of the classical Yoga—a God who has no function except to serve as a focus for concentration—to that of the Highest Person who is supreme Lord and Creator of the universe—not indeed out of nothing but out of the Brahman which is His womb.[3] The God of the Gītā, as Person, then combines the classical Yogin idea of God as object of contemplation with the more ancient idea of the primal *Puruṣa* or Person who, as sacrificial victim, is both the material and efficient cause of the universe.[4]

The undoubted confusion that exists in the first six chapters of the Gītā is due also to the fact that Sāṁkhya-Yoga and Vedāntin terminologies are inextricably mixed. What the Sāṁkhya calls *puruṣa* and *prakṛti*, is all included by the Vedānta under the one category of Brahman. *Prakṛti*, in its original

[1] Cf. *Bṛhadāraṇyaka* Up., 3. 8. 8.
[2] Gītā, 11. 38.
[3] 14. 3.
[4] Rig-Veda, x, 90.

'unmanifest' state, is one aspect of Brahman, being the indestructible basis of the phenomenal world, but the word *Brahman* is also used in the sense of an eternal mode of existence outside time and unaffected by change. This is the meaning of such phrases as *brahma-nirvāṇa*, *brahma-bhūta*, etc. In *this* sense Brahman is the totality of the *puruṣas* of the Sāṁkhya system. In cosmological as opposed to psychological passages in the Gītā, then, Brahman means what the Vedāntins of Śankara's school understand by *māyā*, something that is not absolutely unreal like the 'son of a barren mother', i.e. a logical impossibility, but something that is real from the empirical point of view, though wholly unreal as far as the Absolute is concerned, 'neither being nor not-being',[1] i.e. contingent being or the world of becoming.

To sum up: Brahman, in the Gītā, is cosmologically primal matter (*prakṛti* or *māyā*); psychologically it is the realization of immortality. The confusion is appalling.

These introductory chapters, then, as Rāmānuja rightly saw, are concerned primarily with self-realization, 'becoming Brahman' in the Buddhist sense of experiencing immortality. Secondarily these chapters reinterpret an essentially Sāṁkhya ontological scheme in Vedāntin terms. Brahman thus becomes the combination of the objective universe on the one hand and the sum-total of human souls on the other. This grand combination is what Rāmānuja calls 'the body of the Lord'. However, although Rāmānuja's interpretation of *brahma-bhūta* as 'each established in his own form' (*sva-svarupenāvasthitam*)[2] almost certainly conveys the thought of the Gītā, he probably misinterprets § 29 of chapter vi which states that the *ātman* is in all things and all things in it, thereby identifying it with the Krishna of §§ 30–31. This Rāmānuja interprets as meaning that all souls are of one and the same form as being rational (*jñānaik'ākāratayā*). Brahman still means the eternal element in the human soul *and* the eternal 'law' in Nature. The purpose of the later chapters of the Gītā is to demonstrate that there is One who is both Law-giver and the Supreme Soul, Person, or Spirit.

[1] Gītā, 13. 12. [2] On 6. 27.

'The first six chapters dealt with the essence (*yāthātmya*) of the individual soul (*pratyag-ātman*). The aspirant was seen to obtain [direct] knowledge of this soul by previously practising works [while detaching himself from their "fruits"]. This is a department of the [higher] knowledge and leads up to the adoration (*upāsana*) of, that is, the means of attaining to, Him who is the highest goal, the Highest Brahman, the indestructible sole cause of the entire universe, omniscient, all-Being, who wills the real (*satyasaṅkalpa*), God (*Nārāyaṇa*) the Glorious, the all-pervading.' So does Rāmānuja introduce the seventh chapter of the Gītā. From this chapter up to the twelfth—with the exception of chapter viii which again reverts to the Yogic theory of achieving an immortal state independent of God—the subject-matter of the Gītā is the nature of God.

In the eighth chapter, which is largely a repetition of what has gone before, there is a marked difference. The classical Yoga, as we know, recommended contemplation of the 'Lord' as the one ever-undefiled *puruṣa*; but the idea that it might be possible to approach that Person and commune with him was not for a moment entertained. Yet, in the eighth chapter, even those self-centred Yogins who merely use God as a focus on which to concentrate their meditation and whose ultimate aim is only to isolate their own souls in their eternal essence,[1] will be helped by God and brought near to Him in return for their good intentions.

'He who utters the monosyllable 'Oṁ', which is Brahman, yet keeps Me in mind the while, who leaving his body, passes away, goes on the highest course. If a Yogin who has reached a state of constant integration, constantly bears Me in mind with no thought for aught else, then can he easily attain to Me. Having come near to me, these great souls will have reached supreme fulfilment (*saṁsiddhi*) and, never born again, will never return to this impermanent abode of pain.'[2]

Integration of the personality, then, which Yoga techniques

[1] See Rāmānuja on 8. 11. [2] 8. 13–15.

produce, is only the first stage on the mystical path to God. By realizing oneself as an integrated (*yoga-yukta*) personality, the soul is now open to the grace of God. The preliminary realization of self has not been in vain.

To know God does not mean to sink oneself into an Absolute which is devoid of quality. It means getting to know Him as He is. Since I have already spent longer than I had intended on the Gītā, I will not attempt to give a detailed description of all the Gītā has to say about God, but will confine myself to those passages which are not commonplaces in other theistic systems, whether Hindu or otherwise. God is, of course, creator, sustainer, and destroyer of the universe, its beginning, middle, and end,[1] transcendent as the Highest Person as well as immanent, and, dwelling in the hearts of men,[2] the essence of all things[3] and their seed.[4] On the subject of the divine immanence the Gītā is not consistent. There are purely pantheistic passages ('I am the ritual, I am the sacrifice', etc.)[5] as well as passages in which God is described as the most essential quality in any given substance or the highest representative in any given species ('I am the taste in the waters, I am the light in the sun and moon', etc.).[6] These are probably later accretions or derive from extraneous sources because, in one or two key passages, the Gītā does try to state with precision how it understands immanence. Of the three *guṇas* or inherent characteristics of which all Nature is made up, Krishna says: 'Know that these are *from* Me; I am not in them but they are in Me.'[7] Similarly God sustains all creatures but does not subsist (*-stha*) in them. 'All creatures subsist in Me, but I am not established in them. And yet creatures do *not* subsist in(side) Me—Behold My sovereign power (*yoga*). My own self sustains creatures without subsisting in them; it causes them to exist.'[8] 'He is,' in fact, 'in all things as causing the being of all things,'[9] as St. Thomas was later to define the divine immanence. The relationship of the divine immanence to the created world is that of space to the

[1] 10. 20. [3] 7. 8 ff. [5] 9. 16 ff. [7] 7. 12.
[2] 15. 15. [4] 7. 10: 9. 18: 10. 39. [6] 7. 8 ff. [8] 9. 4–5.
[9] *Summa Theologica*, I, viii, I, resp. obj. I.

wind:[1] the second is conditioned by the first and cannot exist without it. Just as the wind is in space and not vice versa, so is creation in God.

In Islam God creates the world out of nothing: He says 'Be' and it is. In Christianity God 'generates' the Word in eternity and creates through the Word in time. In the Gītā God generates the world from Himself, He Himself being the seed.[2] 'The great Brahman is my womb; in that I put my seed, and from that all beings grow together.'[3] God, as 'seed' and therefore son, is begotten of Himself both as the world and as the divine *avatars*.[4] 'Though I am unborn and of changeless substance (*ātman*), though I am the Lord of creatures, yet do I by my creative power (*māyā*) draw near to Nature (as mother) which is of Me and thus grow together (as son):[5] for God is both Father, Mother,[6] and seed, producing the phenomenal world and His own *avatars* by fertilizing Himself. The world is, then, totally dependent on Him while He is utterly independent of the world.

According to Rāmānuja there is no purpose in creation: it is of no use to God except as something to play with. 'No creature is of the least service to Me, its only use is as a plaything.'[7] And this is perhaps the great weakness of the theology of the Bhagavad-Gītā. God has no purpose in creating the world: man is simply hurled into the 'wheel of Brahman', a blindly operating mechanism[8] from which he must at all costs escape; and it is God who keeps the mechanism going since He is apparently obliged to do so by His own Nature (*svabhāva*) which cannot help emanating and absorbing endless universes endlessly. For the Hindus, as for Richard Jefferies, it is not the eternal which is mysterious—one has only to persevere in the practice of Yoga to 'become Brahman'—it is matter, *māyā*, *prakṛti*, the 'unmanifest' which is 'beyond understanding, mysterious, impene-

[1] Gītā, 9. 6. [2] See p. 128, n. 4. [3] 14. 3.
[4] 4. 6 (of *avatars*): cf. 9. 8 (of the world). [5] 4. 6. [6] 9. 17.
[7] On 7. 12: *mama tu tair na kaścit tathāvidha upakāraḥ; kevalam līlaiva prayojanam.*
[8] 18. 61.

trable'.[1] It cannot be explained except as a practical joke that God plays on man.

The game, however, is worth playing, for by involving man in matter God kindles a deep longing in his soul not only for release from this world but for reunion with Himself. The real message of the Gītā does not lie in its philosophy but in its teaching that God is not a passionless Absolute but the lover of man's soul, indeed Love itself. 'I am that love in created things which is not contrary to righteousness', Krishna roundly declares.[2] He is father, comrade, and beloved,[3] and man is a 'fragment'[4] of the divine substance, the divine spark which needs must return to its home.

Here we have reached a position that is very near to that of the Christian mystics. There is a mutual interaction between God and man, not a single human effort as in Buddhism, nor a shaking off of all temporal being with the benign assistance of *a* god in order to realize one's own soul as in the Sāṁkhya-Yoga, nor yet a realization of oneself as the Absolute as in Śankara's Vedānta, but a mutual relationship between an I and a Thou, a relationship of grace and love. 'Listen again to My final word, the most mysterious of all. With strong desire have I desired (*iṣṭo*) thee; therefore shall I tell thee thy salvation (*hitam*). Think of Me, worship Me, sacrifice to Me, pay Me homage: so shalt thou come to Me. I promise thee truly, for I love thee well. Give up all things of the law (*dharmān*), turn to me only as thy refuge. I will deliver thee from all evil; have no care.'[5]

In passages like these we have passed far beyond the philosophico-psychological gropings of the earlier Upanishads. For the first time in the long history of Indian religious experience God seems to be speaking directly to man—a God of love certainly, but not *only* a God of love, for always and in all religions that concern themselves with God rather than with an impersonal absolute there is terror in God as well as mercy: beside *Pie Jesu Domine* there is always *Rex tremendae majestatis*,

[1] R. Jefferies, *The Story of my Heart*, p. 32.
[2] Gītā, 7. 11. [3] 11. 44. [4] 15. 7. [5] 18. 64–66.

beside *Ar-Raḥmān ar-Raḥīm*, 'the Merciful, the Compassionate', there is *Al-Qahhār*, 'He who overwhelms', that terrible God into whose hands it is a fearful thing to fall.[1] For Krishna too has His transfiguration which He reveals to his beloved disciple Arjuna; and Arjuna is overwhelmed and panic-stricken by this vision of God in His all-consuming power.

'As I look upon Thee touching the sky, blazing with many a hue, Thy mouth wide open, Thy blazing eyes expanded, my inmost soul shudders [within me]: I find no sure ground [on which to rest], nor peace, O Vishnu. Looking upon Thy jaws, terrible with their tusks, as into Time's devouring fire, I know no longer where I am and find no resting-place. Have mercy, Lord of gods, Refuge of the world. All the sons of Dhṛtarāṣtra . . . rush headlong into Thy gaping, fearful jaws, terrible with their tusks. Some of these I see caught between Thy teeth, their heads ground to powder. As many rushing torrents hurtle headlong into the sea, so do these heroes in their worldly pride rush into Thy blazing mouths. As in mad haste moths rush into a flaming fire to their own destruction, so do [all] the worlds rush hurtling into Thy mouths to perish there. Devouring all the worlds completely in Thy flaming mouths, Thou lickest them up. Filling the whole world with Thy light, Thine awful brilliance scorches the whole universe.'[2]

Here is a vision of God as fearful as any that the Old Testament can supply, that terrible aspect of the Deity which no non-dualist religion can wholly conceal. The man-God Krishna, so gentle to his beloved disciple, is at the same time that fearful power of attraction that draws all things to itself whether they will it or not; One God always, and always a 'Living Flame of Love', absolutely and totally terrifying to those who reject Him, but more tender than a lover to those who accept Him. Thus after the tremendous vision Arjuna cries out: 'Bowing down and prostrating my body before Thee, I crave Thy grace, Adorable Lord. Bear with me, I pray Thee, as a father with his son, friend with friend, lover with beloved.'[3] To which Krishna

[1] Hebrews, 10. 31. [2] Gītā, 11. 24–30. [3] 11. 44.

replies as Christ did after His own transfiguration, 'Arise and "be not afraid".'[1]

It is difficult indeed for any unprejudiced person to remain unimpressed by the astonishing resemblance between the theophany of the Bhagavad-Gītā and the Christian account of God in the New Testament. In both we have God exhibited incarnate as 'meek and lowly' but exhibited also in His terrible form as an all-consuming flame. Obviously there is a close parallelism here: and we shall try to draw some conclusions from it later.

The theophany is the 'prophetic' core of the Gītā, but it is at the end of the eighteenth and last chapter that the essential teaching of the Gītā is summed up. If man is to encounter his God, he must first of all conquer his own lower nature in order that he may realize his own eternal being, the image of God within him. Only then does his dialogue and his communion with God begin:

'By giving up self (the ego), force, pride, lust, anger, and acquisitiveness, with no thought of "mine", at peace, so is a man fitted to realize his eternal essence (*brahma-bhūyāya kalpate*). Become eternal (*brahma-bhūta*), his soul all stilled, he grieves not nor does he desire. Feeling equanimity towards all creatures, he receives the highest love (*bhakti*) of Me. By his loving devotion he comes to *know* Me as I am, how great I am and Who. Then once he has known Me as I am, he forthwith comes to Me.'[2]

Here the relationship between the mysticism of realizing the eternal oneness of one's own soul and the mysticism of the love of God is more clearly formulated than anywhere else except perhaps in *The Spiritual Espousals* of Blessed Jan Ruysbroeck. The one gives the peace of detachment from all temporal things, the other sets the soul aflame with the love of a God, the infinite depths of whose Being can never be exhausted. So, in the Gītā, the soul, released from the fetters of time and self and at peace, is now ready to respond to the secret workings of grace:

[1] Matt. xvii. 7: Gītā, 11. 49. [2] 18. 53–55.

'Fixing thy thoughts on Me, thou shalt surmount all difficulties through My grace. But if, prompted by thine "ego", thou wilt not hearken, thou shalt perish. Shouldst thou, relying on thine "ego" think, "I will not fight", thy effort is in vain, for Nature will compel thee. Bound by thine own deeds [done in lives gone by] which are born of thine own nature, thou wilt do what, in thy delusion, thou wouldst not, for thou art without mastery.

'The Lord abides in the hearts of all creatures and by his supernatural power, makes them move hither and thither, things caught in a machine. Flee to Him as thy refuge with all thy being. Through His grace thou shalt attain perfect peace and an eternal abode.'[1]

Then Krishna declares the unheard-of secret of God's love for man:

'Think on me, worship me, sacrifice to Me, pay Me homage: so shalt thou come to Me. I promise thee truly, for I love thee well. Give up all things of the law, turn to me only as thy refuge. I will deliver thee from all evil. Have no care.'[2]

This is the 'Highest Word', the 'most mysterious of all', a thing unheard-of in India before—God loves man.

[1] 18. 61–62. [2] 18. 65–66.

CHAPTER IV

Prophets Outside Israel

In the foregoing chapters we tried to show in as brief a compass as possible what Indian religion was about. It is philosophic and empiricist; and except in the eleventh chapter of the Bhagavad-Gītā it makes no claim to be a self-revelation of a personal God who stands outside man, directs him, and leads him on to his destiny. It is rather a revelation of what is latent in man, the revelation of the immortality of his soul—a revelation, it is claimed, which, once experienced, can never more be doubted. For the earlier Upanishads, this sufficed in itself, it was the *paramā gatiḥ*, 'the highest going' or 'final stage' beyond which, it was considered, it was impossible to proceed. Yet despite the discovery of this enormous empirical truth (if truth it is), the Indian mind did not rest content with this. Beyond the soul, they felt, there must be something yet higher, something beyond both the *ātman*, the immortal soul, and the Brahman, the mysterious principle which pervades the whole universe and makes it what it is, something or rather someone who rules the entire cosmos yet who is, in the words of the Qur'ān, 'nearer to man than his jugular vein'.[1] This idea finds its most perfect expression in the Bhagavad-Gītā; and it is characteristic of un-historically-minded India that this unique theophany should form part of the great Epic and should be put into the mouth of a mythical hero who, though he may reflect a real person in remote history, is scarcely a historical

[1] 50. 15.

personage in the sense that the Buddha or Zoroaster are. Krishna, in any case, is no prophet in the Old Testament sense: he claims to be an incarnation of God revealing himself directly to man. Rather, perhaps, we should say he is the idea of God made incarnate in the Indian mind. In India, then, there is nothing corresponding to the prophetic tradition of Israel. For this we have to look to India's sister civilization, Iran.

In Iran we do find a prophetic figure similar in all respects to the prophets of Israel—Zoroaster or Zarathushtra, to give him his proper name. He is one of the most puzzling figures in the history of all religion, and this for several reasons. First, the language in which he composed, though closely akin to Vedic Sanskrit is still only imperfectly understood and all too frequently we can only guess at his meaning. Secondly, although the mythology of the later Avesta shows close similarity to that of the Veda, the hymns of Zoroaster himself stand quite apart, for all the gods have been deposed from their high estate, and there remains only Ahura Mazdā, the Wise Lord, who is both supreme creator, judge, and God—attended, it is true, by subordinate beings who are, however, not minor godlets, but abstract ideas, the Holy Spirit, the Good Mind, Righteousness, Right-mindedness, the Kingdom, Wholeness, and Immortality. Thirdly there is no reliable tradition in accordance with which his doctrine can be interpreted; and fourthly it is extremely difficult to fit the *Gāthās* or 'Songs' of Zoroaster into the other sources of early Iranian religion, particularly the Achaemenid inscriptions and the account of the religion of the Persians given by Herodotus. Anything, then, that I should say about Zoroaster's own religion as distinct from the Zoroastrianism of the post-Christian era should be treated with some reserve.

The very date of Zoroaster is a matter of speculation. Recent research has, however, shown that the traditional date, that is, '258 years before Alexander' can be accepted with good reason. 'Before Alexander' could only mean to the Iranian mind the extinction of the Persian Empire and the death of Darius III in 330 B.C. If we take the date to refer to the beginning of the Prophet's mission when he was granted his first revelation, his dates would be fixed at B.C. 628–551; and this would make him a contemporary of the Buddha and probably also of the middle stratum of the Upanishads. His field of operation seems to have been ancient Chorasmia, that is to say, somewhere within the wide area now occupied by Persian Khorasan, Northern Afghanistan, and what is now the Turkmen Republic of the Soviet Union.[1]

Of his life we know only what he tells us himself, and this amounts to very little. It is clear that he was forced to flee from his native land[2] where his preaching was actively opposed by the upholders of the traditional and probably polytheistic religion, whom he habitually refers to as 'the followers of the Lie': thence he appears to have wandered in search of a protector, one who would accept both him and the new teaching of which he claimed to be the prophet. Such a protector he found in King Vishtāspa, possibly the paramount prince in Chorasmia, and it was under his auspices that Zoroaster was able to develop his doctrines.

In coming to Zoroaster from the Bhagavad-Gītā we are immediately conscious of a wholly different religious climate. In the Gītā we meet with Krishna, the mythological charioteer of Arjuna, revealing himself gratuitously to the latter as supreme Lord and God of the universe. It is a wonderful story of divine grace woven into the fabric of India's great Epic. With Zoroaster things are quite different. Here we are in the presence of an historical character who, like the prophets of Israel, became acutely conscious of God as a living presence, a God alternately concealing and manifesting Himself according to His inscrutable will. To Zoroaster the revelation of God comes gradually. At the beginning of his mission he still doubts whether God has the power to shield him from the violence of his enemies. 'When shall I come to know,' he asks his God, 'whether Thou hast power over all those who threaten me with destruction? . . . When will the warrior take note of my message? When wilt

[1] For the date and place of operation of Zoroaster see W. B. Henning, *Zoroaster, Politician or Witch-Doctor?*, Oxford, 1951, pp. 35–43.

[2] *Yasna* (abbreviated hereinafter to Y.), 46. 1.

Thou strike down this filthy drunkenness with which these priests evilly delude [the people] as do the wicked rulers in full consciousness [of what they do]?'[1] Here we have the genuine voice of the prophet crying to his God to put down the idolaters with their debauched sacrificial rites.[2] Here is the same prophetic intolerance of all worship that is not exclusively directed to the one true God which is so utterly typical of the Old Testament and is so foreign to the spirit of Indian religion. Zoroaster sees no good in the old religion, it is directed to the *daēvas*, the ancient Indo-Iranian gods, whom he now regards simply as demons who lead astray mankind. Between them and him there can be no compromise; they follow the lie, he alone follows the Truth. 'They, the followers of the Lie, have rejected the Holy Spirit, not so the followers of Truth. Whether a man be lord of little or of much wealth, he should do good to the followers of Truth, evil to the followers of the Lie.'[3]

However, this is not only a matter of religious principle; the struggle has economic causes too. Zoroaster's community is a community of settled herdsmen, his opponents are the marauding nomads who prey on his people's flocks and herds. The two ways of living are seen by the Prophet as the reflection of two contrary principles—*Asha*, Right Order, both in the cosmos as a whole and here on earth, righteousness and truth, and *Druj*, the principle that thwarts and upsets this Cosmic Order, wickedness and falsehood. Thus it is 'the follower of the Lie, ill-famed and reprobate in his deeds' who 'would prevent the supporters of Righteousness from making their kine to prosper in their district or their land. Whoso deprives him of his sovereignty or life,' says the Prophet, 'shall, leading the way, tread the path of the good doctrine.'[4] For the supporters of the ancient religion are Zoroaster's declared enemies as they were to be Muhammad's in Mecca twelve centuries later; and since Zoroaster is convinced that God has revealed the truth to him, he *cannot* leave his countrymen to follow the old ways. It is a matter of the salvation of souls: if the enemy will not be con-

[1] Y., 48. 10.
[2] But see below, p. 152.
[3] Y., 47. 4.
[4] Y., 46. 4.

verted he must be overcome. 'He who, by word or thought or with his hands, works evil to the follower of the Lie or converts his comrade to the good, such a man does the will of the Wise Lord and pleases Him well.'[1]

How different from the Indian spirit! For Zoroaster religion is a matter of life and death: it is deadly serious, anything but a game that God is playing with man. It is something in which not only man but also God is vitally concerned, the question of the choice that must be made between good and evil, Truth and the Lie. The Prophet hungers and thirsts after righteousness. For Krishna, on the other hand, though there may be only one religion which is perfect—his own—yet other religions are nevertheless at least approximations to it, and he therefore encourages them all. 'Those whose minds are distracted by manifold desires,' he says, 'worship other gods performing different rites, constrained by their own nature. Whatever form a religious man chooses to worship with unwavering faith, his faith do I confirm. Firm in that faith he seeks to propitiate his god, and from that god he obtains his desires though these are really apportioned by Me.'[2] This, to the prophet, is always unthinkable, for it compromises the truth. He can accept, certainly, the idea that the followers of false religions go to what they worship, but what they worship is evil, and their mead is therefore Hell, called by Zoroaster the 'house of the Lie',[3] where there is unending torment. With Zoroaster, as with all prophets, there are no nuances: religions are not, as for Krishna, approximations to the truth. They are either true (his own) or false (all others). There can be no compromise. How could there be? For Zoroaster sees himself as the chosen prophet of God 'from the beginning',[4] 'the Prophet who raises his voice in veneration, the friend of Truth'[5] and of God,[6] and therefore 'a powerful support to the followers of Truth' and 'a true enemy of the followers of the Lie'.[7] So too in a late Zoroastrian catechism we read: 'I declare that I have received the Good Religion of

[1] Y., 33. 2.
[2] Gītā, 7. 20–22.
[3] Y., 49. 11: 51. 14, etc.
[4] Y., 44. 11.
[5] Y., 50. 6.
[6] Y., 46. 2.
[7] Y., 43. 8.

the worshippers of the Wise Lord and have no doubts concerning it. . . . I neither approve of, nor respect, other religions, nor do I lend them credence.'[1] The catechumen here is fully faithful to the spirit of the Prophet.

But what is this strange power that gives the Prophet his overwhelming conviction that he serves the Truth? It is the realization, which seems to have come to him in a vision, that God is holy, righteous, and good. 'As holy[2] did I conceive Thee, Wise Lord', forms the refrain of *Yasna* 43, and in the same hymn the agent of inspiration is the *Good* Mind. This is the Prophet Zoroaster's great theme, the core of the revelation he claims to have received from God, a message that we find neither in India nor in Israel. God is not only Righteousness and Truth: He is also Good. 'There is none good but one, that is, God',[3] Christ was to say later: and in this He takes up the teaching of the Iranian Prophet rather than that of the Hebrew prophets.

This emphasis on the goodness of God was to lead the followers of Zoroaster into a cut-and-dried dualism never, perhaps, foreseen or intended by the Prophet himself. For Zoroaster God is above all the friend of the good and the enemy of the wicked, distributing rewards to the one and punishments to the other.

'As holy did I conceive Thee, Wise Lord,' the Prophet exclaims, 'when I saw Thee, the Eternal (*paourvīm*), at the birth of existence, appoint a recompense for deed and word, an evil lot for the wicked, good for the good, through Thy virtue at the last turning-point of creation.'[4]

But if God is good and righteous and holy, how did evil come into the world?

Everyone knows that in later times Zoroastrianism came to be the classic dualistic religion, but does this reflect the mind of

[1] See R. C. Zaehner, *The Teachings of the Magi*, London, 1956, p. 23.

[2] The meaning of this word (*spenta*) is not wholly certain. It may perhaps mean 'creative' or 'who gives increase'.

[3] Matt. xix. 17.

[4] Y., 43. 5.

the Prophet himself? This is far from certain. In the later religion the dualism is between Ahura Mazdā, the Wise Lord or Ohrmazd as he later came to be called on the one hand, and Angra Mainyu, the Evil or Destructive Spirit, Ahriman, on the other. This is not so in the *Gāthās*. There the basic opposition is between Truth, Righteousness, or order (*asha*) on the one hand, and the Lie, unrighteousness, or disorder on the other. God or Ahura Mazdā, though the creator of all things, must Himself choose between the opposing tendencies at work in His creation. As supreme Lord and Judge he is approached by the opposing parties, the ancient gods dispossessed by Zoroaster themselves asking for His almighty blessing:

'Family and village and tribe, and the godlets too, like me, asked bliss of the Wise Lord [saying]: "Let us be Thy messengers that we may keep at bay those who hate Thee." To them did the Wise Lord, united with the Good Mind and in close companionship with Truth, make answer from His Kingdom: "Holy and good Right-Mindedness do We choose; let it be ours." '[1]

God has decided: He has pronounced in favour of 'Right-Mindedness' (*ārmaiti*) which here seems to refer to the Prophet's community as against the ancient cult.

God, then, *chooses* righteousness as against the Lie; but how these themselves arose is not clear. And what is the relationship between the Wise Lord and the two spirits of good and evil, the Holy Spirit and the Destructive Spirit as they are called. In the later texts Ahura Mazdā, the Wise Lord, is actually identified with the Holy Spirit, and the two terms become interchangeable; but this is not true of the *Gāthās*. There the Wise Lord is once called the father of the Holy Spirit.[2] Again in the later texts the Wise Lord or the Holy Spirit who by this time have become one and the same being, is identified with light and the Destructive Spirit with darkness, whereas in the *Gāthās* the Wise Lord creates both light *and* darkness.[3] It is then more than likely that Zoroaster regarded his supreme God as being the

[1] Y., 32. 1–2. [2] Y., 47. 2–3. [3] Y., 44. 5.

author of all things including the Destructive Spirit who is, or at least became, the Devil. This surely must follow from the fact that the Wise Lord is the father of the Holy Spirit and the latter is referred to as the Destructive Spirit's twin. Yet Zoroaster's God, Ahura Mazdā, abhors for ever the Evil Spirit and the Lie, even though, ultimately, it would seem, they must have proceeded from Him just as Satan proceeds from God in the Old Testament. Zoroaster recognized, as few have done before or after, that there is only one true God, whose will is Righteousness, whose spirit is the Holy Spirit, and whose mind is the Good Mind. Nevertheless he is acutely conscious of the problem of evil and of the essential blasphemy of attributing evil directly to God. So he leaves this problem as yet unsolved though in places he seems to suggest a fully dualist solution which later was to become Zoroastrian orthodoxy. This incipient dualism is affirmed in two celebrated passages:

'I will speak out,' the Prophet proclaims, 'concerning the two Spirits of whom, at the beginning of existence, the Holier spoke to him who is Evil: "Neither our thoughts, nor our teachings, nor our wills, nor our choices, nor our words, nor our deeds, nor our convictions, nor yet our souls agree." '[1]

Here good and evil face each other in stark opposition, two Spirits who are different in all things and can never agree. The theme of the two Spirits is further developed in another *Gāthā*:

'In the beginning the two Spirits who are the well-endowed (?) twins were known as the one good and other other evil in thought, word, and deed. Between them the wise chose the good, not so the fools. And when these two Spirits met, they established in the beginning life and death, that in the end the evil should meet with the worst existence but the just with the Best Mind. Of these two Spirits he who was of the Lie chose to do the worst things; but the Most Holy Spirit, clothed in rugged heaven, [chose] Righteousness (or Truth) as did all

[1] Y., 45. 2.

those who sought with zeal to do the pleasure of the Wise Lord by [doing] good works.' But 'between the two the ancient godlets did not choose rightly; for, as they deliberated, delusion overcame them so that they chose the Most Evil Mind. Then did they, with one accord, rush headlong unto Wrath that they might thereby extinguish (?) the existence of mortal man.'[1]

Now this passage, which is so often quoted as being conclusive for Zoroaster's dualism, is nothing of the kind. Rather the reverse: for not only are the two Spirits called twins—which can only mean that they have a common father—but the 'most Holy Spirit' is also clearly referred to as being other than the Wise Lord. He it is who first chooses Righteousness along with all others who choose 'to do the pleasure of the Wise Lord by doing good works'.

The Holy Spirit is, then, the first to seek to do the pleasure of the Lord. We can, then, hardly resist the logical conclusion that both the Spirits—the evil one as well as the good—are 'sons' of the Wise Lord. This does not, however, mean that God created evil, for Zoroastrianism is the religion of free will *par excellence*. The Evil Spirit *chooses* to do the worst things: his initial act of *will* is evil, not necessarily his nature. In Zoroastrianism no rational being, whether human or angelic, is created with an unfree will, and this must be true of the Evil Spirit too. He chooses evil of his own accord, and once he has chosen, his choice is irrevocable. He becomes the Destructive Spirit who brings death into the world. For the Zoroastrians as for the Jews man was created immortal in body and in soul. But physical death is not due to man's own sin as in the Jewish legend, but to the wickedness of a more than human power which seeks to blot out the 'existence of mortal man'. For the Zoroastrian salvation does not consist in extricating the soul from the body before death as it does for the Buddhist: it consists in reuniting soul and body after they have been separated. This is expressed by the words 'wholeness' (*haurvatāt* from the same root as *salva*-tion) and 'immortality'; and there can be no

[1] Y., 30. 3–6.

wholeness if one half of a man, even the less noble one, has perished for ever.

The doctrine of the two Spirits as being subordinate to God thus seems to emerge clearly enough even from the two texts which are supposed to be conclusive in favour of Zoroaster's dualism. There is, however, a passage in the *Manual of Discipline* from the literature of the Dead Sea sect which shows that this very idea had made its way into Judaism. The closeness of the parallel between the texts we have just quoted and the *Manual of Discipline* leaves us in no doubt that the Dead Sea sect must have borrowed the idea from a Zoroastrian source. Here we find a qualified dualism that is almost identical with that of the *Gāthās*, not with the later dualism of the Sassanian period. The idea, of course, is dressed up in Jewish garb, but is none the less unmistakably the same idea as what we have seen to be the Prophet's own:

> God 'created man', we read, 'to have dominion over the world and made for him *two spirits*, that he might walk by them until the appointed time of his visitation; they are the spirits of *truth* and of *error*. In the abode of light are the origins of truth, and from the source of darkness are the origins of error. . . . And by the angel of darkness is the straying of all the sons of righteousness . . . and all the spirits of his lot try to make the sons of light stumble; but the *God* of Israel and his *angel of truth* have helped all the sons of light. For he created the spirits of light and of darkness, and upon them he founded every work and upon their ways every service. *One of the spirits God loves* for all the ages of eternity; as for the other, *he abhors its company, and all its ways he hates for ever.*'[1]

In this passage the Gāthic myth is almost exactly retold in an Hebraic idiom. The identification of truth with light, and error with darkness is, of course, Zoroastrian too, but does not necessarily go back to the Prophet himself. Once the myth is trans-

[1] See Millar Burrows, *The Dead Sea Scrolls*, New York, 1956, p. 374: Theodor H. Gaster, *The Scriptures of the Dead Sea Sect*, London, 1957, pp. 53–4.

planted on to Jewish soil, however, there is a notable change in tone. The evil spirit of the Dead Sea sect is created evil by God, and God abhors his handiwork. With Zoroaster, on the other hand, the origin of the Evil Spirit can only be deduced by comparing different texts; it is never explicitly stated. And the Evil Spirit is evil not through any act of God's but through his own will. For God is good; and this is not a matter on which the Iranian Prophet was prepared to compromise.

God is good: and He is hypostatized as *Holy* Spirit, as Righteousness, Truth, or Justice (*asha*), and the *Good* Mind. Paternity of all three is ascribed to the Wise Lord,[1] but the paternity envisaged is far more akin to the Christian idea of the 'generation' of the Word than it is to the purely sexual imagery of the Indian myths. For Zoroaster generation means creation through thought: God thinks Righteousness and Righteousness therefore is. So He is the father of Righteousness[2] and also its creator by His will or wisdom (*khratu*).[3] Not only Righteousness but the whole of God's creation is regarded as being the result of God's thought and will, not of His forming of primal matter of which there is no trace in the *Gāthās*: 'He, the primeval, first *thought*, "Let the goodly empyrean be filled with light." '[4] And again: 'Physical life (*gaēthā*), conscience (*daēnā*), and will were created at the beginning by God's *mind*.'[5] Here there is no primal matter, no chaos as in the first chapter of Genesis; things simply come into being by being thought and willed by God. Outside Israel Zoroaster is perhaps alone among Gentile thinkers before Christ in declaring that God creates *ex nihilo*, from nothing.

The Holy Spirit, Righteousness, and the Good Mind are God's first exteriorized thoughts: of these He is the 'mental' father, and the Holy Spirit is the power through which He is the creator of all things.[6] The divine economy in the act of creation is best summed up in this remarkable stanza:

'He, the primeval, who first thought: "Let the goodly em-

[1] Y., 47. 2–3: 44. 3: 31. 8.
[2] Y., 44. 3.
[3] Y., 31. 7.
[4] Ibid.
[5] Y., 31. 11.
[6] Y., 44. 7.

pyrean be filled with light", He it is who is the creator of Righteous Order (*asha*) by which He sustained the Good Mind. These twain hast Thou increased by that Spirit which up to now remains ever the same.'[1]

So too man as an entity possessed of body, mind, conscience, and free will comes into being out of the thought of the Wise Lord:

'Since in the beginning Thou didst fashion for us physical life, consciences, and wills, since Thou didst give us bodily life too, and deeds, and doctrines, so that man might freely put his choice into effect, one man speaking truly, another falsely, one wise, another unwise, [speaking] from their hearts and minds, may Right-Mindedness, going from one to another, search out by the Spirit all those places where there is error.'[2]

Man, then, is created a moral being, with will, and conscience, and complete freedom to choose between good and evil, right and wrong. The body is the organ by which he puts into practice his free decisions. So far from being a useless drag on the soul, it is its outward expression, through which the good or evil character of the soul becomes manifest. It is an essential part of man as a moral being.

When all is said and done, this was the outstanding achievement of Zoroaster which sets him apart as a prophet and which separates him out from the whole mystical tradition in India and indeed from all mystical traditions. Man is not simply a soul imprisoned in the 'body of this death'[3] from which he pines to escape; he is a created being destined by God to live as an indissoluble unity of body and soul, destined to work out his own salvation here on earth, endowed with complete freedom of will, and asked to make his choice and define his position between righteousness and falsehood, between good and evil. As a reward for choosing rightly he is promised 'wholeness and immortality', states of being which belong to God properly but in which man is also called to share.

[1] Y., 31. 7. [2] Y., 31. 11. [3] Rom. vii. 24.

'The best lot shall belong to that wise man (*mazdāi*) who, knowing My true doctrine, shall proclaim it—the doctrine of Wholeness and Immortality [which are] of Righteousness: his shall be the Kingdom which shall wax ever greater for him in accordance with the Good Mind.'[1]

Man, like God, the two primeval spirits, and the ancient gods too, is faced with the choice between good and evil which none can avoid. If he chooses rightly he will regain that wholeness and immortality of which the Evil Spirit had robbed him by introducing death into the world. The choice, however, rests entirely with him; he is master of his own destiny, capable of gaining eternal life in body and in soul in the House of Song[2] in union with the Good Mind,[3] or of going down to the House of the Lie[4] where there is lasting torment.[5] God, in His justice and goodness, judges men in accordance with their deeds since man is wholly responsible for his own choices. No religion, perhaps, has accorded to man so much dignity and therefore so much moral responsibility. The rewards and punishments that man must expect are magnificently proclaimed in the following strophes:

'I shall speak out the word which the Most Holy One declared to me—the best of all words for men to hear: "Whoso shall hearken even unto him (the Prophet) for My sake, shall attain to wholeness and immortality by performing [the works] of the Good Mind." [Thus spake] the Wise Lord' . . . 'from whom all men who live [today], who have been or are yet to come, shall receive their lot of weal [or woe], for He apportions both. Powerful in immortality shall be the soul of the follower of Truth, but lasting torment shall there be for the man who cleaves to the Lie. So does the Wise Lord dispose through His sovereign power.'[6]

The judgement is in accordance with the holiness of the Lord.

[1] Y., 31. 6.
[2] Y., 45. 8: 50. 4: 51. 15.
[3] Y., 28. 8: 46. 12, 14.
[4] Y., 46. 11: 51. 14.
[5] Y., 31. 20: 45. 7, etc.
[6] Y., 45. 5, 7.

Life is not a meaningless concatenation of events endlessly recurring in the same automatic pattern as it is in India: it is a straight-line development of which the goal is conditioned by man's own free choices. The world has a beginning, middle, and end—creation, testing-time, and consummation, 'the last turning-point of this created world'. Life on earth is deadly serious, because it has a purpose and a goal, and man is made acutely aware by God's Prophet that his sojourn on earth is anything but a joke. He is not the plaything of the Deity as so often in Indian religious literature, but subject to an all-powerful, omniscient, just, and *good* God; and in God's moral rectitude Zoroaster recognizes His holiness:

'Then did I realize, Wise Lord, that Thou wast holy,
When I saw that in the beginning, at the birth of existence
Thou didst ordain that deeds and spoken words should meet with [just] requital—
Evil for the evil, but good reward for whoso is good
At the last turning-point of this created world. So far doth Thy power extend.'[1]

Not only does Zoroaster foresee the judgement, but he also looks to the establishment of the Kingdom of Righteousness on earth; and he seems to have hoped that he would be able to establish this kingdom himself. So he prays that 'it may be *we* who shall make existence perfect (excellent, *frasha*) . . . 'when [all] minds shall agree [even] among those for whom false teaching prevails.'[2] He must soon have realized, however, that this was not to be, and he therefore looked forward to a 'second'[3] or 'renewed'[4] existence in which wholeness and immortality should reign.[5]

From this germ developed the later doctrine of a new heaven and a new earth, referred to in the later literature as the *frashkart*, the 'making excellent' or rehabilitation of all things in wholeness and immortality, the 'Final Body' when the dead will be raised and men will enjoy everlasting bliss with Ahura Mazdā,

[1] Y., 43. 5. [2] Y., 30. 9. [3] Y., 45. 1.
[4] Y., 34. 6, 15. [5] Y., 45. 5, 10.

the Wise Lord. This 'new existence' will be inaugurated by the Saoshyans, who will be born from the seed of Zoroaster miraculously preserved in a lake. This Saoshyans, often translated as 'Saviour', would be better rendered as 'he who will bring benefit'. He it is who, by God's gracious permission, raises the bodies of the dead and inaugurates the new era when man will be immortal in body and in soul, as he was in the beginning before the Evil Spirit introduced death into this earth. Thus 'the victorious Saoshyans and those others who help him . . . will make the world most excellent, unageing, undecaying, neither passing away nor falling into corruption; for ever shall it live and for ever prosper, [each man] rangeing at his will. The dead shall rise again and the living shall be visited by immortality, and [all] existence shall be made most excellent in accordance with its will. . . . The material world will no more pass away . . . and the Lie shall perish.'[1]

These, then, were the fundamental doctrines proclaimed by Zoroaster six centuries before the coming of our Lord, doctrines which have subsequently become part and parcel of our Christian heritage:

(1) There exists One God, creator and sustainer of the universe who grants complete freedom of the will to all His rational creatures.

(2) This God is just and *good.*

(3) There exists also an evil spirit who must derive from God but who is evil by choice rather than nature. He it is who brings bodily death into the world.

(4) Man was designed by God to live an immortal life in body and in soul, and only when the Evil One is finally vanquished and man receives his body back, can he realize his destiny as *man.*

(5) Man is essentially a moral being, composed of body, conscience, and will: as such he must choose between good and evil.

(6) In accordance with his choice he will be rewarded or punished in heaven or hell.

[1] *Yasht*, 19. 89–90.

(7) All men will receive their bodies back at the end of time, and (according to later doctrine, though probably not according to the Prophet himself) all the denizens of hell will be released at the end of time and brought into the new paradise where all without exception will live on for ever in body and in soul—whole men, lacking nothing and united in the praise of their Creator.

How much, if anything, of this remarkable body of doctrine existed before Zoroaster, it is impossible to say; but even if some of it goes back to a remoter past, the Prophet's achievement is none the less outstanding. His affirmation of the unity and goodness of God is almost certainly new, as is the deep moral earnestness of his tone, his thirst after righteousness and abhorrence of evil. His message is in direct antithesis to Indian religion; for his voice is the voice of prophecy, not the voice of philosophy. Except the theophany in the Bhagavad-Gītā there is nothing that can be compared to his message in all Indian religion; but that theophany and the message that Zoroaster brought from his God complement each other. God is both just and good and a hater of evil, as the Iranian prophet proclaimed, but He is also the lover of the human soul as Krishna, the Man-God of Indian folk-lore, announced.

These were, then, the main doctrines enunciated by Zoroaster; but later Zoroastrians, while remaining true to the Prophet's insistence on the goodness of God, pushed to the limit doctrines which were only implied in the *Gāthās*. Thus in the matter of the godhead later orthodoxy was to adopt a fully dualistic position and make Ahura Mazdā and Angra Mainyu, the Wise Lord (now identified with the Holy Spirit) and the Evil Spirit, or Ohrmazd and Ahriman as they came to be called, into two co-eternal principles of good and evil—a radical cleavage of the unity of the godhead which seems far from the Prophet's own doctrine and was never accepted by the heterodox.

Zoroaster had faced squarely up to the problem of evil, and he seems to have solved it by attributing complete freedom of will to all created and subordinate spirits. The Evil Spirit was evil because he 'chose to do what was worst'. God did not stop him doing so any more than He stops evil men from choosing evil. He permits evil because He had granted His creatures freedom. Later Zoroastrianism would not, however, countenance even this. For them God is all goodness and all light: Ahriman or the Devil is all evil and all darkness. The one is good *by nature*, the other evil by nature; the one a good substance, the other an evil one, and it is one of the properties of a substance, that it cannot change.[1] To attribute evil, however indirectly, to God was, for the later orthodoxy to attribute to Him devilish qualities. These the Jews and the Muslims did quite openly since they did not believe that God was absolutely and wholly good—the Jews, it may be said, quite as much as the Muslims, for does not Yahweh say by the mouth of Isaiah: 'I make peace, and *create evil*; I the Lord do all these things'?[2] This, for the Zoroastrians, is either blasphemy or sheer madness. How can one worship such a God, they would say.

Hinduism and Buddhism, on the other hand, are not vitally interested in the problem of evil. Like Jung Hindus were prepared to accept it as the 'negative' side of either the human or the divine personality. For the Upanishads at least the concepts of good and evil lose all meaning once an eternal mode of existence has been realized. Zoroaster and his followers went to the other extreme: they were quite obsessed by the idea and indeed by the existence of evil. This for them was *the* inescapable fact and as such it had to be faced. Facing it squarely the medieval Zoroastrians came to the radical conclusion that there must be a separate principle beside God who was substantial evil, the creator of death, disease, suffering and sin. 'I must have no doubt,' their catechism says, 'but that there are two first principles, one the Creator and the other the Destroyer. The Creator is Ohrmazd who is all goodness and all light: and the Destroyer is the accursed Destructive Spirit who is all wickedness and full of death, a liar and a deceiver.'[3]

[1] See R. C. Zaehner, *Zurvān, A Zoroastrian Dilemma*, Oxford, 1955, pp. 157 and 164 n. D.

[2] Isa. xlv. 7.

[3] See R. C. Zaehner, *The Teachings of the Magi*, London, 1956, pp. 22–3.

For medieval Zoroastrianism, too, the world has a purpose. It is a deadly serious battle between good and evil—a battle in which the scales are not quite equally balanced. The good has the advantage, not because it is more powerful, but because it is orderly and wise. Evil on the other hand must ultimately be annihilated because it is a disorderly motion, brutish, foreseeing nothing, and therefore carrying the seeds of its own destruction within itself. Creation, otherwise so great a mystery, is not only no mystery to these rationalistic epigones of the Prophet; it is a sheer necessity imposed on God as a measure of self-defence against the diabolic attack which cannot fail to materialize since Ahriman, the Devil, is by nature an aggressor. The conflict, once joined, must finally be won by Ohrmazd since the anarchy inherent in the diabolic camp must finally destroy itself. After the inevitable defeat of the Devil the millennium will set in, in which heaven and earth are made anew and man enjoys eternal fellowship with God.

Zoroastrianism has much in common with Judaism in that it sees eternity not as a state to be enjoyed here and now, but as the end of an historical process. In 'classical' Zoroastrianism the process is set in motion by the Devil's attack on God's creation. Had God not foreseen this attack, there would have been no creation; for what sense could there be in a perfect being making an imperfect world? The Devil's attack makes creation necessary, and the world process, in its turn, is also necessary in that it represents the slow but sure grinding down of the powers of evil. Man's reward, when the victory is won, is literally life everlasting, that is, life lived as he lives it now, in body and in soul, though no doubt in a greater glory. 'It will be permitted me to possess the truth in a soul and a body', the French poet Rimbaud says at the end of the *Saison en Enfer*. Without knowing it he was thereby enunciating again the message of Zoroaster, a message that was later to be one of the articles of the Christian creed.

Nobody who has borne with me so far will have failed to be impressed by the extraordinary similarity between the main tenets of Zoroastrianism and some of the principal Christian doctrines. We shall have more to say about this later. Here we would merely stress the fact that Zoroaster, in his consciousness of the near presence of God as his friend and helper, must be accounted fully as much a prophet as the prophets of Israel: more, perhaps, since despite the difficulties of the language his message is far more coherent.

One quite arresting resemblance between Zoroastrianism and Christianity remains to be noticed. This is the Haoma sacrifice and sacrament which seems to foreshadow the Catholic Mass in so strange a way.

We have seen (p. 137) that Zoroaster fulminated against the sacrificial ritual of the older religion in which an ox was slaughtered and the fermented juice of a plant called Haoma drunk. This must have been an ancient ritual common to India and Iran, for the same rite appears in the Rig-Veda and it is quite clear from the description of the god Indra when under the influence of this beverage of immortality, that it was very intoxicating.[1] Zoroaster condemned the ox sacrifice out of hand, but he seems to have retained the Haoma rite, probably with partially fermented juice. He never attacks the Haoma rite as such, only drunkenness[2] and the use of the fermented Haoma as an accompaniment to the ox sacrifice.[3] On the contrary, the Haoma rite with partially fermented juice became the central act of Zoroastrian worship, and it is difficult to believe that this could have been so had the Prophet ever formally condemned it. The use of other intoxicants is indeed condemned in the post-Zoroastrian hymn addressed to Haoma as being 'accompanied by fury', whereas the exhilaration produced by the Haoma is commended as being 'accompanied by Righteousness'.[4]

Haoma is both a plant and a god. As a plant it seems to have been yellowish in colour, and it grew in the mountains. At the sacrificial ceremony it was 'slain' by being pounded in a mortar, and the juice that oozed out of it was consumed by priest and faithful as an elixir of immortality. As a god Haoma was the

[1] Rig-Veda, x, 119. [2] Y., 48. 10. [3] Y., 32. 14. [4] Y., 10. 8.

son of Ahura Mazdā, the Wise Lord,[1] and by Him he was established as the first priest of the cult of which he was himself, as plant, the victim.[2] We thus have the strange spectacle of a son of God offering himself incarnate as a plant to his heavenly father. And the purpose of the sacrifice is to confer immortality on all those who drink of the sacred liquid—the life-juice of a divine being pounded to death in a mortar. The god dies in his humble incarnate form in order to confer immortality on those who partake of the fluid which flows from him. As priest this strange god offers perpetual sacrifice to his father, and as victim, he enables man to participate in the very life of God.

Zoroaster delivered his message in ancient Iran some 600 years before Christ, and much of his teaching has been incorporated into Christianity. Some 600 years after Christ another prophet of even greater stature arose in Arabia, a prophet whose followers today number some three hundred and fifty millions. This was, of course, Muhammad.

For us Christians Muhammad is, perhaps, the greatest stumbling-block to our faith; and for this reason Christian writers—and particularly missionaries—have sought to belittle the stature of the Prophet, or, worse still, have cast doubt on his sincerity. To my mind any doubt about Muhammad's sincerity, at least during the period in which he was persecuted in Mecca, can only be attributed either to ignorance or to prejudice; and this over-simplication of a very real problem has, fortunately, now been abandoned by all Christian scholars of repute. One has only to read the early *Sūras* of the Qur'ān with their urgent and passionate appeal to repentance and the earliest accounts of Muhammad's life, to realize that this is no impostor, but a man driven on by a power far greater than himself to deliver a message, at once terrifying and unpopular, to a people most unwilling to receive it. That Muhammad was literally constrained to proclaim a new religion, seems clear enough from the earliest accounts.

"The beginning of the revelation for the Messenger of God,"

[1] Y., 11. 4. [2] *Yasht*, 10. 89.

Al-Zuhrī says,[1] "was a true vision. It used to come like the breaking of dawn. Afterwards solitude became dear to him, and he would go to a cave on Hirā" to engage in devotional exercises there for a number of nights before returning to his family, and then he would return to them for provisions for a similar stay. At length unexpectedly the Truth came to him and said: "O Muhammad, thou art the Messenger of God."

'The Messenger of God . . . said: "I had been standing, but I fell to my knees; then I crept away, my shoulders quaking; then I entered Khadīja's[2] chamber and said: 'Cover me, cover me,' until the terror left me. Then he came to me and said: 'O Muhammad, thou art the Messenger of God.' "

'Muhammad said [further]: "I had been thinking of throwing myself from a mountain crag, but while I was so thinking, he appeared to me and said: 'I am Gabriel and thou art the Messenger of God.' "

'Then he said: "Recite." I said: "I cannot recite" (or "What shall I recite?"). Muhammad said: "Then he took me and squeezed me violently three times until exhaustion overcame me." Then he said: "*Recite in the name of thy Lord who created.*" And I recited.'

Muhammad's experience was one of overwhelming terror. Wholly unprepared, he suddenly found himself constrained by the divine command to proclaim God's message, though he felt himself utterly unqualified to do any such thing. So awful did this charge appear to him that for a long time he contemplated committing suicide. These are not the reactions of an impostor or an ambitious man. Muhammad certainly never asked to be a prophet; he was overcome by what later writers were to call the 'prophetic spirit' from which he could not escape. 'Recite', 'Speak forth', was the first command he received:

> 'Recite in the name of thy Lord who created,
> Created man from clotted blood.
> Recite, for thy Lord is most generous,

[1] See W. Montgomery Watt, *Muhammad at Mecca*, Oxford, 1953, p. 40.
[2] Muhammad's first wife.

Who taught by the pen,
Taught man what he did not know.
Nay, but verily man acts presumptuously,
Because he thinks himself independent.
Verily, to thy Lord is the return.[1]

In these verses, traditionally the first revealed of all the 'verses' that were later to be put together in the form of the Qur'ān, Muhammad's conception of God is already all there in embryo. God is the Lord, Creator, and Judge: to Him must all return. He is utterly and entirely transcendent, and man is wholly dependent on Him. God is the Lord, and man is His slave (*'abd*). Like the God of the Old Testament prophets He is the One True God, One without a second, unique and indivisible even in thought.

'Say, He is God, the One, God, the Eternal: He did not beget, neither was He begotten; and like unto Him hath there never been anyone.'[2]

This is classic affirmation of God's absolute oneness, a refutal possibly of the Christian Trinity, but more probably directed against Arabian polytheism. For Muhammad the deadliest possible sin was to associate others with God; and even if these verses do not refer to the Christians, he was later to accuse them of doing precisely this.

Muhammad was fully aware that both the Jews and the Christians claimed to be in possession of earlier revelations from God, though his knowledge of these religions seems to have derived from oral sources of a bewilderingly heterogeneous nature. In past times, then, revelation had only been vouchsafed to the Jews; and Muhammad therefore considered himself as primarily the prophet of the Arabs who had hitherto been lost in polytheism. This is how he puts it: 'Verily it is a revelation of the Lord of the worlds, Which the faithful spirit hath brought down Upon thy heart that thou mayest be a warner In clear Arabic speech.'[3] His message, he claimed, was the same message that had been delivered to Moses for the Jews

[1] Qur'ān, 96. 1–8. [2] Ibid., 112. [3] Ibid., 26. 192–5.

and to Jesus for the Christians, and the Qur'ān is full of stories from the Old and New Testaments, their apocrypha, and ancillary writings which are usually used to support Muhammad's claim to be a true prophet of God. Yet after his flight to Medina when the Prophet learnt to know the Jews at first hand and where he had closer contact with Christians, he was perplexed and hurt to find that neither community was disposed to see in him an authentic prophet in the line of the Jewish prophets the last of whom, according to Muhammad, had been Jesus. Closer acquaintance with Jews and Christians convinced him that what had been revealed to him in his recitations (that is the Qur'ān) did not tally in some fundamental respects with Jewish and Christian doctrine as interpreted by the orthodox. For though Muhammad was prepared to accept a very great deal of what Christians claimed on behalf of Jesus—in sharp contradistinction to the Jews who preferred to ignore Him—there were some things he could simply not accept. Jesus he accepted as Messiah, though it is not at all clear what he understood by that term, as the Word of God or a Spirit from God. He accepted further His birth from a Virgin and His wholly exceptional miraculous powers (Muhammad himself never claimed to work miracles). Jesus, moreover, had reaffirmed the one true religion and attested the ancient Law while relaxing some of its prohibitions. This, for Muhammad, was the truth about Jesus, the last of the long line of prophets before himself who was the 'Seal of the Prophets', the bringer of the Qur'ān, which Muslims were to come to regard as the very Word of God, uncorrupted and undefiled by any human agency.[1]

So much does Muhammad concede about Jesus—and it is a very great deal: but the essentials of Christianity he could never consciously accept since they ran counter to the very essence of his faith—the absolute transcendence and 'otherness' of God which placed an unbridgeable gulf between Him and man, his slave or, as Ghazālī puts it, his chattel or property.[2] Thus

[1] On the Qur'ānic view of Jesus see the appendix.

[2] E.g. *Mishkāt al-Anwār*, tr. W. H. T. Gairdner, Lahore, reprint 1952, p. 102.

though the Muhammadans pay the greatest reverence to Jesus and are justifiably irritated by the contemptuous attitude to their Prophet so often exhibited by Christians, they cannot possibly accept the Incarnation; nor do they accept the historical fact of the Crucifixion[1] which, as for the Gnostics, seemed altogether too degrading a fate for the last and greatest of the prophets before Muhammad. About the Ascension, however, they had no difficulty at all, nor did they deny the second coming.

The Muhammadan attitude towards Christ is, in fact, the exact reverse of that of the rationalists: for they accept all that is miraculous and 'absurd', the Virgin birth, the miracles, and the Ascension, but deny, out of their very veneration for Jesus, the one fact that is admitted by all historians to be authentic, the Crucifixion. Outside the Christian body itself there is no one who has gone further to meet Christianity half-way: for in the Qur'ān itself Jesus is accepted as both Messiah and the Word of God, but not as the Son of God, 'for God neither begat nor was He begotten'. That Muhammad should not have understood the central doctrines of Christianity—the Incarnation and the Trinity—is scarcely surprising. Firstly he was very ill informed about them; and secondly Christians, for all their nice formulations, as often as not understand them as little as did he.

The strength of Islam's claim to be the true religion rests, in the last analysis, on the fact that historically Muhammad is the last or 'Seal' of the prophets and that the Qur'ān supersedes all other written revelations as being the very Word of God, the original of which dwells eternally with God, inscribed on the *lawḥ al-maḥfūẓ*, 'the preserved tablet', the eternal examplar from which all copies of the sacred text on earth derive. The theory underlying these claims is that although one and the same true religion was revealed to the prophets of Israel, the last of whom was Jesus, this one religion was, in the process of time, distorted and corrupted by both Jews and Christians. In neither case was

[1] Some Muslim modernists do now accept the Crucifixion but not the Atonement.

the authentic message written down early enough. This view Muhammad derived, indirectly no doubt, from Mānī, the founder of the Manichaean religion, who flourished in the third century A.D. From Mānī too he seems to have borrowed the idea that his coming had been foretold by Jesus: Muhammad was the promised Paraclete—a title which Mānī, who was far better instructed in the Christian religion than was Muhammad, had formerly claimed for himself. Muhammad certainly knew that the Christians believed that the coming of Christ had been foretold by the prophets who had gone before; and he seems also to have known that Jesus had promised to send the 'Paraclete' after him: so as evidence that he is indeed the promised Paraclete, it is written in the Qur'ān:

'And when Jesus, son of Mary, said: "O Children of Israel, I am God's Messenger to you, confirming the Torah which was before me, and announcing the good tidings of a messenger who will come after me, bearing the name Aḥmad." '[1]

This passage seems to be a garbled version of John xiv. 16 ('and I will pray the Father, and He shall give you another Paraclete, that he may abide with you for ever'); and it has been generally assumed that 'Aḥmad' is a translation of περίκλυτος which may have been confused with the word παράκλητος Paraclete) which stands in the text. Even so this does not explain why the Qur'ān should speak of Aḥmad rather than Muḥammad. Certainly the two names derive from the same root *ḤMD*, but they are not the same name any more than are, for instance, Maḥmūd or Ḥamīd. However the very strong probability that the Qur'ānic passage rests on a misreading of a New Testament text has about as much relevance to the Muslim as the argument that many of the Old Testament stories recounted in the Qur'ān are garbled versions of Talmudic texts imperfectly understood. For him to argue thus is simply beside the point. There can be no question of the Qur'ān being wrong since it is God's *ipsissima verba* in which there can, by definition, be no error. If there are discrepancies between it and the Old

[1] Qur'ān, 61. 6.

and New Testaments, then it is the latter that are at fault, and the discrepancy is due to the assumed fact that the Jews and Christians had tampered with the sacred text to serve their own purposes. The so-called higher criticism of the two Testaments has done much to confirm the Muslim in this belief.

Doctrinally the strength of Islam's claim lies in its dogma that the Qur'ān is God's Word finally delivered through Muhammad for all time to come. It is not a new revelation, but an unadulterated restatement of the religion of all the prophets which had since become corrupted. Because the early Muslims believed this to be so, the early Caliphs set about collecting and putting together the scattered fragments of the Qur'ān at a very early period, and the third of them, 'Uthmān, ordered a definitive text to be drawn up about twenty years after the Prophet's death. All other versions were destroyed.

Because Muslims believe the Qur'ān to be the word of God, they have never submitted it to the searching criticism to which Christian scholars have submitted the New Testament. Such a process would appear to them sheer blasphemy. No doubt sooner or later this operation will have to be faced; and when it happens it may well have a more shattering effect on Islam than ever it had on Christianity: but so long as Muslims continue to believe that the Qur'ān is what tradition claims it to be, no argument from the Christian side is likely to have the slightest effect.

It may be argued that the mere fact that Muhammad appeared after Christ is no argument that his revelation was a true revelation. Of course it isn't, any more than it is a valid argument to say that Christ fulfils the Messianic promises of the Hebrew prophets. The Jews rejected Christ as Messiah very largely because they did not see how He fulfilled the Messianic promises. *This* was not at all what they had been led to expect. Similarly Muhammad was rejected by both the Jews and the Christians—by the first because a gentile prophet could scarcely be of direct concern to the chosen people, by the second because there could be no *new* revelation after the Incarnation of the Son of God. The fact remains, however, that both Muhammad himself and his early followers were fervently convinced that he was the Messenger of God, just as much as were the first disciples of Jesus convinced that He was the promised Messiah.

It is often claimed for Christianity that the original spreading of so paradoxical a Gospel was miraculous; and I should be the first to agree. Yet by what token, I wonder, would I be entitled to deny that the spread of Islam was equally miraculous? In his Meccan days Muhammad too was persecuted and was fighting against what seemed overwhelming odds; and if later he triumphed by fraud and force, this does not, to my mind, of itself invalidate the truth of his message: for the God of Muhammad is the God of the Old Testament rather than the New. He is the same God who hardened Pharaoh's heart and 'who make[s] peace and create[s] evil': He is not the God than whom none other is good. 'And [the Jews] were crafty,' says the Qur'ān, 'and God was crafty and God is the best of the crafty Ones.'[1] If, then, God resorts to guile, who are we to blame His Prophet for doing likewise?

Muhammad's character has often been used as an argument against the truth of his message, and particularly its deterioration in his period of success and conquest in Medina. The Muslims themselves seem to have been well aware of the defects in his character, and in later ages they did everything in their power to transform him into a paragon of all the virtues, many of which he possessed in very small measure. This seems to be rather a futile proceeding, for there would seem to be as little reason for Muslims to whitewash Muhammad as there is for Protestants to whitewash Luther, or for Catholics to whitewash Alexander VI and the whole amazing cavalcade of abominable Popes who, by their open wickedness, made all attempts to reform the Church from within impossible. If God is as arbitrary as the Qur'ān depicts Him, then the fact that He should have chosen not a saint but a man possessed of the prophetic spirit as few had been before him and who at the same time was a political genius, should not surprise us. Indeed the Muslim should see in the very imperfections of Muhammad the sign of

[1] 3. 47.

God's sovereign power to use what vessel He will, however imperfect, for the furtherance of His own inscrutable purpose. Nor should we be shocked by the fact that Islam was spread by the sword, for had not a burning faith preceded the sword, Muhammad would never even have been in a position to draw the sword.

Both Christianity and Islam spring from a Jewish stem; and the spirit of this uniquely chosen people hangs over them both. So the Christian Church claims to be the second or true Israel —a claim that must seem a trifle fanciful to the Jews—and Islam, a Semitic though not a Hebraic religion, claims to be a restatement of the true religion revealed by God to Abraham before Israel ever was. All three claim to be direct revelations from God. Christ claims that He came to fulfil the Law, and Muhammad claims to re-establish a truth that had become obscured. The result is not that you have one continuous revelation, but that you have three revelations, all deriving from one religious tradition, and all claiming alone to be true. 'The Gods love the obscure, as it were, and hate the obvious',[1] a Brahman seer once said long long ago; and our consideration of the rival claims and clashing doctrines of the world religions has gone far to persuade us that he was right.

Yet, whatever we may think of Islam, it is *the* prophetic religion *par excellence*; and even Christians, when they speak of *the* Prophet usually mean Muhammad: for the Qur'ān, of which Muhammad was the mouthpiece is for Islam what the Law and the Prophets are for Israel. In it is revealed the whole of religion as understood by Muslims—everything, that is, that pertains to this world and post-mortem events in time, nothing concerning the essential nature of the soul. Theology, man's destiny, his religious duties, and the legal code according to which he must regulate his life—all is there in embryo. The Prophet too is law-giver in his own right, and when the Qur'ān does not speak with a clear voice, the sayings of the Prophet are called upon to supplement it. The whole religious life of the Muslim is regulated by the Qur'ān and the Tradition. God is a distant law-giver, and His relation to man is that of Lord to

[1] *Aitareya* Up., 3. 14=*Bṛhadāraṇyaka* Up., 4. 2. 2.

slave: it is not for man to have 'a choice in the affair'. 'When God and his Messenger have decided an affair, it is not for a believing man or a believing woman to have a choice in their affair; whoever opposes God and His Messenger, has strayed into manifest error.'[1]

Zoroaster spoke to God as a free man, and as friend to friend; and Krishna too is represented as speaking to his beloved disciple Arjuna as a friend. Between Allah and His Prophet there can be no question of friendship, because friendship implies congruity, and nothing exists that is in any way comparable to God. He is utterly withdrawn from man, inscrutable, unaccountable, arbitrary. Certainly He is the Merciful, the Compassionate, but the attributes that the Qur'ān constantly emphasizes are those of absolutely uninhibited power: He is utterly transcendent. So Islam and the Hinduism of the Upanishads represent two radically opposed conceptions of the Godhead. In the Upanishads the Deity becomes so radically immanent that it is sometimes indistinguishable from the universe on the one hand and the human soul on the other. In Islam God is so utterly transcendent that no effective communion with Him is possible. In the one man comes to identify himself with God: in the other man's dependence on God is so complete that he scarcely dares to claim existence at all.

We saw that in India the theistic cults of Śiva and Vishnu to some extent restored the balance between immanence and transcendence; and the history of the higher religions shows that whenever a 'revealed' text overstresses one pole of the deity, then there is bound to be a reaction towards the other. Similarly in Islam, in the second century of the Hijra, a pietistic movement arose under the name of Ṣūfism. Its beginnings were humble and owed much to Christian monasticism. The Ṣūfīs withdrew to the desert to practise interior prayer, and there they were astonished to find that it *was* possible to have a direct experience of God independently of the outward observances of their faith. Slowly the movement developed into a fully-fledged mystical movement which based itself on man's yearning for

[1] Qur'ān, 33. 36.

God and on God's love for man—a concept, the very possibility of which was hotly denied by the orthodox.

Under the influence of Ṣūfism not only was the character of Muhammad shorn of its rough edges, not only did he become the ideal man, perfect in every respect, whose every action must be imitated—he became not only the last of the prophets in time (which indeed he was) but the first of them in eternity: he became identified with the very creative Word of God 'through whom all things are made'. This astonishing development was due in the first place to Ḥallāj, that wild apostle of the love of God who was crucified for this and other heresies in A.D. 922; but it was later taken up by Ghazālī himself,[1] the great eleventh-century theologian who tried—with what success only Muslims can judge—to wed a rigid orthodoxy to an inward-looking mysticism which taught that God dwelt in the human heart. After Ghazālī Ṣūfism threw aside all restraints and, particularly in Persian hands, became more and more brazenly pantheistic. The unbridgeable gulf between man and God was not only bridged; it became increasingly difficult to say whether there was any distinction at all. This astonishing transformation within Islam was certainly due in large measure first to Christian influence seeping in through the conquered peoples, secondly to Indian influence making itself felt in much the same way, and thirdly to the influence of Neo-Platonism by way of semi-mystical philosophers like Al-Fārābī and Avicenna; but the transformation could never have been so radical, had not Islam over-emphasized to such a tremendous degree the transcendence at the expense of the immanence of God, His majesty at the expense of His tenderness.

Ṣūfism, then, not only transformed the whole nature of the Prophet's message, it transformed the Prophet himself. For just as the latter-day Buddhists exalted that gentle sage who believed in neither God nor Absolute into the principle and source of the universe, so did the Ṣūfīs transform Muhammad, the rough Prophet of Arabia, who regarded the Christian claim that their Founder was divine with abhorrence, into the uncreated Word

[1] In the last section of the *Mishkāt al-Anwār*.

of God, the unknown God's manifestation of Himself to man. Transformations such as these are not easy to explain; and for the present we must leave them unexplained, yet somehow they seem to fit into the general pattern of prophetic and mystical religion which we have tried to trace. Perhaps they point to a just balance between the two. 'Fate and effort are like two bales of a traveller's baggage on the back of a mule,' a Zoroastrian text tells us. 'If one of them is heavier and the other lighter, the load falls to the ground, and the back of the mule is broken, and the traveller suffers embarrassment and does not reach his destination. But if both bales are equal, the traveller does not need to worry, the mule is comfortable, and both arrive at their destination.'[1] If for 'fate and effort' we substitute 'prophecy and mysticism', it is possible that we may be somewhere near a solution.

[1] See R. C. Zaehner, *Zurvan, A Zoroastrian Dilemma*, p. 405.

CHAPTER V

Consummatum Est

In the second century A.D. when Christianity had become thoroughly involved in the Graeco-Roman world, it became necessary to adapt the Christian message to current Greek philosophy; and it was to this task that Clement of Alexandria, among others, particularly addressed himself. The Christian revelation he saw not only as the fulfilment of Old Testament prophecy, but as the natural completion of the philosophy of the Greeks. The advent of Christ was not only prepared among the Jews, it was prepared in a different manner also among the Greeks. For, according to Clement, 'We shall not err in alleging that all things necessary and profitable for life come to us from God, and that philosophy more especially was given to the Greeks, as a covenant peculiar to them, being, as it were, a stepping-stone to the philosophy which is according to Christ.'[1]

Clement was a citizen of the Roman Empire, and for any Roman citizen the οἰκουμένη or inhabited world meant principally the Empire. The great civilizations of Asia, that is, India and China were almost unknown to him, and his knowledge of even Iranian religion can only have been second-hand at best. It would then be natural for him to seek for the traces of revelation in those traditions only which were fully accessible to him —the prophetic tradition of Israel and the philosophic tradition of Greece, the latter no less a 'covenant' than the former. It would, however, be more natural for us, who during the last

[1] *Protrepticus*, vi, 8.

two centuries have become aware of the sacred literature of the Asiatic peoples, to look for the *praeparatio evangelica* not so much among the Greeks as among the nations of Asia; for it is Asia that is the birthplace of every single religion that has withstood the test of time, whereas Europe is the home rather of rational and scientific inquiry—and with Plato, if you like, of metaphysical speculation too—but not of religion; for religion, as distinct from theology, is concerned not with any metaphysical system, not even with what some modern esoteric writers would call 'metaphysical truth', but rather with the deep-down places of the human soul which metaphysics and psychology can rationalize but can neither reach nor understand, the non-rational sub- and super-structure of the human psyche which normally adopts a defiantly hostile attitude towards the rationalizing ego and which Jung has conveniently labelled the 'collective unconscious'.

In the Christianity of Clement of Alexandria Hebrew prophecy and Greek philosophy meet and, except in the more extreme forms of Protestantism of which the 'Biblical realism' of Dr. Kraemer is a notable example, they have never parted company since.

Today it would be utterly unrealistic, un-catholic in the widest sense of that word, and absurd to persist in confining ourselves to the legacy of the Graeco-Roman world alone. Since Christianity claims to be a universal faith, it can only survive by showing that it can assimilate not only what is digestible to the Christian constitution in Plato and Aristotle, but also whatever in Oriental religion seems to point the way to Christ. It is true that Christ said that 'Salvation is of the Jews';[1] but by this He did not preclude the possibility that the faith He was to found should be as much a fulfilment of the religions that had preceded Him in distant Asian lands as it was of the religion in which He had been brought up. 'Salvation is of the Jews' for no other reason than that God in Christ became incarnate as a Jew and was crucified as a Jew by the will and at the instigation of orthodox Jewry. Salvation is of a Jew who was rejected by

[1] John iv. 22.

the Jews because He came to 'fulfil' (πληρῶσαι) the Law and the Prophets: that is, by rejecting the orthodox and purely Jewish interpretation of the Messiahhood and opening the doors of salvation to the Gentiles, He filled out what was lacking in the traditional teaching and laid the foundations of a new Israel which the old Israel, out of very faithfulness to 'the works of the law',[1] could not and would not herself enter.

In our earlier chapters we tried to show that the Indian approach to religion is wholly different from the Hebraic. It is much more comparable to the Greek; but whereas Greece rose to the idea of God through a philosophy that became ever more sharply divorced from popular religion, it was popular religion itself in India which forced the idea of a personal God, distinct from both the universe and the human soul, on to the attention of the metaphysician. The weakness of God's 'covenant' with the Greeks was that in it philosophy was divorced from worship just as in His covenant with the Jews it might be said that an intense consciousness of the presence of God called forth no rational attempt to account for it. In India, on the other hand, religion starts with a more or less crude polytheism, passes through a quest of immense significance both for a unifying principle of the universe and for that in the human soul which the Indians instinctively felt to be immortal, to an apperception, more or less clear but never clear-cut, of a God who transcends both the Brahman and the *ātman*—that principle by which all things cohere and which indwells the human soul as its finest essence. In India, except in the purely popular cults, religion is never divorced from philosophy: religion means primarily the realization of immortality while philosophy is only the rationalization of this felt immortality of the human soul and its relationship to the totality of existence. So it is that because Indian religion is so thoroughly preoccupied with the experience of an eternal mode of being rather than with a direct encounter with an eternal, objective 'Thou' manifesting Himself through power, it has never felt the need of any particular divine revelation through a prophetic agency.

[1] Rom. ix. 32.

'If a person knew the Self with the thought, "This am I", then with what desire, for love of what would he cling to the body?'[1] What indeed could be the point of worrying about the phenomenal world and what goes on there, if one has passed beyond it into an immortal mode of existence?

This seems to be—I will not say the weakness of Indian religion, for it is, rather, its strength—but what makes it incomplete; for no religion can wholly satisfy which is based fundamentally on the total rejection of the phenomenal world either as an illusion or as a prison in which the immortal spirit is held helplessly captive. Modern Hindu writers like Śrī Aurobindo, Hiriyanna, and Radhakrishnan have felt this acutely; but it is open to doubt whether they would ever have felt it, had they not been faced with the Christian challenge which claims that this world is no illusion but rather a testing-ground in which man works out the *quality* of his own immortality.

Any Christianity which denies the dignity of the body and therefore of matter seems to me to be no Christianity at all; for it is to deny the basis of all Christian faith, the resurrection of the body of Christ Jesus from the dead. The immortality of the soul is not a peculiarly Christian doctrine: it is a doctrine of all the great religions with the notable exception of the Judaism of Moses. What distinguishes Christianity from the whole way of thought of the Indians is: 'I believe in the resurrection of the body': and this must be, to my mind, what marks Christianity most sharply off from all those Gnostic religions, whether of Mediterranean or Indian origin, which see in the body nothing more than the prison of the soul.

Primarily Christianity is a Jewish religion. It is the heir to a prophetic tradition in which man is, one might say, a chemical compound, not a mixture, of soul and body. The immortality of the soul is certainly preached by Christianity, but the immortality of the soul is not the immortality of man. It may approximate to the mode of existence of the angels, but man is not an angel, and in seeking to be one, he deprives himself of

[1] *Bṛhadāraṇyaka* Up., 4. 4. 12.

something that is essential to his being. Without making himself an angel, he makes himself something less than man.

The Buddha, who inherited the dualistic conception of man from his Brahmanical predecessors, understood this clearly and carried it to its logical conclusion; for by denying any permanence to the human personality, whether in body or in mind, he wholly and completely dehumanized man and made this the goal of all our striving. The living man as we know him he declared to be a mere agglomeration of ever-changing atoms, not, as the Vedāntin held, a permanent substance to which these atoms became attached and from which they fell away, but simply an impermanent, evanescent, ever-changing assortment of accidents unattached to any identifiable substance. Brahmanism had asserted that man, as he lives in the body, consisted of an immortal substrate on which impermanent adjuncts were superimposed, and his beatitude consisted in the separation of the permanent and eternal from the impermanent and perishable—the latter being only real in a very relative sense, if at all. The Buddha denied that there could be any personal *substrate* to the human person because the latter is no more than a mental construction derived from false premisses. He therefore was generally content to assert only the existence of a permanent something, the nature of which he declined to define as not belonging to the proper sphere of religion, that is, as being outside the realm of what the mental construction called man can actually experience. In actual fact, however, by deliberate vagueness he evades the central issue; for the 'deathless' itself must be the object of experience and must therefore be experienced by someone or something. So the Buddha does, on occasion, allow himself to speak of a 'self' which, like *dhamma* and *brahman*, is a permanent something, though apparently quite unconnected with any of the combinations of atoms that constitute what is generally understood by man.

Mr. Frithjof Schuon, in his *Transcendent Unity of Religions*, has tried to show that there is a fundamental unity underlying all the great religions. The attempt was worth making if only to show that no such unity can, in fact, be discerned. M. Schuon would perhaps, have had more chance of producing a plausible case if he had been content to treat Buddhism as he treated Protestantism, that is to say, as a heresy. For if one is dealing in orthodoxies, as M. Schuon claims to do, and if one is prepared to dismiss the whole Protestant movement simply as heresy, by the same token, one would have thought, one would have to dismiss Buddhism as a heresy of Brahmanism and Shī'a Islam as a heresy of Sunnī Islam. If there is anything corresponding to what we understand by revelation in India it is to be found in the Upanishads and the Bhagavad-Gītā which all Hindus acknowledge as authoritative, whereas the Buddha rejected the whole of the Vedas, of which the Upanishads form a part, out of hand. Nor can any of the Buddhist canons be justly claimed as revelation, since they do not agree among themselves. Buddhism is, in fact, exactly parallel to Protestantism in this, that it rejects much of what it considers superfluous in the older faith and keeps only what it considers to be the hard core of essential truth—in the case of Buddhism, the possibility of escaping from the transitory to the eternal and the way by which that escape may be achieved.

However, if revelation means anything at all, it means the revealing not only of something about God which the unaided reason cannot attain to, but also of something which man's soul cannot experience out of its own resources. Assuming, then, that the spiritual potentialities of man, when unaided by divine grace, are no different today from what they ere in ancient India, it seems clear from all the evidence that it was just as possible for man then as now, if not more so, to realize by his own unaided efforts the immortality of his own soul as Proust did in this twentieth century, or to identify his own 'soul-stuff' (as the anthropologists sometimes call it) with that 'power more subtle than electricity' described by Richard Jefferies and which is felt to pervade the whole universe. To anyone who has been privileged enough to have either of these experiences, the teachings of the Upanishads come not as a revelation, but as a *confirmation* of something already experienced. The Upanishads are the classic textbook of Jungian psychology: they teach us how and where we can discover the immortal substrate that underlies our mortal frame; but with the single exception of the *Śvetāśvatara* they teach us very little that is significant about God. They are strongest where the Old Testament is weakest and weakest where it is strongest. The Old Testament has nothing to teach us about the immortality or rather timelessness of the soul; and this is absolutely astonishing when we consider that this doctrine had become a commonplace to the Indians as a fact to be experienced rather than as a dogma to be proclaimed. Further, immortality had been proclaimed, not as an experience this time, but as a revelation by Zoroaster in Iran, while in Greece it had been the incessant preoccupation of the philosophical schools. How is it that among all the races on this earth it should be God's chosen people that was so peculiarly blind?

If mysticism is the key to religion, then we may as well exclude the Jews entirely from our inquiry: for Jewish mysticism, as Professor Scholem has so admirably portrayed it, except when influenced by Neo-Platonism or Ṣūfism, would not appear to be mysticism at all. Visionary experience is not mystical experience: for mysticism means, if it means anything, the realization of a union or a unity with or in something that is enormously, if not infinitely, greater than the empirical self. With the Yahweh of the Old Testament no such union is possible. Pre-Christian Judaism is not only un-mystical, it is anti-mystical, as is the main stream of Protestantism—and for the same reason: each is exclusively obsessed by the transcendent holiness of God and man's nothingness in face of Him. The Jews rejected the Incarnation and, with it, the promise that as co-heirs of the God-Man they too might be transformed into the divine likeness; and it is therefore in the very nature of the case that Jewish 'mysticism' should at most aspire to communion with God, never to union.

The Protestant suspicion of mysticism is perforce less radical, since to reject it outright would amount to rejecting Christ's prayer 'that they all may be one: as Thou, Father art in Me, and I in Thee, that they also may be one in Us'.[1] One cannot,

[1] John xvii. 21.

however, escape the conclusion that much of this Protestant mistrust of mysticism is due to an uneasy feeling that if what the mystics say is true, then there is nothing particularly arresting or unique in the Christian revelation. Such a view seems to be based on a singularly superficial reading of the mystics, pardonable no doubt in view of the fact that the great majority of writers on mysticism have attempted to reduce this complex of related but dissimilar phenomena to a single pattern, but regrettable none the less—and rather un-Christian, in that it leaves quite out of account the whole mass of Pauline and Johannine teaching which is mystical to the core.

Neo-Calvinism, in particular, with its stark emphasis on the 'prophetic' side of 'Biblical realism', merely carves out of the full Christian heritage that part which is most suited to its own uncouth and rugged temperament. It would then seem to be both arrogant and misinformed to accuse 'the mystic who triumphantly realizes his essential oneness with God, or the World-Order, or the Divine'—and the author of these lines seems to draw no distinction in this context between God and the World-Order—of committing 'in a sublime way the root sin of mankind—"to be like God". In other words, *he repeats the Fall*'.[1] Of course, in nine cases out of ten, he does nothing of the kind, and Dr. Kraemer might have considered whether there is or is not a real distinction between the following attested types of mystical experience: (a) the Sāṁkhya-Yogin type, in which the mystic does nothing but realize the eternal nature of his own soul; (b) the nature mystic or pan-en-henic who feels himself to be in some mysterious way identified with Nature, not with God; (c) the theistic mystic, who seeks to enter into a direct 'I-Thou' relationship with God; and (d) the genuine monist who, in realizing the ground of his own soul, thinks that he has reached the soul of the All. Only the last could possibly be accused of 'repeating the Fall', and even that would be unjust since Adam fell even though he *knew* God, and, according to Dr. Kraemer, it would seem that no one can *know* God except through the revelation of 'Biblical realism'. This he himself

[1] Hendrik Kraemer, *Religion and the Christian Faith*, London, 1956, p. 335.

seems to acknowledge, for he adds on the same page: 'this is the dishonouring and non-knowing (*avidyā!*) of the living God.' That neither the man who realizes his own soul nor the monist who takes his own soul for God, knows the Christian God, scarcely needs emphasizing; but in view of the fact that original sin is said to have severed man's relationship with God, the poor Indian mystic is scarcely to be blamed for being ignorant of the 'living God' since he is by Kraemer's definition excluded from His presence. One might have thought that he might have been allowed some credit for finding out as much about himself and about God as he did without the advantages and privileges enjoyed by the Biblical realists. To accuse him of *dishonouring* a God who, according to Kraemer himself, he has not known, is cruelly and wantonly unjust. A less superficial acquaintance with such non-Christian mystics as Rāmānuja and Martin Buber who draw the sharpest distinction between the realization of the ground of one's own soul on the one hand, and the subsequent dialogue between the soul and God which self-realization may promote on the other, might lead to a more balanced approach to the subject among the Protestant *fronde*.

Mysticism, however, *pace* Dr. Kraemer, is part and parcel of the Christian tradition—of the Christian faith, and not merely of what he likes to call historical Christianity; and it is in its mystical element precisely that Christianity may be a 'light to lighten the Gentiles' and the fulfilment of their hopes. Here, and nowhere else, can it enter into a dialogue with Indian religion in terms that the latter can understand.

Plato, in the *symposium*, puts into the mouth of Aristophanes a strange myth according to which originally man was androgynous, complete in himself, satisfactory to himself, autarkic. As such he becomes a menace to the gods, and Zeus thereupon hits upon the idea of bisecting him into separate male and female components. Once the operation has been performed, man is no longer sufficient unto himself: he is only half a being and is for ever in search of his lost half which he all too rarely finds. For the Platonic Aristophanes this dreadful dichotomy of man was caused by the jealousy of the gods. For Christians the mutilation of man is due to original sin, however we may conceive that doctrine. As a result of this primal catastrophe man is separated from God, separated too from his fellow-men, and divided within himself and against himself. Thus, according to this specifically Christian doctrine, there could be no communion between God and man until the ancient disaster could be repaired; nor could effective communion be established between man and man, or man and woman, since even if a man 'cleave unto his wife; and they shall be one flesh',[1] after the Fall they are *not* one flesh. The most they can do is to unite for a moment in which their duality seems to melt away and in which they do feel themselves to be one intensely living 'flesh', and then to fall apart into their habitual solitude. So too between fallen men there is no communion of spirit or of mind. The most that we can do is to send out pointers in the hope that they will be understood, but all that we can *know* is that we can never ourselves be known as we know ourselves—and that knowledge is imperfect enough—even by those we love best, nor can we know them. The rift between man and man cannot be healed until the gap between God and man is bridged; for in the fallen state man *naturally* thinks of himself as an independent being, a universe closed to himself and of which he alone holds the key, and he can never know any other human being until the essential unity of all human beings is restored in God.

Small wonder, then, that the Sāṁkhya-Yogin sought salvation in the total isolation of the self. And this was to be no ordinary isolation but a radical isolation, not merely from one's own fellow-men, which was in any case a *fait accompli*, but from everything in himself that had fallen a prey to corruption, everything in him that was less than eternal, his body, his discursive intellect, his senses, feelings, and emotions. The Sāṁkhya-Yogin saw with absolute clarity that fallen man is no united whole, but an uneasy association of an immortal soul and a perishable bodily apparatus.

The distinguished writer on Yoga, Mircea Eliade, has written

[1] Gen. ii. 24.

that Indian religion persistently refuses to accept *la condition humaine*, by which he means the Judaeo-Christian conception of man as a psycho-somatic unity. In this I should say that he had turned the truth upside-down. On the contrary it is we in the West who have attributed to fallen man the nature of Adam as he was before the Fall. Though it is no doubt true that before the Fall Adam possessed 'the truth in a soul and a body', as Rimbaud puts it, this is certainly not true of man in his fallen estate. However we may choose to interpret Aristophanes' myth in the *Symposium*, it does represent in crude and comic form a profound truth. Whether it is because he cannot find his other half, which Zeus so maliciously lopped off from him, in the outside world, or whether this other half is really a lost part of himself, it remains an empirical fact that man is for ever dissatisfied; and were he not so, he would have no use for religion. For religion, in all its manifestations, offers the prospect of healing and of making whole something in man that is wounded and incomplete. Indian religion knows nothing of the doctrine of the Fall; it takes man as it finds him, analyses him, and prescribes the remedy. And what it finds is not a man but two different things cohabiting, unnaturally it seems, in one vessel. It finds a body, perishable and utterly dependent on what is other than itself, and a soul, immortal, and, if freed from the prison of the body, sufficient unto itself. Salvation, then, can only mean release, the isolation of the spirit from all that comes to be and passes away, for 'flesh and blood cannot inherit the kingdom of God; neither doth corruption inherit incorruption'.[1] This is precisely the *condition humaine* as it exists in fallen men. Indian religion along with the *Tao Tê Ching*, Platonism, Gnosticism, and Manichaeanism, diagnoses the disease correctly. Where they err, if err they do, is in thinking that the disease is an incurable disease and that the cosmos is therefore eternally sick, that man is *by nature* a duality and there can be no bridging the gap between body and soul, spirit and matter.

This duality is as essential to the so-called non-dualist Vedānta as it is to the frankly dualist Sāṁkhya. The problem in both

[1] I Cor. xv. 50.

cases is the same: there are two orders of reality, an eternal and a spatio-temporal. Beatitude consists in the identification of the human self with the former, and its separation from the latter as being either a separate principle (as in the case of the Sāṁkhya and Manichaeanism) or as being simply an illusion or a dream. If there is no connecting link between the temporal and the eternal, then it follows either that the one is and the other is not, or that they are separate substances, or again that they are identical—for if we concede any reality at all to the temporal and there is no link with the eternal, then the temporal must be identical with the eternal as some Upanishadic passages imply and the Mahāyāna Buddhists roundly declare. This dichotomy of spirit and matter is basic to all Indian religion, and it is against it that such modern Indian thinkers as Śrī Aurobindo revolt, not because it is a perversion of Hinduism but because it exalts death over life and drains earthly existence of all positive content.

Both the Indian monists and the Buddhists and the Manichees base their teaching on a fact which, to anyone but a Western materialist, should be self-evident, namely, that man is not identical with either his body or his discursive intellect, that immortality is not of the body but of the soul. This is what I believe Mr. Aldous Huxley means by the *philosophia perennis*. It is the teaching of all the ancient religions that have survived with but two exceptions—Judaism and Zoroastrianism. How is it, then, as I had occasion to ask only a few pages back, that among all the races on earth it should be God's chosen people that was so peculiarly blind?

The answer is surely plain; for when a people lives or believes itself to live under the shadow of Almighty God, under Him who alone truly IS, then any personal experience of immortality can no longer have so very much significance. It can indeed have no significance at all, so immeasurable is the gulf between God and His creation.

'The voice said, Cry. And he said, What shall I cry? All flesh is grass, and all the goodliness thereof is as the flower of the field: The grass withereth, the flower fadeth: because the spirit of the Lord bloweth upon it: surely the people is grass. The grass withereth, the flower fadeth: but the word of God shall stand for ever.'[1]

So the Jews alone among the nations of the world—always excepting the Prophet Zoroaster—because they clung to the belief that man is one whole and unfractionable being, could not grasp the doctrine of the immortality of the soul. So obsessed do they appear to have been with the Majesty of God and man's utter insignificance that they forgot that man became a 'living soul' by the fact that God breathed into him the 'breath of life', the Holy Spirit, which is by definition immortal.

Original sin did two things: it separated man from God, and it set enmity between the body and the soul. In other words it brought bodily death into the world, but it could not bring death to the soul because the soul is of the 'breath of life', the Holy Spirit. The consequences of original sin, then, must be, firstly, that without divine grace it would no longer be possible for the human soul to hold communion with God, and secondly that, being thus detached from God and attached to a mortal body, it could conceive of no salvation except release from the 'body of this death'[2] which prevents it from realizing itself. The dualism of soul and body is now a fact; and it is no accident that the fact is realized by all the great Asiatic religions except Zoroastrianism: for these religions are largely empirical; and the empirical religion of India discovered that man, as now constituted, is not a whole; he is not at one with himself, and the best that he can do is to liberate what of him remains immortal from what is subject to death. Indian religion is never concerned with reconstituting the whole man for the sufficient reason that he can have no knowledge of the whole man except by a special revelation. The Jews of the Mosaic dispensation whose temporal misfortune it has been to be the chosen people of God, could only conceive of man either as wholly immortal as Adam was before the Fall or as wholly mortal. They lost

[1] Isa. xl. 6–8. [2] Rom. vii. 24.

sight of the immortality of the soul as distinct from the body and thereby overstressed the consequences of original sin.

Indian religion, then, preserved intact the cardinal doctrine that the spiritual essence of man cannot die, while Judaism preserved the opposite truth, if truth it be, that man's true immortality must make room for the body as well as the soul. God who 'at sundry times and in divers manners spake in time past unto the fathers and the prophets' meanwhile spoke out in Iran through the Prophet Zarathushtra; and Zoroaster, for the first time in Āryan lands, gave men the hope that the dead should rise again in body and in soul.

Unlike the Indian sages Zoroaster sees man's salvation as consisting in wholeness and immortality, eternal life conceived of as a prolongation of earthly life in soul and in body for ever and ever. Further he proclaims that life here on earth is what predetermines the nature of the life hereafter: 'Powerful in immortality shall be the soul of the follower of Truth, but lasting torment shall there be for the man who cleaves to the Lie.'[1] The future life for Zoroaster is not an eternal, depersonalized existence open to all men irrespective of divine grace: it is immortality in soul and in body in the presence of God in what he calls the House of Song. Zoroaster was no more a mystic than the Hebrew prophets, for, like them, his relationship with God is of person to Person, and between persons, at least as commonly understood, there can be no union or fusion. This is the distinction between the prophetic vision of God on the one hand and the mystical experience of immortality on the other. The two can only meet in a specifically theistic mysticism which recognizes the absolute existence of God on the one hand and the separate and real existence of the creature on the other. Prophecy affirms God as the one true reality, standing apart from His creation, ruling it, and guiding it towards Himself. The mysticism of fallen man, on the other hand, of which early Upanishadic speculation, the Sāṁkhya-Yoga technique, and the parallel Buddhist development are the finest examples, affirms nothing significant about God, but does affirm the im-

[1] *Yasna*, 45. 7.

mortality of the human soul as distinct from the body, mind, and will. In the one man meets God in an 'I-Thou' relationship, in the other there is no encounter at all.

Between the extremes stand Zoroaster on the prophetic side and the Bhagavad-Gītā on the mystical side. Both make known a God who is distinct from His creation and who is approachable as a friend. For the first time in Indian religion since the Rig-Veda love makes its appearance as a possible relationship between God and man. For Zoroaster too it is possible to speak of God as a friend because He is good as well as righteous and holy. The originality of the Gītā within the Indian tradition is that it recognizes God as someone distinct from man with whom union is at least possible; but it can only be possible if and when the human soul has shaken off all attachment to the things of this world, that is, to the body and to matter. And this too agrees with the doctrine of original sin, for so long as the body is mortal and is not 'raised up incorruptible', so long must it be excluded from the kingdom of heaven, as St. Paul teaches. The soul, on the other hand, free even after the Fall to enjoy its own immortality if it can but find it, cannot take the further step and unite with God, its source and Maker, until God reveals Himself to it. So, in the Bhagavad-Gītā, God declares Himself to the human soul as the goal beyond personal immortality, the source and fountain-head of all life, with whom transforming union is possible. The Gītā, however, only points to the possibility: it is not a mystical treatise in the sense that the *Cloud of Unknowing*, for example, or the *Living Flame of Love* of St. John of the Cross are. The Gītā—and indeed almost all the devotional writing of India—speaks of love and the possibility of union; it does not actually describe the dealings of God with the human soul in the language of lived experience as the Christian mystics do. The Gītā offers the promise, not yet the fulfilment.

Similarly Zoroaster enunciates the doctrine of personal survival after death and a second existence in which body and soul will be reunited in eternal bliss; but he can bring no guarantee in support of the truth of such a doctrine, unheard of in the sister civilization of India, and manifestly at variance with the observed facts of human existence. The mere fact, however, that Zoroaster can put forward such a claim and that he should link the quality of the promised immortality with the kind of life we lead on earth, shows that he had already bridged the gulf between time and eternity which we have seen to be one of the results of original sin as that doctrine appears to us in the light of comparative religion.

Unless I am greatly mistaken, all the strands we have been trying to bring together in the different religions, meet only in one place, and that is in the religion of Jesus Christ. In the Person of Christ the two traditions meet and are reconciled. Judaism, alone among the great religions, could not conceive of immortality except as the immortality of the whole man. That the soul could lead an independent and immortal life in separation from the body, did not originally enter into their way of thinking at all, though very early this became almost an axiom in India. Hence God could only convince His chosen people that they were called upon to share in His eternal life either by obliterating the effects of original sin altogether by making the whole human being immortal in body as well as in soul here and now, or by Himself becoming man and taking on a body with all its needs and imperfections, that, in conquering physical death, He might show man his ultimate destiny, which is to possess himself in soul and in body in a restored union with God from whom he originated and to whom he must return.

'Think not that I am come to destroy the law, or the prophets: I am not come to destroy, but to fulfil.' Christ indeed comes to fulfil not only the law and the prophets of Israel, but also the 'law and the prophet' of the Āryan race. He fulfils or rounds out the conception of God independently revealed to the Hebrew prophets and to Zoroaster, and by His Crucifixion, Death, Resurrection, and Ascension He points to the type of mystical path the soul must tread if it is to rise beyond the *ātman* or higher self to its predestined reunion with God.

It could be said that much of recent Protestant Christianity, in sharp contradistinction to the great Reformers, has laid undue stress on the Christian ethic as propounded in the Sermon on the Mount, on works rather than on faith. Yet Christian ethics is not what makes Christianity unique, for the ethics of self-denial had already been preached by the Buddha, who, no less than Christ, taught a universal charity that should comprise all mankind, including our enemies. What makes Christianity what it is, as St. Paul clearly saw, is the scandal and the foolishness of the Cross, the doctrine of atonement by bloody human sacrifice and the Resurrection of the body.

To modern man the doctrine of the atonement is perhaps the hardest of all Christian doctrines to swallow. It was rejected out of hand by the Muhammadans who considered it to be derogatory to the majesty of God and therefore blasphemous. Let us consider what it means in the light of what has already been said. Man was created by God, so the Christian legend runs, a perfect and immortal being composed of an immortal soul and an immortal body, united in an indissoluble harmony. This inner harmony reflected the harmony that existed between the whole man and God in whose image he was made. The relation of the whole man to God was similar to that of his own body to his soul, one of loving dependence and obedience. Man lived in and by God just as his own body lived in and by his own soul, the principle of his own immortality. God, however, made man free; and man, wishing to be like God, that is, wishing to become a pure spirit in separation from his body, disobeyed the commandment of God and ate of the Tree of Knowledge. It is perhaps not too far-fetched to say that before eating of the tree, the fruit of which brings self-awareness, man was conscious of himself only in his relationship to God; he was not conscious of his individual existence as it might be apart from God at all. He ate of the tree and realized himself as an individual. As the Upanishad says: 'Looking round he saw nothing else than himself. He said first: "I am." . . . He was afraid.'[1] This was the result of the Fall: man found himself alone. 'Verily he had no delight: and henceforth man who is alone has no delight. He desired a second. In size he was as great as a man and a woman in close embrace. He split himself in two; and from thence man

[1] *Bṛhadāraṇyaka* Up., I. 4. I.

and wife came to be. Hence a human being is like a half-fragment.'

As I have repeatedly stressed in previous chapters the sacred books of the Hindus reveal not so much God as the essence of man; and the passage I have just quoted seems to me to depict exactly the predicament of fallen man. He is alone, and desiring a second, woman is separated out from him: 'therefore shall a man leave his father and his mother, and shall cleave unto his wife'.[1] Adam had done just this: rebelliously he had cast off the obedience he owed to his Father, God, and contemptuously he cast off his mother, the humble clay that God had brought to life for his sake. He was alone and afraid, and had no alternative but to cling to his wife. Marriage may well be an image of the love of God for the soul; but in man's fallen estate it is a poor enough image and a miserable substitute for the reality.

By sin the essential connexion and link between man and God was cut. Similarly within man himself the inner connexion between soul and body was severed, and henceforth the mortal body was to be at war with the immortal soul. Both the external harmony between God and man and the internal harmony between body and soul had been shattered. God withdrew His presence from the world, revealing Himself only 'at sundry times' to the patriarchs and prophets, and, it must be said, if we accept God's revelation of Himself in Christ as being true, revealing Himself so gradually and so obscurely that fallen man can but hope to be forgiven if he has misread the signs.

The spirit of God, however, which had been infused into Adam at his creation had not been wholly withdrawn. Even when separated from God man was still free to find his own immortal soul, and this is precisely what the Indian sages did. Without God man was free to seek his beatitude in one of two ways. Either he could isolate his soul from that part of him which original sin had handed over to death, or he could let it float and dissolve in that spirit which pervades all natural things, the spirit called the World Soul by the Neo-Platonists, *prāṇa* or 'breath' by the Hindus, 'a force more subtle than

[1] Gen. ii. 24.

electricity' by Richard Jefferies, the 'Universal Mind' by Rimbaud, or simply *prakṛti* or Nature by the Sāṁkhya-Yoga. What the nature of this spirit can be I find it impossible to say. Perhaps it is the Spirit of God in its relationship to the subrational order for which the moral law does not apply, the spirit in Nature which quickens all natural things, as against the same Spirit operating in the moral sphere among rational and responsible beings as conscience and the 'natural' moral law. That such a spirit exists seems to be attested by the experience of all nature mystics, and it is something they feel to be 'beyond good and evil'. The Upanishads explored to the full these two capacities still left to fallen man—the isolation of the self and the merging into the All.

It is only in the *Śvetāśvatara* Upanishad and much more in the Bhagavad-Gītā that we are allowed a glimpse of the God who stands above Nature and above the immortal soul. Neither the Upanishad nor the Gītā is now content with the purely negative descriptions of the supreme principle so dear to the earlier Upanishads; for they realize that 'it is not enough to know only that [God] exists, but one must know His nature and His will':[1] and how can one know His nature and His will except by prophetic revelation? and if by prophetic revelation, by what particular prophetic revelation?

Plainly the only revelation that could lay claim to universal acceptance would have to be a revelation that confirmed all that had been revealed before 'at sundry times and in divers manners' and which enabled these partial revelations to fall into their due place in God's revelation of Himself not only in Israel but also among all nations. Of the revelations outside Israel the most impressive is undoubtedly the progressive revelation in India which showed to man first that there is one principle which informs both the cosmos and the human soul, secondly that the human soul is immortal, and finally that there is a personal God who not only informs and directs all things but who also becomes incarnate 'for the protection of the good,

[1] *Shkand-Gumānīk Vichār*, ed. P. J. de Menasce, O.P., Fribourg, 1945, 10. 37, p. 117.

for the destruction of the wicked, and for the establishment of the law'.[1] Secondly there was the revelation through the Iranian Prophet Zoroaster, who taught first that God is righteous and good, that men will rise again in body and in soul, that their will is free, and that evil will ultimately be destroyed. Thirdly there was the gentle Buddha himself who broke with Brahmanism because he could not see that any useful purpose was served by metaphysical speculation and who preached a selfless love for all creatures though, in a world that was still under the ban of original sin, he knew nothing at all of God. Thus among the Gentiles both Hinduism and Zoroastrianism had already declared something essential about God, whereas the Buddha, who as an atheist can scarcely be claimed as an author of revelation, proclaimed a doctrine of dying to self for no other reason than that the very idea of self was a delusion. I will not now stress the extraordinary fact that the man Buddha, the sceptical empiricist who yet loved all men with a passionless love, was transformed by his later disciples into the incarnation of a triune God, for this is no part of my thesis: for my thesis is this, that Jesus Christ fulfils not only the law and the prophets of Israel but also the Prophet of Iran and the sages of India.

What, however, I will and must stress is the amazing *Umwertung* of all Buddhist values that the Mahāyāna brought with it. The Mahāyāna sensed uneasily that, despite the Buddha's attempts to prove that there was no such thing as a 'self', there was something essentially selfish about the *arhant* ideal; for there is an unbridgeable contradiction in all Buddhist thought. Its philosophical psychology, which denies even relative permanence to all compounded things, does not and cannot fit in with the Buddha's reverence for all living things down to the very gnats that torture us, and his compassion with the suffering of the world. The Theravādins or Hīnayānists, as they are usually called, thought it sufficient for a man to achieve his own Nirvāṇa, to pass quietly out of his earthly bondage into the 'unborn, not become, not made, not compounded', there to enjoy 'deathlessness, peace, the unchanging state of Nirvāṇa'. Once

[1] Bhagavad-Gītā, 4. 8.

this was achieved, 'destroyed is birth, lived is the Brahma-faring, done is what was to be done, there is no more being such-and-such'. Salvation is achieved and this world, that conglomerate of senseless suffering, is left behind for ever.

The Mahāyānists realized that this must be all wrong, for it made nonsense of the Buddha's own compassion. They discovered—and it was a discovery of enormous significance—that there is after all such a thing as the higher selfishness—the selfishness not of the ego, the 'I' that governs the body, mind, and senses, and is in turn dependent on them, but of the 'self', the *atta-ātman*, that is, the centre of immortal life. They realized too that primitive Buddhism, in refusing to define Nirvāṇa except as the 'unborn, not become', etc. was begging the question. For, however much you may deny philosophically that there is any specific entity which might properly be said to experience Nirvāṇa, the empirical fact remains that once you have entered this unqualifiable state, it is *your* bliss, *your* salvation, *your* Nirvāṇa, *your* deathlessness, not your neighbour's. This is the selfishness peculiar to the *puruṣa*, *ātman*, or eternal self, not to the poor matter-bound ego, and of the two it is by far the worse: it is spiritual pride, the besetting sin of all monists, both those who are consciously so and those who are not.

The Mahāyānists were not alone in perceiving this. That prince of Christian mystics, Blessed Jan van Ruysbroeck, observed the same phenomenon in the Christian Middle Ages and denounced it unsparingly:

'Now understand that whenever man wishes to have rest in emptiness without an inward yearning impulse towards God, he makes himself apt to every error. For he is turned away from God, and is inclined towards *himself* through *natural* love. . . . The man who thus lives in merely natural love always possesses himself, unhindered, with all his own attributes.'[1] And this natural love 'is inclined towards itself and its enjoyment, and *always remains alone*'.[2] 'For according to their way of thinking,'

[1] Blessed Jan van Ruysbroeck, *The Spiritual Espousals*, tr. Eric Colledge, London, 1952, p. 168.

[2] Ibid., p. 169.

Ruysbroeck continues, 'they possess everything that they might pray or yearn for. And thus they are poor in spirit, for they are without desire, and they have forsaken everything, and live without any choice of their own, for it seems to them that they have passed beyond everything into an emptiness where they possess that for the sake of which all the exercises of Holy Church are ordained and set. And thus, according to them, no one is able to give to them or to take from them, not even God Himself; for it appears to them that they have advanced beyond all exercises and all virtues. And they have attained, they think, to a perfect passivity in which they are finished with all virtues. And they say that greater labour is needed to be finished with virtue in passivity than to attain to virtue.' For 'according to their way of thinking they are exalted above all the orders of saints and angels and above every reward, which one can in any way deserve. And therefore they say that they can never increase in virtue, that they can never deserve a greater reward, and also that they can never sin again.'[1]

This is rather what the Mahāyānists thought, though they did not express themselves quite so forthrightly; for selfishness is not the prerogative of the dweller in *saṁsāra*, there is an even more subtle form of selfishness in Nirvāṇa, a 'worm' that 'dieth not'.[2] So in place of the more ancient *arhant*, the released soul who simply fades away into *his* Nirvāṇa, they put the Bodhisattvas, those saintly beings who postponed their own Nirvāṇa in order to enable others to reach that blessed estate. The Bodhisattva, unlike the realized Buddha, is completely suffused with a boundless compassion for all souls still bound to the wheel of phenomenal existence. 'He radiates great friendliness and compassion over all beings, and gives his attention to them, thinking: "I shall become their saviour, I shall release them from all their sufferings." '[3] This is the tremendous vow he takes

[1] Ibid., p. 171.

[2] Mark ix. 44, 46, 48.

[3] *Aṣṭasāhasrikā*, 22, 404, *apud* E. Conze, *Buddhist Texts through the Ages*, p. 128.

upon himself—not to enjoy the eternal bliss that is within his grasp but to accept a bitter crucifixion on the cross of this world until *all* souls enter before him into the peace of Nirvāṇa. The whole idea recalls the Manichaean conception of the *Jesus patibilis* crucified not once on Calvary but for ever on the great cross of this world. Mahāyāna Buddhism would seem to lack one thing only—and this it inherits from the Buddha—it refuses to say in what Nirvāṇa consists. The goal is still only to escape from time and space, and so void of content is this condition believed to be that it can only be called 'emptiness'. Here there is communion with neither the Bodhisattva nor with other souls. It is a blessed state but still lacks all that the Bodhisattva himself represents. Communion and union with *such* a being, one would have thought, would have been worth all the Nirvāṇas that could possibly exist.

The Bodhisattva ideal is perhaps the most grandiose that the Indian mind has ever conceived; and it finds its fulfilment as nowhere else in the figure of the Crucified. But whereas the Bodhisattvas are mythical beings thought out by man in his desperate longing that such beings might exist, Christ is the true Bodhisattva, God made Man, suffering with man, and crucified by man and for man that He might release him—not indeed from the suffering of this world, but from the burden of sin that causes that suffering.

When his tremendous task is accomplished and his vow fulfilled, the Bodhisattva, like the countless souls he has helped out of this world of suffering, himself disappears without name or trace into the 'emptiness' of Nirvāṇa. Christ, however, does not disappear: on the third day He arises again in body and in soul, a whole Man who is also God, thereby fulfilling the hope of Zoroaster. And as He rose from the dead, so shall all men rise from the dead as the Prophet had foretold. For Christ's Resurrection is the earnest of all men's resurrection, 'Christ the firstfruits; afterward they that are Christ's at His coming.'[1]

The idea of divine incarnation was well-known to India, and Krishna in the great Epic is so regarded: he is the incarnation

[1] 1 Cor. xv. 23.

of the supreme God Vishnu. This second characteristic Indian hope is once again fulfilled in Christ; for wonderful though the myth of the incarnate Krishna is, it is still only a myth, though a myth full of meaning and a prefiguration of the historical Incarnation of the God who is at the same time love. In Christ the good news brought by Krishna that God loves man, and the more tragic self-sacrifice of the Bodhisattvas, meet. God enters the world and 'abhorreth not the Virgin's womb', even as the Buddha did not shrink from entering the womb of his mother Māyā, whose very name means *materia prima*.[1] But the good news of God's love for man in the Bhagavad-Gītā remains a promise only, the hope that was to be expressed in countless forms throughout the Indian peninsula from the Indian Middle Ages up to the present day. Just as Zoroaster's prophecy of the resurrection of the dead remains a hope only until the Man-God, Jesus, Himself rises from the dead, so does Krishna's revelation of the secret of God's love for man remain a promise only, to be accepted by faith alone, until God Himself becomes man and shows man the total quality of His love. Just as Krishna's original message is that God, the greater than Brahman, the higher than the passionless Absolute, not only stoops to man but even yearns for him, so with the actual historical Incarnation of God in Jesus Christ, Christ takes upon His shoulders the sins of the world 'being made a curse for us';[2] and although 'His nature' was 'from the first, divine . . . yet he did not see, in the rank of Godhead, a prize to be coveted. He dispossessed Himself, and took the nature of a slave, fashioned in the likeness of men, and presented Himself to us in human form; and then He lowered His own dignity, accepted an obedience which brought Him to death, death on a cross.'[3] This, then, was the demonstration of what God's love for man really meant—to die an agonizing death, becoming a 'curse' for man's sake, that man might be delivered from the bondage of sin. 'Greater love hath no man than this, that a man lay down his life for his friends.'[4] This is God's love for man, the reality

[1] *Mahāvastu*, ii, 3 ff.
[2] Gal. iii. 13.
[3] Phil. ii. 6–8 (Knox's translation).
[4] John xv. 13.

foreshadowed surely, but foreshadowed only, in Krishna's dialogue with Arjuna.

In the beginning 'the Lord God formed man of the dust of the ground, and breathed into his nostrils the breath of life; and man became a living soul'.[1] And because the spirit of God was within him, Muslims hold, the angels were bidden to fall down and worship him, Iblīs, the Devil, alone refusing.[2] Adam, however, sinned and the divine spirit withdrew from his body, abandoning it to death. Soul and body were henceforth to be at war, the 'law in my members warring against the law of my mind, and bringing me into captivity to the law of sin which is in my members'.[3] Man's unity could not now be restored without another divine intervention; but this time God did not form Christ, the second Adam, 'from the dust of the ground'. He, the Almighty, approached a human girl and asked to be allowed to dwell awhile within her. Mary, the *materia prima* of the second Adam, accepted all without question: 'Be it unto me according to thy Word.'[4]

Zoroaster had proclaimed that God had created man's will absolutely free, and it was by the free will of the first man and woman that man fell and sin came into the world, and it was by the free will of Mary that the ancient rift between soul and body, between God and Man, that sin had caused, was to be healed. The Indians had sensed rightly that the body, because it is mortal, is in some sense an evil thing, but they did not understand, nor indeed could they, that it is only the *locus* or effect of sin, not sinful by nature. By entering the Virgin's womb God sanctified the whole of matter, raising our mortal bodies to a new dignity which they had not before possessed, calling upon matter to partake of spirit. For this is surely the meaning of the Incarnation and the Resurrection, of the sacrament of water and the sacrament of bread and wine which *are* the body and blood of Christ. There is nothing so very wonderful about the redemption of the human soul and its reunion with the God from whom it sprang but from whom sin separated it; but there

[1] Gen. ii. 7.
[2] Qur'ān, 15. 28 ff.
[3] Rom. vii. 23.
[4] Luke i. 38.

is something utterly mysterious about the redemption of the body. Yet it is fundamental to the Christian faith, and even St. Paul, more obsessed perhaps than any other early Christian writer with the body's heaviness, intractability, and downright sinfulness, sees that redemption cannot be complete until the body shares in the immortality and incorruptibility of the soul. 'For we know that the whole creation groaneth and travaileth in pain together until now. And not only they, but ourselves also, which have the firstfruits of the Spirit, even we ourselves groan within ourselves, waiting for the adoption, to wit, the redemption of our body.'[1] For St. Paul that pain which the Buddha saw as the basis of all transitory existence, was not the pain of an incurable disease but the birth-pangs that announced an incorruptible world, the firstfruits of which was the risen Christ. The great Muslim poet, Jalāl al-Dīn Rūmī, was later to take up the same theme and exclaim:

'All around us one vast hubbub,
Candles blazing, torches hurled;
For to-night the world's in travail,
Bringing forth the eternal world.'[2]

So too does the Persian mystic look forward to the resurrection of the body which must come if man's redemption is to be complete.

By the Incarnation, then, God redeems the material world from its isolation from spirit, and to confirm the reconsecration of matter He rises from the dead and ascends into heaven in bodily form. And this, too, is no doubt one of the reasons why the Assumption of our Lady was recently declared a dogma by the Catholic Church; for all that is material in the Man-God, Christ, derives from Mary: it is she who is the *materia prima* of the second Adam, and through her Assumption all matter is thereby sanctified. The definition of this dogma is the assertion in the clearest possible tones that Christ's incarnation closes

[1] Rom. viii. 22–3.

[2] *Dīvān-i Shams-i Tabrīz,* ed. R. A. Nicholson (reprint), Cambridge, 1952, pp. 142–3.

once and for all the gap that existed between soul and body and kept the latter in perpetual subjection to death.

However we conceive of the resurrection of the body 'sown a natural body' and 'raised a spiritual body',[1] this at least we know, that the body which is the *locus* of mind and character, is what distinguishes one man from another; and it is this distinction that the monistic mystic would abolish. Krishna, however, did not ask Arjuna to be other than he was in order that he might draw near to him; no more does Christ ask us to renounce anything but sin. Changed we shall certainly be, but changed because purged from sin, and therefore incorruptible, but not deprived of our creaturely individual being which is God's unique gift to us. For entrance into the Christian heaven does not entail loss of personality but its infinite enrichment in communion and union not only with God through Christ, but also with all our fellow-men in what is called the Communion of Saints. This again is the fulfilment of the Zoroastrian vision of paradise in which men are whole and immortal in body and in soul, walking together and glorifying God.[2]

Yet though Christianity may be said to be the obvious fulfilment of Zoroastrianism because it has borrowed so much from that religion, is there any sense in which it fulfils Hinduism and Buddhism? We have already seen that Christ crucified is the perfect fulfilment in this world of ours of the Bodhisattva ideal; but there is more to it than this. I have likened the Crucifixion elsewhere[3] to a parable of the crucifixion of the ego and the rising from its ashes of the immortal soul or 'self'. I was wrong: for if this were the whole message of the Cross to the Indian soul, it would be no fulfilment, for it would merely re-enact in physical form a psychological truth which was already well known.

What the Cross does teach is what the Mahāyāna Buddhists instinctively felt, namely, that the realization and isolation of the eternal essence of one's own soul is simply a more subtle kind of selfishness, the last and ultimate self-love which must be

[1] 1 Cor. xv. 44.
[2] See R. C. Zaehner, *The Teachings of the Magi*, London, 1956, p. 148.
[3] *Mysticism, Sacred and Profane*, Oxford, 1957, p. 207.

purged away. The way to realize the soul, the Gītā along with the whole of the Indian ascetic tradition teaches, is through complete detachment from all worldly things; and this seems to be what St. John of the Cross calls the Dark Night of the Senses, and it brings what seems to be a perfect peace. This is the peace (*śānti*) of the *ātman*, but it is not the peace that passeth all understanding.

Christ, being sinless, is of necessity what the Indians call a *jīvanmukta*, 'one who has attained to salvation or release in this life', from the moment of his conception. But since, Christians hold, Christ takes upon Himself all the sins of the world and is made a 'curse' as the representative of sinful man, He must, in the Crucifixion, undergo all the purgation that belongs by right to man if he is to be reunited to the Divine. On the Cross Christ atones not only for the carnal pride of man's ego but also, and much more essentially, for his immortal soul which, in realizing *itself*, so often thinks it has passed beyond the realm of good and evil. Peace is what the *ātman* finds within himself; and this too it must give up. For 'it behoves the soul to abandon all its former peace. This was in reality no peace at all, since it was involved in imperfections; but to the soul aforementioned it appeared to be so, because it was following its own inclinations, which were for peace. It seemed, indeed, to be a twofold peace —that is, the soul believed that it had already acquired the peace of sense and that of spirit for it found itself to be full of the spiritual abundance of this peace of sense and of spirit—as I say it is still imperfect. First of all, then, it must be purged of that former peace and disquieted concerning it and withdrawn from it.'[1] Thus only when the immortal soul itself has been purged of a selfishness of which it had thought itself incapable, can it arise again with Christ, a new man, ready to ascend to the Father. In essence the Cross of Christ as related to the mystical ascent to God the Father is the fulfilment of what Rāmānuja saw must be the soul's approach to God. *Ātmabodha*, 'self-realization', is all very well, for in it 'rest is sufficient and great',

[1] St. John of the Cross, *Dark Night of the Soul*, II, ix, 6; p. 400 in the translation of E. Allison Peers, new edition, London, 1953.

but it is a rest out of which the soul that thirsts for God will be violently shaken, for the love of God demands an absolute and total purity, a total denudation not only of 'I' and 'mine', but of the eternal 'self' too, for the 'living flame of Love' burns up all that is not fit to approach the unutterable holiness of God. 'God's mouth, a blazing, destroying fire, burns up the whole world in its brilliance.'[1] This fire, which appears as the instrument of the divine Wrath to those who are still defiled by sin but as an ardent flame and 'sweet wound' of love to the perfected, 'would have no power over' men 'even though they came into contact with it, if they had no imperfections for which to suffer. These are the material upon which the fire of purgatory seizes; when the material is consumed there is naught else that can burn. So here, when the imperfections are consumed, the affliction of the soul ceases and its fruition remains.'[2]

And what is the soul's fruition? To rise united with the Son of God into the full life of the Trinity—Father, Son, and Holy Ghost—Being, Thought, and the fruition of Love, the *sat*, *cit*, *ānanda* of the Hindus, Three in One as the non-dualist Vedānta itself confesses; for by knowing and rejoicing in Himself, the Eternal Being, though always One, is none the less Three.

In Christianity, then, it would appear that the highest insights of both the Hindus and the Buddhists are fulfilled, and in the Incarnation and Resurrection of Christ which is the 'first-fruits', the resurrection of the body which Zoroaster had seen as inevitable because he could not conceive that man had been *created* a duality, is guaranteed; for man's *final* end is neither isolation nor disintegration into Nature but the realization of his creaturely self in union with the Godhead. And the way to this is, as always, the way of paradox, of 'scandal' and of 'foolishness'; for if man would realize himself in God, he must deny himself utterly, abandoning everything to God, for it is only then that God creates a new man in a new glory 'changed into the same image from glory to glory, even as by the Spirit of the

[1] Bhagavad-Gītā, 11. 19.
[2] St. John of the Cross, op. cit., II, x, 5; Peers, p. 404.

Lord'.[1] Only so is he fit for the transforming union which will bind him indissolubly to God in an eternal I-Thou relationship of person to Person, and through God he will be 'oned' with all that he has ever loved selflessly on earth, for that is surely the meaning of the Communion of Saints.

Christianity, then, does, fulfil both the mystical tradition of India as finally expressed in the Bhagavad-Gītā and the Bodhisattva doctrine, and the hopes of Zoroaster, the Prophet of ancient Iran. In Christ the two streams meet and are harmonized and reconciled as they are nowhere else: for Christ fulfils both the law and the prophets in Israel and the 'gospel according to the Gentiles' as it was preached in India and Iran.

[1] 2 Cor. iii. 18.

APPENDIX

The Qur'ān and Christ[1]

In the lectures which I delivered in Aberystwyth in 1957 of which this book is an expanded version, I had no time to consider the very special case of the Prophet Muhammad. While it would be impossible fully to make good this omission here, our thesis would not have been complete and indeed the main stumbling-block at which it is likely to be shattered would have been quietly ignored, if nothing further were said about the Arabian Prophet.

This seems to me to be the great weakness of almost all works on the great religions of the world written by Christians. They tend to deal in some detail with the Indian contribution to the world's religious heritage—as well they might—but to side-step the very far from negligible factor constituted by Islam. Dr. Kraemer, for instance, whose books are valuable precisely because he makes no attempt to be impartial, but takes Biblical Christianity as the absolute standard against which he judges all religions including historical Christianity, does not seem to be worried by the fact that Muslims have a precisely similar absolute standard against which the religions, including Dr. Kraemer's own Biblical realism, must be judged. If Dr. Kraemer thinks fit to judge and condemn from the point of view of the Bible as interpreted by himself, the Muslims also have their divine norm by which to judge and condemn the religions of

[1] For a full discussion of the divinity of Christ in Islam see I. di Matteo, *La Divinita di Cristo a la Dottrina della Trinità*, Rome, 1938.

which, for them, Christianity is but one, since there is only one religion that is uniquely true, and that is Islam.

Further, if we persist in basing our faith on a book (*biblos*), if we advertise our religion as *Biblical*, then we are logically obliged to consider the claims of Islam as the religion of the Book *par excellence*, for these claims far outshine those of Biblical Christianity. In the case of Islam the Qur'ān received its definitive shape through the executive action of the third Caliph, 'Uthmān, some twenty years after the Prophet's death. Moreover, it was from the beginning agreed what the new revelation consisted in, namely, those utterances of Muhammad which were considered to have been directly inspired by God; and it is remarkable that these utterances never seem to have been confused with the Prophet's own pronouncements on religious matters which were later collected as *ḥadīth* or Tradition. In the case of Christianity things were very different, the Canon of the New Testament not being finally defined until the fourth century A.D. Islam, then, is the religion of the Book *par excellence*, and may, above all other religions, claim to be the authentic *Biblical* realism.

Again when Christians argue against Hinduism and to a lesser extent against Buddhism that they are religions based largely on myth and not on historical fact, they are in a very weak position once they turn their attention to Islam; for although there is a vast deal that is obscure in the early history of the Prophet's career, the story of the first Muslim century works itself out in the full light of history because it was itself making history in a tremendous way. This can scarcely be said of the first Christian century. The credentials of Islam, then, both as an historical and as a 'biblical' religion are very much stronger than are those of Christianity.

As against Islam Christianity would seem to have only one really effective argument, and that is that Jesus Christ, whom Muhammad recognized as the last of the prophets before himself, was God incarnate and claimed to be the 'Son of God'; and that if this is so, His word and its continuation in the Church He founded must take precedence over any merely prophetic revelation. The Muhammadan answer to this is, of course, that Jesus never made any such claim and that the Christians had falsified His message.

I have said earlier that there appears to be no valid reason for rejecting Muhammad's claim to be a prophet if we accept the claims of the Hebrew prophets to be such. Indeed, from the purely monotheistic point of view, Muhammad's claim would appear to be the stronger, for whereas the Hebrew prophets build on a monotheistic foundation which is already there, Muhammad proclaims the absolute Oneness of God among a people which was far from prepared for such a revelation. Nor need we be swayed by the argument that there is practically nothing in the Qur'ān which cannot be traced to the Old or New Testaments, their apocrypha, the Midrash or Talmud. It is certainly probable that Muhammad absorbed all this material in more or less chaotic form in the years preceding his call, and that much of it came bubbling out afterwards in his prophetic utterances which he at least was convinced were inspired by God. All religions, including Christianity, are influenced by external trends, and though Islam shows practically no originality in detail, it is nevertheless, despite the incoherence of the Qur'ān, one of the most coherent of existing religions.

For the purpose of this appendix I assume that Muhammad was what he claimed to be—a prophet sent by God. This does not, of course, mean that I am unimpressed by the arguments against such an assumption as, for instance, the 'abrogated' verses of the Qur'ān and the apparent falling off of inspiration in the later Medinan period when Muhammad speaks rather as a law-giver than as a prophet. This second objection, however, seems to me to lack all validity, for in this Muhammad is following exactly the pattern traced by Moses. As to the first objection, this involves what has become a cardinal Muslim dogma, namely, that the Qur'ān, or at least its heavenly archetype, is uncreated; and if this dogma is accepted, then the 'abrogated' verses are extremely difficult to explain away.

Muslim theology, however, in its orthodox development, is only one of many possible interpretations of the Qur'ān, and many of its accepted dogmas have no basis whatever in that Book. One of these is the dogma of the uncreate Qur'ān which not only lacks all authority in the Book itself, but also runs directly counter to the root-doctrine of the whole Qur'ānic revelation, the absolute unity of God. Muslim orthodoxy, by accepting the dogma of an uncreate Qur'ān, is itself guilty of the unforgivable sin in Islam, *shirk*, 'association of other beings with God'. Moreover, it seems to be generally agreed[1] that the idea of an eternal Qur'ān developed as a direct counterblast to the Christian interpretation of God's eternal Word as being incarnate in Christ. Muslim orthodoxy, while setting itself up as the champion of the absolute unity of God, nevertheless saw nothing incongruous in the 'incarnation' of the Word of God in a Book, which itself had suffered change by the abrogation of revealed verses in the very process of being revealed. This point is made very clearly by the Nestorian Catholicos, Timothy, who counters the Muslim charge that the Christians had tampered with their sacred books with the telling counter-charge that in Islam it is the Qur'ān itself which abrogates earlier Qur'ānic revelations.[2]

The history of the relations between Christianity and Islam has been one of increasing misunderstanding and estrangement, and Muslim theology developed one-sidedly because it was less interested in eliciting the true meaning of the Qur'ān than it was in building up a counter-theology against the already developed Christian system. For the Word made flesh Muslim theology substitutes the Word made Book. Similarly the Qur'ānic evidence for the life, mission, and nature of Christ is always interpreted in a way that is farthest removed from Christian theology: it seeks to reduce the figure of Christ to that of a purely human prophet, though this is scarcely in accordance with the text of the Qur'ān, as we hope to show.

In this appendix I wish to make one main point, that any fruitful approach to the problem of Islam from the Christian side must be made through the Qur'ān itself; for if ever there

[1] See *Encyclopaedia of Islam*, s.v. *al-Ḳur'ān*.

[2] See J. W. Sweetman, *Islam and Christian Theology*, Part I, vol. i, p. 80.

were a case for 'Biblical realism', it is that of Islam, not of Christianity. For Islam is, of all religions, the religion of the Book (Bible!), whereas in Christianity the Book originally depends on the Church which alone had the authority to draw up the Canon and to decide what was genuine revelation and what was spurious. Even so the Church was in no hurry to do so until its hand was forced by the appearance of what it considered to be an unorthodox canon of scripture, the canon drawn up by the heretic Marcion in the second century A.D. In Christianity, then, the Book depends on the Church as the Church depends on Christ who is the Word Incarnate: it is therefore strictly of tertiary importance. In Islam things are very different: it is the Book that is the Word of God, and the Prophet, so far from claiming divine status, is merely the human channel through which God's Word is transmitted to man—more specifically to Arabian man. The Qur'ān claims to be the confirmation of what was revealed before. It might be called the 'testament' of the Arabs just as the Torah was the testament of the Jews. According to the Qur'ān the content of the two 'testaments' is the same:

'And before it is the Book of Moses, a model and a mercy; and this is a Book confirming it in Arabic speech, to warn those who have done evil, and good tidings to those who do good.'[1]

In essence the Qur'ān contains the same message as was previously sent down to the Jews in their scriptures:

'Verily it is revelation (*tanzīl*) of the Lord of the worlds, brought down by the Faithful Spirit upon thine heart that thou mayst be a warner, in clear Arabic speech. Verily it is in the Psalms (*zubur*) of the ancients. Was it not a sign to them that the doctors of the children of Israel know it?'[2]

The Qur'ān indeed seems to be regarded as specifically the ful-

[1] Qur'ān, 46. 11: cf. 12. 2: 13. 37: 20. 112: 39. 29: 41. 2: 42. 5: 43. 2. Unless otherwise stated all further references in this appendix are to the Qur'ān.

[2] 26. 192–7.

filment of the Old Testament rather than of the New. It is indeed coupled with the Gospel in three Medinan passages,[1] but it is not stated that it is the direct fulfilment of it as it is of the 'Book of Moses' and the Psalms.

What causes more friction than anything else between Muslims and Christians is undoubtedly the refusal of the latter to concede that Muhammad can be considered to be a prophet sent by God. Christians find it impossible to concede this first because there would seem to be little point in sending a Prophet after the Incarnation, and secondly because the message contained in the Qur'ān is alleged to deny certain essential Christian doctrines, viz. the Divinity of Christ and His Sonship, the Trinity, the Atonement, the Crucifixion, and the Resurrection. It would therefore seem worthwhile to examine the disputed Qur'ānic passages in question.

On the subject of the divinity of Christ Early Christian apologists could point to passages in the Qur'ān which seemed to assert or at least to imply precisely this. Perhaps the most important of these is 4. 169 where Muhammad is specifically warning the Christians against exaggerating their claims on behalf of Christ:

> 'O people of the Book,' he exclaims, 'exceed not all bounds in your religion and say nothing about God but the truth. The Messiah, Jesus, son of Mary, is but a messenger of God and His Word which he cast upon Mary, and a spirit from Him. So believe in God and His messengers and say not "Three". Refrain, for it will be better for you. God is only one God; far be it from His glory to have a son.'

It remains a mystery to this day from what source or sources Muhammad derived his Christological ideas. He was, however, aware of the differences that split Eastern Christianity in his day[2] when the great bulk of the Semitic Christian world was already no longer in communion with the Byzantine Church, but was either Monophysite or Nestorian. The first great

[1] 3. 2.: 5. 110: 9. 112.

[2] 19. 38. 'But the sects disagreed among themselves.'

Christian schism was already a fact. It does then seem likely that when speaking of Christ he is speaking against a Christian theological background, using Christian terminology without, probably, understanding its meaning. The terminology used, indeed, is too close to that of Christianity to be interpreted without reference to a Christian context.[1]

What, in fact, is Muhammad denying in this passage? Nothing more, it would appear, than that God was physically the Father of Jesus. Muhammad, though he certainly knew of the Christological controversies that had been raging during the last centuries, was not a trained Christian theologian, and for anyone who was not just that, the whole concept of the 'generation' of the Word must either have been incomprehensible or implied that God had taken on a human form and cohabited with Mary rather as the ancient gods did in pagan legend. Such an idea was rightly abhorrent to the Prophet. In this passage he in fact affirms not only the Virgin Birth on which the Qur'ān always lays great emphasis, but also that Christ is 'only' God's messenger and His *Word* (*kalima*)[2]—a spirit from Him, that is to say, not carnally conceived, but conceived by the divine afflatus and the divine *fiat*[3]—exactly, then, what orthodox Christianity means by the 'Word made flesh'.

This would seem to be corroborated rather than denied by 19. 35–36: 'That is Jesus the son of Mary—a statement (? so the Muslim tradition) of the truth wherein they are in dispute. It is not for God to take to Himself a son. Glory be to Him! When He decrees a matter, He only says, "Be", and it is.'

It has frequently been pointed out that if the pointing of *qawla'l-ḥaqqi* ('word or statement of truth') is changed to *qawlu-'l-ḥaqqi*, we obtain this sense: 'That is Jesus, son of Mary, the Word of Truth'[4] or 'the Word of God'. There is no means of

[1] For a modern Muslim defence against a Christian interpretation of the Qur'ānic references to Christ see the commentary of Maulānā Muhammad 'Alī, Lahore, 1951.

[2] See also 3. 40.

[3] See the following quotation.

[4] Cf. John xvii. 17, 'Sanctify them through Thy truth: Thy Word is truth.'

telling which version stood in the original Qur'ān since that was not pointed. In any case even if we follow the standard pointing it is still possible to translate: 'That is Jesus (in his capacity of) the Word of Truth,'[1] and this in fact agrees amazingly well with the similar text 3. 52–53.[2] This point does not, however, require to be laboured further here as we shall be returning to it later. Moreover, it is not a matter of dispute that Jesus is actually called the 'Word' (*kalima*) of God in the first passage quoted.

But what of the statement: 'It is not for God to take to Himself a son'? The operative word here is surely 'take to Himself' (*yattakhidha* meaning literally 'acquire'). God, according to this passage, then, does not *acquire* a son in the course of time; and this again is consonant with orthodox Christian teaching and actually opposed to the Arian heresy which held that God the Son was created in or before time. God does not acquire a 'son' because the 'Son' or, as the Qur'ān prefers to call Him, the 'Word', is co-eternal with God.

In another passage the Prophet roundly condemns those who identify God (Allah) with the Messiah. After chiding the Christians for their disunity[3]—'for they have forgotten part of that of which they were reminded and We (God) have stirred up enmity between them[4] and hatred until the Day of Resurrection'—he goes on to say 'surely they have disbelieved who say that God is the Messiah, the son of Mary.'[5] This passage again does not represent any insuperable difficulty for 'Allah' would naturally refer to God the Father, not to the 'Word'. So far, then, there is nothing in the Qur'ān which is obviously contrary to orthodox Christianity. 9. 30, however, is not nearly so easily explained away:

[1] For the construction see W. Wright, *A Grammar of the Arabic Language*, vol. ii, p. 114 B., *wa-hādhā ba'lī shaykhan*, 'and this is my husband, an old man'.

[2] See below, pp. 207–8.

[3] 5. 17: cf. 43. 65.

[4] This, however, may refer to the enmity between the Christians and the Jews.

[5] 5. 19.

'The Christians say that the Messiah is the Son of God. . . . God fight them! How they lie!'

This verse was apparently 'revealed' before Muhammad's expedition to the North, the first time he engaged a Christian enemy, and it was therefore necessary to excite the anger of the Muslims against them. Even so the words need mean nothing more than that Jesus, 'the Messiah', is not the son of God according to the flesh, and this is almost certainly the meaning of the famous Sūra 112: 'Say, God is One, God the Eternal; He did not beget, nor was He begotten, nor hath there ever been anyone like unto Him.' Muhammad was, after all, preaching to Muslim converts from paganism to whom the 'Son of God' could only mean one thing, namely, the son of God by cohabitation with a woman. That this is not what Christians mean by the term goes without saying.

Muhammad, however, does seem to have been aware of the controversy concerning the two natures of Christ, and the propositions he condemns unreservedly are (a) that Mary is the Mother of Allah, and (b) that the 'Messiah' is the son, rather than the Word, of God. Even though Allah must mean God the Father (if we allow ourselves to use Christian terminology at all with reference to the Qur'ān), the denial that Mary is the mother of Allah (God) would seem to be in direct support of the Nestorian position which denied to Mary the title of Mother of God. She could not even be said to be the mother of the Word that was 'cast upon' her since this pre-existed her, and if motherhood implies origination, then Mary is not the mother of God, though she is the mother of the 'Messiah', who, in some way not defined by the Qur'ān, is united to the eternal Word. The Qur'ānic position, then, with regard to the two natures of Christ would appear to be Nestorian. Whether or not Nestorianism is to be regarded as a heresy would appear to depend on how the terms 'mother', 'person', and 'hypostasis' are defined. For Muhammad, not unnaturally, 'father' meant a physical father by physical insemination. It can, then, be assumed that by 'mother' he meant the physical vessel of reproduction, and when he denies that Mary was the mother of God he probably means that she did not originate God, a conception that he rightly found blasphemous.

We have already seen that, according to the Qur'ān, Christ is both the Word of God and a spirit from Him. He is also the Messiah (*passim*), a messenger (*rasūl*) of God, His prophet (*nabī*), and His slave or servant. All of this accords with the New Testament. Of Himself as Messenger (*rasūl*='one sent') Christ said: 'As Thou hast sent Me into the world even so have I also sent them into the world.'[1] As Prophet he is acclaimed by the multitude on his triumphal entry into Jerusalem: 'This is Jesus the Prophet of Nazareth of Galilee.'[2] As to Christ's being God's slave or servant (*'abd*), this may be no more than the assertion of His humanity, *'abd* being the ordinary word used for man in contra-distinction to God, the Lord (*rabb*). Equally, however, the term[3] may be a faint recollection of Philippians ii. 6–11, where the Incarnate Christ is spoken of precisely as 'slave' (*δοῦλος*), a slave, however, raised to be Lord (*κύριος*) of all. We shall have occasion to return to this text from Philippians which must, in some form or other, have been familiar to Muhammad.

These terms, however, present no difficulty, for Muhammad is very emphatic that Christ was a real human being and *not* just a likeness of a human being. Thus Muhammad emphasizes the fact that Jesus ate[4] since he himself was derided by the Meccans for claiming to be a prophet though he ate and drank[5] whereas they demanded an angelic being unembarrassed by these earth-bound necessities. Muhammad, then, emphasizes the reality of Jesus' humanity in order to justify his own human mission. Yet Muhammad quite obviously considered Jesus to be very much more than a prophet. In Sūra 3. 40 the story of the Annunciation is given in the following terms:

'O Mary, verily doth God give thee good tidings of a Word from Himself whose name is the Messiah, Jesus, son of Mary, illustrious in this world and in the next.'

[1] John xvii. 18.
[2] Matt. xxi. 11: cf. also Luke vii. 16.
[3] Qur'ān, 19. 31: cf. 43. 59.
[4] 5. 79.
[5] 25. 8: 23. 34–35.

This text already seems to imply that Jesus has an eschatological mission as well as an earthly one, and this seems to be the purport of the very obscure verse 43. 61: 'And he is the sign ('*alam*, or differently pointed 'knowledge', '*ilm*) for the Hour.[1] In any case later Muhammadan tradition confidently looked forward to the second coming of Christ in which he would overthrow the *Dajjāl* or Anti-Christ, deny His own followers, and lead the Muslims in prayer as their Imām.

But perhaps the most interesting interpretation of the nature of Christ in the Qur'ān is the comparison made between Him and Adam. The creation of the man Jesus is compared to that of Adam: 'In the eyes of God the likeness of Jesus is as the likeness of Adam (whom) He created from dust and then said to him, "Be", and he is.'[2] Now it is not at all clear in this passage what Jesus' likeness to Adam consists in; for, according to the Qur'ān, Jesus was not created from dust, but, as in the Gospel, He was a special creation in the womb of Mary. The similarity must then lie elsewhere. The story of Adam's creation is told in the following words in the Qur'ān:

> 'And when thy Lord had said to the angels: "Lo, I am going to create a human being of potter's clay, of mud ground down. And when I have formed him and breathed into him of My Spirit, fall down before him in obeisance." So the angels made obeisance, all of them together, except Iblīs, who refused to join in with those who made obeisance.'[3]

Here the Biblical story of the creation of man from the dust of the ground and his being brought to life by the Spirit (*rūḥ*) of God is retold. In the Qur'ānic account it seems clear that Adam is regarded as being a divine being, for it is not lawful to fall down in obeisance to any but God. Thus, had Adam not been divine, God could not have bidden the angels worship him. Iblīs, the Devil, refused and for this he was damned. In this story we have the Muslim version of the creation of Adam

[1] The translation is uncertain: see the notes in Bell's translation.

[2] 3. 52.

[3] 15. 28–31: cf. 2. 28 ff: 7. 10 ff.

in the image of God, and this idea is specifically repeated in the Tradition and is widely developed in Ṣūfī speculation. Christ's 'likeness' to Adam would seem to be, then, that He is a special creation into which God's Spirit is breathed: and on the showing of the Qur'ān itself, it would seem that Jesus, equally with Adam, must be worthy of worship. Moreover, in comparing Jesus to Adam, Muhammad was, no doubt, unconsciously reproducing the Christian doctrine of Jesus as the second Adam. It would therefore follow that Jesus, who was sinless and presumably on that account raised by God unto Himself,[1] was also worthy of worship from the moment that God breathed His Spirit upon Mary, just as Adam was before Him. But whereas Adam lost the divine spirit by sin, Jesus did not and was accordingly raised up to God's own presence where He must remain a legitimate object of worship for all time.

We have seen how strongly the Qur'ān objects to the idea of begetting as applied to God because of its physical connotations. So we read in 2. 110–11:[2]

'They say, "God hath taken to Himself a son." Glory be to Him! Rather, to Him belongs what is in the heavens and the earth . . . when He decrees a thing, He says to it only, "Be", and it is.'[3] The human Jesus, then, is produced *directly* by God's creative Word or *Logos*; He is not a son acquired by God but is brought into existence in the Virgin's womb by the direct action of the divine Word 'Be'. The phrase *kun fa-yakūnu*, ' "Be", and it is', is used to describe a direct creation without intermediary and, except when applied to Jesus, it is only used to describe the mode of God's original creation[4] and the second creation in the final resurrection of the body.[5] The Incarnation of Christ, then, breathed from the Spirit of God, is thus regarded as an event as momentous as the original creation or the universal resurrection at the end of time. This would seem to indicate

[1] 4. 156: see below pp. 211–13.
[2] Almost identical is 19. 36.
[3] Cf. also the account of the Incarnation in 3. 42.
[4] 6. 72: 40. 70.
[5] 16. 42: 36. 82.

that Muhammad must, again unconsciously, be reproducing the Christian idea of Christ as the new Adam and as the 'first-fruits' of the resurrection. The application of the term *kun fa-yakūnu* only to creation, Christ, and the bodily resurrection brings the three events together in what seems to be a redemptive scheme, and can be explained as an echo of 1 Corinthians xv. 20–23:

'But now is Christ risen from the dead, and become the first-fruits of them that slept. For since by man came death, by man came also the resurrection of the dead. For as in Adam all die, even so in Christ shall all be made alive. But every man in his own order: Christ the firstfruits; afterward they that are Christ's at His coming.'

Now it cannot be maintained that in these Qur'ānic passages Christ is regarded as being identical with the *Logos*; but together with the first creation and the final resurrection He is regarded as being the direct and simultaneous effect of that *Logos*, that is, the command 'Be'. Now, in 3. 52–53 the creative Word is thus described: 'He said to him, "Be", and he is—the truth from the Lord.' The creative command 'Be' is thereby equated with the Word of Truth (*qāla la-hu kun . . . al-ḥaqqa*, 'He said to him, "Be" . . . (that is) the Truth, [acc.]). Now, this is an exact parallel to the passage (19. 35–36) we have already quoted in which the words *qawla'l-ḥaqqi* are traditionally translated as 'a statement of truth', although the translation 'Word of Truth' in apposition to Jesus has been suggested as an alternative. The parallel between the two passages is exact because in each we have a form of the root *QWL* (*qāla*, 'he said', and *qawl*, 'the saying' or 'word') governing the word *ḥaqq*, 'truth'. In both passages, then, the 'Word of Truth' must be the creative command 'Be'. The meaning of 19. 35–36 now seems clear:

'That is Jesus, the son of Mary, the Word of Truth wherein they are in dispute. It is not for God to take to Himself a son. Glory be to Him! When he decrees a matter, He only says, "Be", and it is.'

A comparison between the two passages shows that *qawla'l-ḥaqqi* does not mean the banal 'statement of truth' adopted by the Muslim tradition. The parallel passage *qāla kun . . . al-ḥaqqa*, 'He said, "Be" . . . (that is) the Truth', shows that the *qawla'l-ḥaqqi* of 19. 35 must mean 'the Word of Truth' and that this Word is the creative command 'Be'. With this Word or command Jesus is identical.

For the sake of greater clarity let us put the two passages side by side:

Q. 3. 52–53	Q. 19. 35
'In the eyes of God the likeness of Jesus is as the likeness of Adam (whom) He created from dust and said to him, "Be", and he is; it (sc. the likeness of Jesus is) the Truth from thy Lord; so be not of those who dispute.'	'That is Jesus, son of Mary (as) the Word of Truth wherein they are in dispute. It is not for God to take to Himself a son. Glory be to Him! When he decrees a matter, He only says to it, "Be", and it is.'

In the first passage 'the Truth from thy Lord' appears to be the complement of 'the likeness (*mathal*) of Jesus' and this is probably the meaning of the second passage too. The pre-existent Jesus, then, as Word (*kalima*), is the creative command of God, here called the Word (*qawl*) of Truth or 'the Truth from thy Lord'. The incarnate Jesus on the other hand is truly the son of Mary, but the *Word* not the 'son' of God.

The Qur'ānic conception of Jesus is perhaps best expressed in the words that are put into the mouth of the infant Jesus Himself in Sūra 19. 31–37:

'(Jesus) said: "Lo, I am the slave of God; he hath given me the Book and made me a prophet, and hath made me blessed wherever I am, and hath charged me with the prayer and the almsgiving so long as I live; and (he hath made me) kindly towards my mother, and He hath not made me a tyrant, damnable. And peace is (or be) upon the day that I was born, and on the day when I shall die, and on the day when I shall be raised up alive." That is Jesus, the son of Mary, the Word of Truth, wherein they are in dispute. It is not for God to take to Himself a son. Glory be to Him! When He decrees a matter He only says, "Be", and it is. Verily God is my Lord and thy Lord, so serve Him. This is a straight path.'

Here the Qur'ān would appear to accept Christ's divinity as the 'Word of Truth', while laying great stress on His true humanity. Christ is God's slave and His prophet and confesses that God is His Lord and 'your Lord'—a recollection, perhaps, of the risen Christ's words to the Magdalene: 'I ascend unto My Father, and your Father, and to My God, and your God.'[1]

Christ, then, in the Qur'ān, would appear to be both the Word of God and therefore divine, and truly man; but He is not the 'son' of God for reasons we have already explained. He is both God-Word and man *bi-lā-kayf* (without inquiring further as to how this can be); and it is at least arguable that the Qur'ān has herein followed a more prudent course in allowing the divine mystery to remain a mystery rather than attempting to explain it in logical terms which vary enormously from language to language, which are more often than not a source of confusion and contumacy, and which are in any case incomprehensible to the mass of the faithful.

Muslims, of course, agree in denying the divinity of Christ; but this is the result not of a close and impartial study of the Qur'ān but of an anti-Christian tradition that can already be discerned in the later Sūras of the Qur'ān itself. The development of a growing hostility to the Christians is fairly marked in that Book, and it is undeniable that this growing hostility is reflected in the Prophet's Christology. However, when arguing on the *religious* level rather than on that of exact scholarship, we must take the Qur'ān as it stands and as a whole, and try to reconcile the contradictions that exist in it in the same way that Dr. Kraemer, quite justifiably, takes the Bible as it stands and ignores the findings of recent Biblical criticism. The point of view of this appendix, then, is to accept all the Qur'ānic state-

[1] John xx. 17. Cf. J. W. Sweetman, op. cit., p. 32.

ments as being of equal validity and to attempt to reconcile them where they conflict. We shall now have to proceed to study the Qur'ānic evidence on the subject of the Crucifixion.

Muslim tradition, of course, rejects the Crucifixion out of hand, but accepts without reservation the story of the Ascension. This rather unhistorical view was probably due to the most generous motives, for to any non-Christian it must seem intolerable that one of the elect of God should suffer so shameful a death. However, whatever their motives may have been, the Muslims responsible for this tradition thereby abolished the very centre of the Christian message, the redemptive sacrifice of Christ on the Cross. It now remains for us to see whether in fact the Muslim tradition is faithful to the Qur'ān in this.

There are three references to the death or crucifixion of Jesus in the Qur'ān. The first of these we have just quoted where the infant Jesus is represented as saying that there is peace on the day of His birth, His death, and His being raised up alive (*ub'athu ḥayyan*). This obviously refers to the death that all men must die and not to the second death that Muslims believe Christ will die after His second coming.[1] Similarly in 3. 47–48 we read:

'(The Jews) plotted, and God plotted; and God is the best of those who plot, when God said "O Jesus, I purpose to cause thee to die (*mutawaffiyu-ka*)[2] and to raise thee up to Myself and to purify thee from whoso hath disbelieved; and I will exalt those who have followed thee above those who have disbelieved until the day of the Resurrection." '

Both these passages are quite clear: Christ was caused to die by God and was then raised up to Him. By 'raised up' is not meant the bodily resurrection, which is expressed by the root *B'TH* and applied to Jesus in 19. 34, but Christ's physical Ascension into Heaven (root *RF'*). Taken together, however, the two texts state clearly that Christ both died, was raised up alive,

[1] Cf. Q. 4. 157.

[2] The normal meaning of *tawaffā* in the Qur'ān is 'to cause to die'. Cf. 32. 11, 'The angel of death who is given charge over you, will cause you to die (*yatawaffā-kum*)'. So. 39. 43. Cf. 6. 60: 8. 52: 10. 104: 16. 72, etc.

and was 'assumed' by God into His presence. Yet only the Ascension is accepted by orthodox Islam.

In the early centuries of Islam Christian apologists invariably used these two texts to prove from the Qur'ān itself that Christ's crucifixion was a real death and his resurrection a real resurrection from the dead.[1] Muslim polemists as invariably retorted by quoting Q. 4. 156 where one of the charges against the Jews is 'for their saying: "Lo, we slew the Messiah, Jesus, son of Mary, the Messenger of God; yet they did not slay him, nor did they crucify him, but doubt was sown among them (?)." And those who differ therein are in doubt because of him. They have no knowledge concerning him, but only follow an opinion. In truth they did not slay him, but God raised him up to Himself, and God is sublime, wise.'

Muslim tradition, which has been followed by many European translators of the Qur'ān, takes the words *shubbiha la-hum* which I have provisionally translated as 'doubt was sown among them', to mean that Jesus was crucified only in appearance—the old docetic heresy, but it is extremely doubtful whether the words can mean this. Bell translates, 'he was counterfeited for them' which seems to stretch the meaning of *shubbiha* unbearably. *Shabbaha* means (a) 'to cause to resemble', and (b) 'to cause doubt'. In the context it is more natural to take *shubbiha* in the sense of 'doubt was caused for them', for the following sentence ('And those who differ therein are in doubt because of him') seems to be a gloss on the unusual phrase. If, however, we take Jesus as the subject, we must translate, 'he was made a likeness to them', which seems meaningless unless it is a reference to some other text. Now, such a text exists in Philippians ii. 7 where Jesus 'being in the form of God' was '*made in the likeness* of men' (ἐν ὁμοιώματι ἀνθρώπων γενόμενος). The Qur'ānic passage is very possibly, then, an unconscious memory of this text, and we may therefore translate 'and he was made in their likeness',[2] i.e made a man like them, but as the text goes on to

[1] See J. W. Sweetman, op. cit., p. 79.

[2] For *shabbaha li-* in this sense see Dozy, *Supplément aux dictionnaires arabes*, vol. ii, p. 725.

say, unlike them, God raised him up to Himself. The whole passage is, indeed, explicable in terms of Philippians ii, as we shall see. Maulānā Muḥammed 'Alī, in his translation, realizes that 'counterfeiting' will not do and renders 'he was made to appear to them as such'; and in the long note he appends to the passage he takes the line that Jesus was indeed crucified, but was still living when he was taken down from the Cross. His arguments from the Gospels in support of this view are ingenious, but he does not mention the other two Qur'ānic passages in which Jesus' death is referred to in no uncertain terms.

In actual fact the three passages do not contradict one another. In 3. 48 God causes Jesus to die and raises him up to Himself, whereas in 4. 156 it is roundly asserted that the *Jews* neither slew nor crucified the Messiah, Jesus, son of Mary, but that God raised him up to Himself—the implication being that it was God Himself who slew and crucified Jesus. The Jews took the credit for what was in reality God's own initiative. Exactly the same idea occurs in Q. 8. 17 where the first Muslim victory at Badr is ascribed directly to God, not to the participants in the battle:

'Ye slew them not, but God slew them; and when thou (Muhammad) didst throw, then didst thou not throw, but God threw, and (this was) that He might confer on the believers a benefit from Himself. Verily God is one who hears, knows.'

The idea seems to be precisely the same in both cases. In the second case the Muslims presumptuously claim the credit for their first victory over the infidel, a great 'benefit' to them, but it was in reality God who devised the victory and inspired the conquerors. Similarly the Jews presumptuously claimed the credit for crucifying the Messiah, but it was not they who slew Him, but God who raised Him up unto Himself.

Now, the word *rafa'a*, 'raised up', can be interpreted in two ways. The most natural interpretation is that God raised Jesus up into Heaven at the Ascension—and this agrees with Philippians ii. It can also mean, however, that He raised Him up on the Cross; and one may compare John iii. 14: 'And as Moses lifted up the serpent in the wilderness, even so must the Son of man be lifted up.' In both Philippians and John the Greek word is ὑψόω, the natural Arabic translation of which is the *rafa'a* which stands in the Qur'ānic text. If we take it that the word is used in both senses, we obtain this admirable, because logically consequent, sense: '(The Jews said): "Lo, we slew the Messiah, Jesus, son of Mary, the Messenger of God; yet they did not slay him, nor did they crucify him, but he was made like unto them (a man), and (it was) God (who) raised him up (upon the Cross and) to Himself." ' Thus it would appear that the Crucifixion is regarded by the Qur'ān as being an act performed by God Himself in order that He might exalt Jesus to the very rank of deity: 'God raised up or exalted him unto Himself.'

If read without reference to the Muslim tradition, then, the three crucifixion passages in the Qur'ān state (a) that Christ was caused to die by God, (b) that he was resurrected alive, and (c) that he was raised up on high to God. What little the Qur'ān does say about the Death, Resurrection, and Ascension of Christ, fits neatly into St. Paul's classic formulation of the abasement and exaltation of Jesus in Philippians ii. 6–11 and must surely derive from it:

> Jesus Christ 'being in the form of God, thought it not robbery to be equal with God, but He emptied Himself, taking upon Him the form of a slave (cf. *'abd*), being made in the likeness of men (cf. *shubbiha la-hum*); and being found in fashion as a man, He humbled Himself, and became obedient unto death, even the death of the Cross (cf. God caused Him to die). Wherefore God hath highly exalted Him (cf. *rafa'a-hu*), and given Him a name which is above every name, that at the name of Jesus every knee should bow, of things in heaven, and things in earth, and things under the earth; and that every tongue should confess that Jesus Christ is Lord, to the glory of God the Father.'

Of course the Qur'ān nowhere speaks of Christ as Lord or God, but in saying that God exalted Him *to Himself*, it practically admits the divinity of Christ which it anyhow attests in its description of Him as the Word of God, the Word of Truth, and apparently the creative command 'Be'.

Muslims, then, in denying the Crucifixion—and Islamic modernists are at long last attempting to make good this centuries-old error—are rejecting the very words of the Qur'ān: and in denying the divinity of Christ because they are unable to reconcile it with His humanity, they appear to be doing the same. How rightly do they describe themselves as *ahl al-sunna*, 'the people of the tradition', and not as *ahl al-kitāb*, 'the people of the Book'. They, of all people, seem to have forgotten that 'God over all things hath power'.[1]

So too in the matter of the Holy Trinity it is always assumed that the Qur'ān flatly denies It, so tremendous is its emphasis on the absolute unity of God. But the trinity that the Qur'ān explicitly denies is not that of Father, Word, and Holy Spirit, but that of God, Jesus, and Mary,[2] which no orthodox Christian has ever professed. Nor can the Prophet's warning, 'Say not, "Three". God is only one God', be taken as a condemnation of the Christian conception of the Trinity. That there are actual traces of *a* trinitarian doctrine in the Qur'ān has long been recognized, and the whole question has recently been subjected to a close and impartial scrutiny by Fr. Thomas O'Shaughnessy, S.J.[3]

The Qur'ānic Trinity, if so we may call it, is that of God (Allah), His Command (*amr*), and the Spirit (*rūḥ*). The most important of the texts which deal with this triad was later to assume enormous importance in Islamic mystical theology, for the Qur'ānic *amr* was equated with the Neo-Platonic *Nous*, and the *rūḥ* with the Universal Soul of the same system. In the Qur'ān the whole affair is swathed in mystery. The verse runs as follows:

'And they ask thee concerning the Spirit. Say, "the Spirit is

[1] Q. 2. 19, etc.

[2] 5. 116: cf. 5. 76 ff.

[3] In *The Development of the Meaning of Spirit in the Koran*, Rome, 1953. The same author's *The Koranic Concept of the Word of God* is equally valuable.

of the *amr* of my Lord; and of knowledge you are given but a little".'[1]

Now, the word *amr* means either the (divine) command or simply an 'affair'; but in these passages where it is connected with *rūḥ*, the 'Spirit', it is generally agreed that the word reproduces the Hebrew *memrā*, deriving as it does from the same root. The Hebrew word corresponds to the Greek *Logos* and means 'Word'. This idea seems to have percolated through to the Prophet who does not, however, attempt to explain it.

'The Spirit is of (or from) the Word (*amr*) of my Lord.' The sentence, as it stands, can actually be interpreted as a statement of the Catholic (rather than the Eastern Orthodox) interpretation of the Trinity: the Holy Spirit proceeds from the Word of God (*qui ex Patre* Filioque *procedit!*).

The second passage in which the collocation of *amr* and *rūḥ* occurs, is more definite:

'He sends down the angels with the Spirit from His *amr* to whom He will of his servants that they may give warning that there is no God but Me.'[2]

The Spirit, then, is that Spirit which testifies through the prophets to the unity of God, the Spirit who in the very words of the Christian Creed *locutus est per prophetas*, 'spoke through the prophets'. Thus again in 40. 15 the same Spirit from God's *amr* gives warning through 'His servants' of the 'day of meeting', and in 42. 52 God inspires Muhammad with a Spirit from His *amr*, 'for thou didst not know what the Book and the Faith were; but we made it (sc. the Spirit) a light by which we guide whomsoever we please of our servants, and verily thou wilt guide to a straight path.'

The Spirit or Holy Ghost—elsewhere so called in the Qur'ān, three times in connexion with the story of Jesus,[3] and once claimed by the Prophet as the guarantor of his own revelation[4] —is thus regarded as the authentic Spirit of God which inspires

[1] Q. 17. 87.
[2] 16. 2.
[3] 2. 81, 254: 5. 109.
[4] 16. 104.

the prophets. *Mutatis mutandis* He is the Spirit of Truth[1] promised by Jesus to His disciples.

It is quite certain that, in speaking of God's *amr* and His *rūḥ*, Muhammad had no intention of formulating a Trinitarian doctrine, but the Qur'ān itself is wide open to such an interpretation. It was, moreover, developed in Islam itself along Neo-Platonic lines by the Ṣūfīs, and the Christian doctrine of the Incarnate Word which the Qur'ān does not deny as being present in Jesus, was later transferred to the Prophet himself who thereby became the creative principle of the Universe. That such views were vigorously rejected by the orthodox is not surprising, for Muhammad never made any claim except to be a divinely inspired prophet: the Word and the spirit were the especial prerogatives of Jesus.

The Qur'ān, then, as opposed to traditional Muslim orthodoxy, does not explicitly *deny* any specific Christian doctrine except that Christ is the *son* of God, and this for obvious reasons that have already been pointed out. For, except to those well coached in Christian theology, sonship implies physical procreation and this is unthinkable in God who is a pure Spirit. The Christian interpretation of the eternal *Logos* has room for both the Muslim conception of God's *amr*, *kalima*, and *qawl*—His Word—and for the Hindu conception of God's eternal generation of the 'seed' (=Arabic *walad*, 'offspring', which the Qur'ān utterly denies to God) which we have met with in the Bhagavad-Gītā and which is basic to the theology of the worshippers of Śiva.

So far as his Christology is concerned, Muhammad, in the Qur'ān, nowhere denies and sometimes affirms specifically Christian beliefs; and so far as his sublime conception of the unity and transcendence of God is affirmed, he may justly claim to be the 'Seal of the prophets'. He adds nothing new to what had been previously revealed because he is a prophet, and no more than a prophet. The mystical bond of love which Christ, in His own Person, brings to 'fill out' the hopes of the prophets before Him, is lacking, as it was bound to be, in the one Prophet

[1] John xv. 26.

who came after Him. And it was left to the great Muslim Persian poet, Sanā'ī, to reaffirm within Islam itself that the way of union with God lies only through the Cross:

> 'How shouldst thou gain the fruit of thy divinity
> Until thy humanity has been raised up upon the Cross.
> So long as thou and thy being exist, Reason is clouded;
> The eye of thine intelligence is distracted from the next world.
> For on the road towards divinity
> Thy Jesus must pass by the Friday of Crucifixion.'[1]

[1] Sanā'ī *Ḥadīqat al-Ḥaqīqa*, ed. Teheran, A. H. (solar), 1329, p. 112.

Index

INDEX

INDEX

God and Absolute, 97; no revelation in, 22, 170; primitive—, 15, 16, 18, 39, 97, 185; use of Yoga, 39. Cf. Mahāyāna, Zen

Byzantine Church, 200

Calvary, 187

Calvinism, 14

Catholic Church, 190. *See also* Roman Catholic Church

Catholicism, Catholics, 29, 49, 72, 152, 160, 215

Chāndogya Upanishad, 52 n. 1, 54 nn. 3 and 5, 64 n. 2, 66 n. 1, 71 n. 4, 72, 77 n. 3, 86, 92, 105

China, 26, 83, 165

Chorasmia, 136

Christ, 9, 21, 23, 116, 132, 139, 144, 153, 158, 159, 180, 182, 189, 190, 191, 192; claims of, 196; contrasted with Buddha, 21, 103; divinity of, 200, 214; fulfils all prophecy, 180, 184, 194, and India's hope, 188, 194, and the Law, 161, 167; in the Qur'ān, **195–215**; incarnate Word, 198, 199, 204; incarnation of, 117, 157, 206; Muslim attitude to, 157, **200–14**; Oriental religions and, 166; preparation for His coming, 165; resurrection of, 168, 180, 187, 200; true Bodhisattva, 187, 191. *See also* Jesus

Christianity, 11, 13, 14, 15, 16, 18, 19, 20, 23, 24, 27, 28, 30, 57, 68, 73, 79, 83, 84, 103, 104 n. 1, 113, 117, 129, 132, 144, 151, 152, 159, 160, 161, 180, 181, 192, 195, 196, 197, 199, 201, 202, 214, 215, 216; and dignity of body, 168; and Greek philosophy, 165, 166; and Islam, 155–7, 198, 200; and Indian religion, 173, 193, 194; dogmatism in, 56; fulfils Zoroastrianism, 191, 193, 194; mysticism, 43, 130, 173, 179, 185; view of man in, 22; Zoroastrian doctrines in, 148–9, 153

Clement of Alexandria, 165, 166

collective unconscious, 49, 52, 88, 166

Communion of Saints, 191, 194

Comparative Religion, 11–12, 30, 180

consciousness, 77, 78; 'higher' form of, 54; inseparable from breath, 64, 65; stilling of, 49; transformation of, 37–8, 77

Coomaraswamy, A., 36 n. 2, 98, 99

Corinthians I, 28 n. 2, 187 n. 1, 191 n. 1, 207

Corinthians II, 194 n. 1

cosmic consciousness, 49, 52

creation, 34; *ex nihilo*, 32, 129, 144; purpose of (Zoroastrian), 151; purposeless (Rāmānuja), 129–30

Cross, 21, 181, 187, 188, 191, 192, 210, 212, 213, 217

Crucifixion, 157, 180, 187, 191, 192, 200, 217; in Qur'ān, **210–14**

daēvas, 137

Dajjāl (Anti-Christ), 205

Darius III, 135

Dasgupta, Surendranath, 36

Dead Sea Scrolls, 12

Dead Sea sect, 143, 144

desire, 95–6

Destructive or Evil Spirit (Angra Mainyu), 140, 146, 148, 150; chooses evil, 142, 144, 148, 149; origin of, 144; relationship to Wise Lord, 141–2; twin of Holy Spirit, 141–2. *See also* Angra Mainyu, Ahriman

detachment, 21, 120, 122

deva, 104, 105

dhāman, 31, 120, 124, 125

dhamma, 100–2, 169

Dhammapada, 99, 100 nn. 1–3, 101 n. 3

Dharma-body, 104

dharman, 31

dialectical materialism, 63, 64
Dīgha-Nikāya, 97 n. 1, 100 n. 4, 101 nn. 1, 2 and 6
di Matteo, I., 195 n. 1
dream, 56, 87, 90
dreamless sleep, 89–90
Druj, 137. *See* Lie
dualism, 139, 141, 142; in *Manual of Discipline*, 143; in Sassanian period, 143; of soul and body, 177; qualified in Zoroaster, 143
Dupont-Sommer, 12

Eastern Orthodox Church(es), 28, 56, 215
Eckhart, Meister, 113
'ego', 40, 42, 43, 44, 53, 61, 101, 133, 166, 185, 191, 192; and 'self', 44–7, 49, 73; denial of, 24, 95, 99; dissolution of, 74; Jung on, 77
Eliade, Mircea, 92, 174
Engels, 63, 86
Enneads, 25 n. 1
'en-stasis', 92
Eternal, the; as God, 26, 69, 112, 139, 193, 203; as state, 30; merging into, 26; relationship to temporal, 176
eternal life, 20, 61, 146, 178, 180
eternal 'now', 23, 44, 46, 50, 73, 80, 81, 82
eternity, 81, 102, 111, 180; experience of, 25, 26, 80; Jewish view of, 151; quest for, 26; two types of, 23; Zoroastrian view of, 151
evil, problem of, 141, 149, 150
Evil Mind, 142

Fall, the, 14, 90, 117, 172, 177, 179, 181; effects of, 174–5
Farmer, H. H., 20, 23
filius philosophorum, 77
'Final Body', 147
food; as Brahman, 59, 61–3
frashkart, 147
free will, 142, 145, 147, 149, 181, 184, 189

Gabriel, 154
Galatians, 188 n. 2
Gardet, Louis, 92
Gārgī, 67
Garutmat, 31
Gāthās, 135, 140, 141, 144, 149
Gauḍapāda, 88, 89, 93 n. 1
Genesis, 29 n. 3, 61, 144, 174 n. 1, 182 n. 1, 189 n. 1
Ghazālī, 12 n. 1, 156, 163; on mystical experience, 13
Gnosticism, Gnostics, 157, 175
God, *passim*
(Hindu), and man, 70, 88; as breath or spirit, 65, 104; as creator, 32; as dreamless sleep, 89–90; as efficient cause, 32, 89–90, 114, 115, 116; as Lord, 69, 70, 105, 114, 115, 116; as manifest in creation, 34; as material cause, 32, 58, 89–90; as personal, 23, 24, 26, 52, 69, 94, 134; communion with, 25, 132; constrained by His own nature, 129; development of idea of— in Upanishads, **104–115**; ensnares and releases soul, 113, 115; excluded in Sāṁkhya system, 73; Hindu idea of, 66–8, 71; His attributes in Gītā, 128–30; identified with soul of man, 39, 55–6, 58, 68, 71, or with world, 55–6, 58, 68, 71; immanent, 59, 65, 105–6, 112, 115, 128, 162; in *Śvetāśvatara* Upanishad, 114–5; in Yoga system, 73; Inner Controller, 58; Lord of Brahman, 110; love of, 130, 131, 132, 133, 149, 179; relationship to Brahman in Gītā, **117–33**; source of Brahman, 108, 109, 114; terrible aspect of, 130–1, 132;

INDEX

INDEX

imago mundi, 76, 77, 81, 88
immortality, 26, 37, 57, 61, 80, 83, 94, 104, 134, 153, 168; elixir of, 152; experience of, 24, 39–40, 43, 44–6, 49, 92, 120, 126, 167, 171; in body and soul, 148, 168–9, 178, 181, 190, 191; in food and breath, 61–5; is Nirvāṇa, 96; Jewish view of, 180; of soul only, 176, 177, 178–9; personal, 23; quality of, 168, 180; realizable without revelation, 170; starting-point of mystic, 81
(Zoroastrian), 135, 142, 145, 146, 147, 178
incarnation; Buddhist, 184; Christian, 117, 132, 157, 159, 171, 187, 188, 189; Hindu, 116, 117, 122, 132, 135, 183, 187
India, Indians, 9, 13, 14, 15, 16, 19, 22, 23, 24, 26, 36, 38, 39, 47, 56, 60, 63, 75, 83, 85, 88, 107, 133, 134, 135, 136, 139, 144, 147, 152, 165, 170, 171, 177, 178, 179, 180, 184, 189, 194; no prophets in, 25
Indian mysticism, 14, 173; four types of, 88
Indian religion(s), 13, 15, 16, 19, 21, 22, 23, 24, 35, 57, 70, 115, 118, 130, 134, 137, 149, 168, 175, 179, 195; and Christianity, 173; and Jungian psychology, 43; and philosophy, 31; concerned with eternal state, 30, 61; development of, 167; dichotomy of spirit and matter in 176, 177; dualist view of man in, 22; indifference to dogma of, 20; predominantly mystical, 25; progress of theological thought in, 64–6; three trends in, 69, 72–9. *See also* Buddhism, Hinduism
Indra, 30, 31, 64, 152
integration of personality, 42, 47, 55, 77; in Indian mysticism, 53–4, 123, 128
Iran, 9, 27, 135, 152, 153, 165, 171, 178, 184, 194
Īśā Upanishad, 104 n. 2, 105 n. 2
Isaiah, 27, 29 n. 2, 150, 177 n. 1
Islam, 13, 29, 129, 170, 195, 197, 198, 199, 211, 214, 216, 217; Christian and Indian influences on, 163; claims of, 157, 159, 161, 196; contrasted with Hinduism, 162; Jewish origin of, 161; prophetic religion *par excellence*, 161; religion of the Book, 196, 214; restatement of true religion, 161; spread of, 160, 161; transformed by Ṣūfism, 163; view of man in, 22
Israel, 15, 25, 26, 27, 69, 135, 136, 139, 144, 152, 158, 161, 165, 167, 183, 184, 194, 199; second or new—, 161, 167. *See also* Hebrews, Jewry, Judaism
īśvara ('the Lord'), 125; in Upanishads, 105; in Yoga system, 41, 110

Jainism, Jains, 21, 38, 41, 42, 48, 69, 72, 73, 79, 97, 98, 102; use Yoga, 39
James, E. O., 11, 19
James, William, 48, 49, 50
Japan, 44
Jefferies, Richard, **79–87**, 129, 130 n. 1, 170, 183; on death, 84; on 'Highest Soul', 84; on the body, 82–3
Jesus, 12, 27, 29, 49, 156, 157, 158, 180, 188, 196, 205, 214, 216. *See* Christ
in Islam: a prophet, 156, 157, 196, 198, 200, 204, 208; ascension accepted, 157, 210–11, 212; born of Virgin, 156, 157, 201; compared to Adam, 205–7; crucifixion, **211–14**, 217; Messiah, 156, 157, 200, 202, 203, 204, 211, 212, 213; second coming of, 205, 210; sonship of God denied, 27, 200 ff., 206,

P

as female principle, 34. *See also* primal matter
matter, 23, 35, 41, 63, 80, 90, 111, 179, 189; consecration of, 190
Matthew, St., 24 n. 2, 116 n. 4, 132 n. 1, 139 n. 3, 204 n. 2
Māyā, 188
māyā ('magic power'), 113, 116, 126, 129; is Nature, 112, 113, 129
Mecca, 137, 153
Medina, 156, 160
Messiah, 156, 159, 160, 167, 200, 202, 203, 204, 211, 212, 213
metempsychosis, 22. *See* reincarnation, transmigration of souls
microcosm, 88, 89–90, 105
Midrash, 197
mirror, 111, 112
Mitra, 31
Mohenjo Daro, 38
mokṣa ('release' q.v.), 39, 43, 74, 94
monism, 39, 66, 68, 71, 94, 107, 172, 191; Buber's refutation of, 91–2; H. Kraemer on, 14; of *Māṇḍūkya* Upanishad, 72; pantheistic—, 55; Rāmānuja's refutation of, 78
Monophysites, 200
Moses, 155, 168, 197, 199, 200, 213
Muhammad, 118, 137, **153–61**, 195, 196, 197, 200, 201, 203, 204, 206, 207, 212, 215, 216; attitude to Jesus, 156; attitude to Jews and Christians, 156, 157; his call, 153–4; his character, 160; his claims, 197, 216; law-giver, 161, 197; promised Paraclete, 158; Prophet of the Arabians, 27, 155; Prophet *par excellence*, 27; 'Seal of the prophets', 156, 157, 216; Ṣūfī deification of, 163, 216
Muhammad 'Alī, Maulānā, 201, 211
Muhammadans, 181. *See* Muslims, Islam
Müller, Max, 30
Muṇḍaka Upanishad, 52 n. 3, 107, 108 nn. 1–3, 118, 124 n. 5
Muslim(s), 150, 156, 158, 159, 160, 189, 195, 203, 205, 208, 209, 210, 211, 212, 216; and Christians, 200, 209; theology, 197, 198. *See also* Islam
mystical experience, 24; univerality of, 25
mysticism, 25, 50, 164, 171; different types of, 43, 172; Jewish, 171; meaning of, 171; theistic, 178; theistic— and self-realization in Gītā, 132

Naciketas, 106
Nature, 34, 35, 41, 42, 48, 81, 101, 112, 119, 122, 123, 124, 125, 128, 129, 133, 183; communion with, 25, 87–8; confused with God, 87; God author of, 112; is *māyā*, 113; Jefferies on, 85–7; laws of, 86, 126; merging of soul into, 49, 66, 74, 76, 78, 172, 193. *See also* *prakṛti*
nature mysticism, 43, 47, 55, 69, 70, 84, 94, 172, 183; basic to Upanishadic thought, 43, 48, 56; claims of, 75; defined, 47–8, 49, 53; explained by Aristotle, 76, and Jung, 53, 78–9, 88; Jefferies on, 81, 87; universality of, 25, 55
Neo-Buddhists, 76
Neo-Calvinism, 172
Neo-Platonism, 163, 171, 182, 214, 216
Neo-Vedāntins, 36 n. 2, 76
Nestorians, 200, 203
New Testament, 132, 156, 158, 159, 160, 197, 200, 204; canon of, 196
Nicolas of Cusa, 76, 88
nirvāṇa, 16, 17, 18, 23, 47, 80, 92, 95, 102, 185, 186, 187; is deathlessness, 96, 98, 184; means 'blowing out', 43; of Brahman, 122, 123, 126
Noble Truths, the Four, 17, 104
Not-Being, 33, 34
Nous, 214

Ohrmazd, 140, 149, 150, 151. *See also* Ahura Mazdā, God (Zoroastrian), Wise Lord
Old Testament, 15, 16, 22, 26, 27, 69, 116, 118, 131, 135, 137, 141, 155, 156, 158, 160, 165, 171, 197, 200
Oṁ, 49, 127
One, the, 33, 34, 89, 90; androgynous, 35
Original Sin, 14, 83, 90, 173, 178, 179, 180, 184; separates man from God, 174, 177, 182, man from man, 174, and soul from body, 177, 182
O'Shaughnessy, T., 214
Otto, Rudolf, 12, 59, 118
Oxford, 93

pan-en-henic experience, 48, 49–50, 56, 73, 172
pantheism, 32, 33, 37, 66, 68, 71, 72, 115
Paraclete, 158
Parmenides, 37
participation mystique, 60, 76
Patañjali, 41, 42, 73
Paul, St., 28, 96, 179, 181, 190, 213
Persia, Persians, 135, 163
Persian Empire, 135
person (*puruṣa* q.v.), 24, 37, 42, 47, 73, 102, 178, 194; = God, 66, 71, 108, 124, 125, 126, 127, 194; = Self, 49, 67, 71, 125, 127
personality, 24; denied by Buddhists, 95; expansion of, 47, 74; illusory, 24; Jung on, 77; loss of, 24, 48, 49, 50, 73, 191; realization of, 73; release of, 43, 74; 'self' and, 44
Pharaoh, 160
Pharisees, 103
Philippians, 188 n. 3, 204, 211, 212, 213
philosophia perennis, 176
Plato, 96, 108, 166, 173
Platonism, 175
Plotinus, 25
praeparatio evangelica, 9; among Greeks, 165–6; in Asia, 166
prakṛti ('Nature' q.v.), 41, 47, 83, 124, 125, 126, 183; is *māyā*, 113
prāṇa ('breath' q.v.), 64, 86, 104, 182; indifference to good and evil of, 86
Praśna Upanishad, 53 n. 3, 55, 56 n. 1, 64 n. 2
pre-Socratics, 36
primal matter, 59, 124. *See also materia prima*
prophecy, prophets, 25, 26, 30, 118, 136, 139, 152, 155, 156, 159, 161, 163, 164, 167, 172, 178, 183, 194, 215; Hebrew, 166, 184, 197; intolerance of, 137; Muhammad, **153–61**, 195 ff, 215, 216; outside Israel, 27, 29; Zoroaster, **135–48**, 149, 184
prophetic tradition, 135; of Israel, 165, 168
Protestantism, Protestants, 29, 72, 160, 166, 170, 173, 180; anti-mystical, 171, 172
Proust, **44–8**, 49, 56, 73, 79, 82, 92, 170
Psalms, 199, 200
puruṣa ('person' q.v.), 60; as soul, 40, 41, 42, 47, 49, 73, 82, 83, 89, 98, 126, 127, 185; as Supreme Self, 89, 105, 125
Puruṣasūkta, 32

Qur'ān, 15, 22, 27, 118, 134, 153, 155, 156, 157, 158, 160, 162, 189 n. 2; abrogated verses, 197, 198; and Christ, **195–215**; and Crucifixion, **210–4**; and divinity of Christ, **200–9**; and Trinity, **214–6**; confirms previous revelation, 199–200; definitive text drawn up, 159; final revelation, 157, 159, 161; uncreated, 197, 198; Word of God, 156, 157, 159, 198, 199

Radhakrishnan, 14, 36 n. 2, 119, 168
Rāmānuja, 75, 81, 119, 120, 121, 123, 126, 127, 173, 192; his refutation of monism, 78; sees no purpose in creation, 129–30
Raphael, 21
Rees, M. G., 9
Reformers, the, 180
Reid, Forrest, 74 n. 2, 75, 79
reincarnation, 23, 41, 96, 121. Cf. metempsychosis, transmigration of souls
'release', 39, 43, 73, 74, 79, 94, 98, 123, 192; as oneness or isolation, 114. See also *mokṣa*
resurrection of body, 23, 187, 191; distinguishes Christianity from Indian religion, 168; in Christianity, 22, 117, 168, 181, 193; in Islam, 22, 206, 207; in Zoroastrianism, 148, 149, 184, 188
revelation, 22, 134, 155, 171, 183, 184; and experience, 57; conflicting revelations, 161; Hindu and Judaic ideas of, 70; in Christianity, 165, 172; in India, 170, 183, 197; in Islam, 156, 157, 159, 197; in Old Testament, 69; in Zoroastrianism, 135, 137, 171; meaning of, 170; no felt need for— in India, 167
rewards and punishments, 139, 146, 147
Rhys-Davids, T. W., 97
Righteousness (*asha*, Truth q.v.), 135, 137, 139, 140, 141, 144, 146, 147
Right-mindedness (*ārmaiti*), 135, 140, 145
Rig-Veda, 30, 31 nn., 32 nn., 33, 34, 35, 104 n. 2, 112, 125 n. 4, 152, 179
Rimbaud, 151, 175, 183
Roman Catholic Church, 28, 56. *See also* Catholic Church
Roman Empire, 165
Romans, 96 n. 3, 145 n. 3, 167 n. 1, 177 n. 2, 189 n. 3
Rosary, 49
ṛta, 31
Rudra-Śiva, 109, 113
rūḥ ('Spirit'), 214, 215, 216
Rūmī, Jalāl al-Dīn, 190
Ruysbroeck, Blessed Jan, 132, 185, 186

Sac-cid-ānanda ('Being-Awareness-Bliss'), 51
Śaivites, 116
śakti ('power of God'), 109
Śāktism, 109
salvation, 24, 97, 98, 137, 192; for the Gentiles, 167; in Buddhism, 96, 142, 185; in Indian religion, 23, 175; in *Śvetāśvatara* Upanishad, 111, 114; in Zoroastrianism, 142, 147, 178; 'is of the Jews', 166–7; technique of, 38; = isolation in Sāṁkhya (q.v.), 58, 73, 174, 175
samādhi, 25, 93; Jung on, 52
Sāṁkhya, 21, 39, 41, 42, 47, 48, 49, 79, 82, 88, 97, 102, 126; dualistic, 41, 58, 175; isolation of soul goal of, 93, 176; no God in, 41; theistic—, 112
Sāṁkhya-Yoga, 39, 41, 42, 43, 47, 48, 49, 58, 69, 93, 94, 96, 109, 111, 120, 124, 125, 130, 172, 178, 183; isolation of soul goal of, 42, 72–3, 174
saṁsāra, 186
Saṁyutta-Nikāya, 17 n. 1, 95 n. 1, 96 n. 4, 100 n. 5, 101 n. 5, 102 n. 3, 103 n. 1
Sanā'ī, 217
Śāndilya-Vidyā, 65, 68
Śankara, 39, 118, 119, 121, 124, 126, 130
Sannyāsa Upanishads, 116
Saoshyans, 148
Satan, 141
Śatapatha Brāhmaṇa, 66 n. 1

INDEX